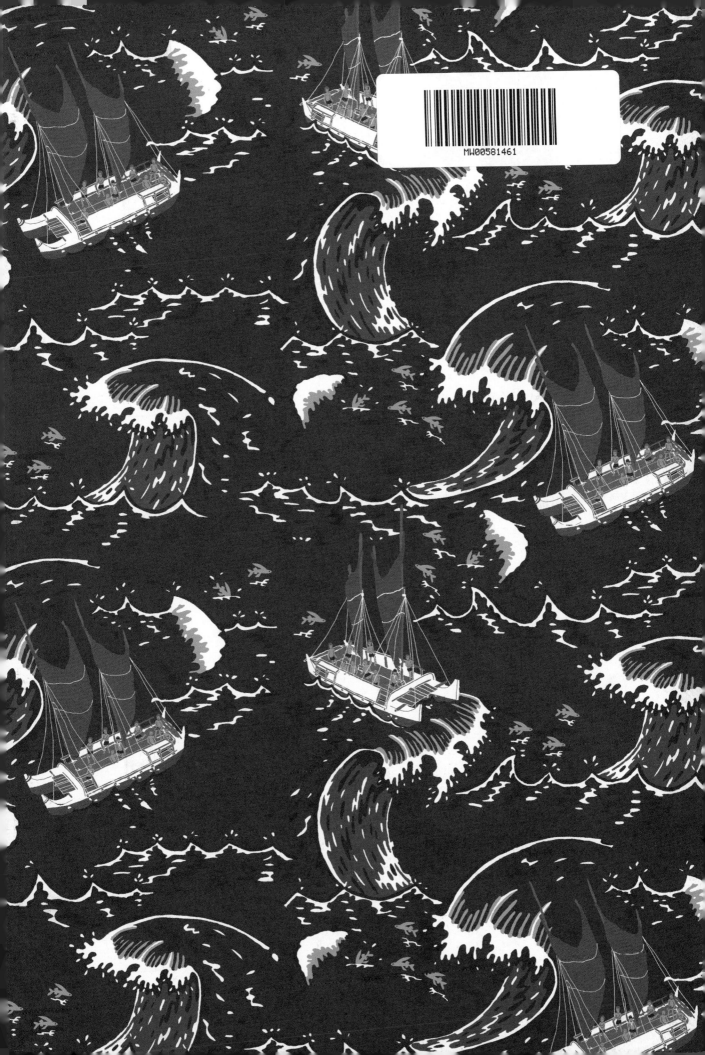

"The voyage is about sailing on the core set of values we believe in. The sail plan of humanity is off course. But there is a movement of kindness and compassion that is happening around the world in response to the damage to our Earth. *Hōkūleʻa* is a needle sewing a *lei* of flowers around the world as an act of peace ... and that is why we sail."

Nainoa Thompson
Pwo Navigator, Captain, and President of the Polynesian Voyaging Society

MĀLAMA
HONUA

Hōkūle'a – A Voyage of Hope

Jennifer Allen

Photographs by John Bilderback

patagonia

CONTENTS

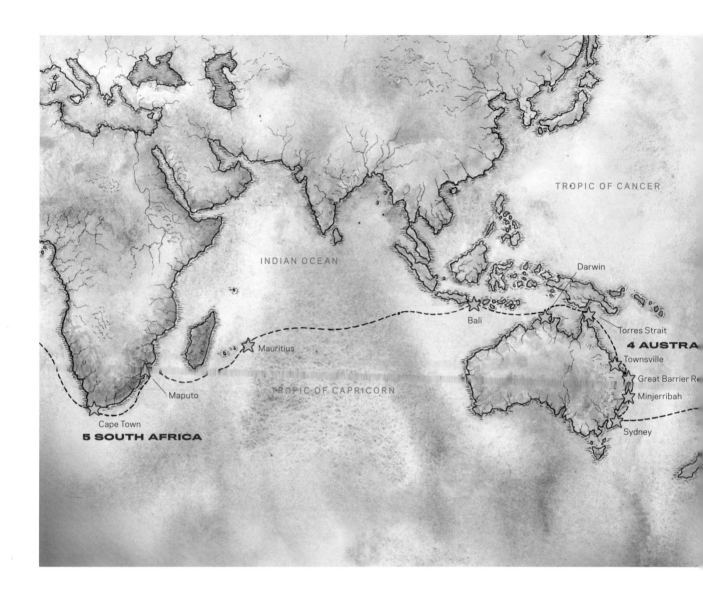

Hōkūleʻa
Mālama Honua Worldwide Voyage

HŌKŪLEʻA IS A PERFORMANCE-ACCURATE double-hull voyaging canoe built in the early 1970s to prove that Polynesians purposely navigated throughout the Pacific to find and settle new lands. The canoe is the inspiration of the Polynesian Voyaging Society—a group founded by Herb Kāne, Ben Finney, and Tommy Holmes. *Hōkūleʻa* is sailed without engine, compass, or GPS. When she was launched in 1975 she was the first of her kind in more than 600 years.

    Since that first voyage, *Hōkūleʻa* has had many miles of ocean pass under her hulls sailing throughout the Polynesian Triangle—Hawaiʻi, Rapa Nui, Aotearoa— and has even gone as far as Japan and California. She has inspired a cultural and

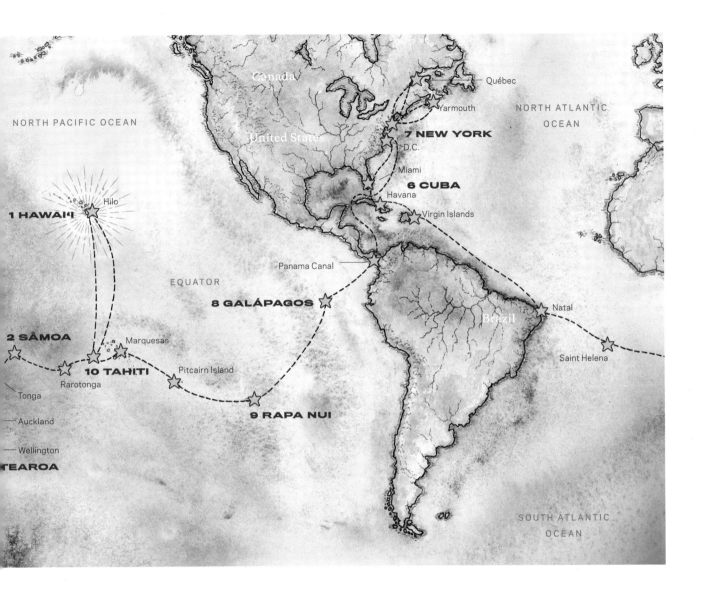

voyaging revival throughout Polynesia, and spawned many like-minded voyaging societies and voyaging canoes.

The Mālama Honua voyage circled the Earth to join the global movement toward a more sustainable world. Begun in 2013 with a Mālama Hawai'i sail around the Hawaiian Islands, it continued (as shown on the map above), arriving back in Honolulu in June 2017. *Hōkūle'a* visited ports around the world, allowing the crew to connect with and honor indigenous communities, and discover local environmental solutions.

In four decades of sailing, this was the first time *Hōkūle'a* voyaged out of the Pacific Ocean, beyond the geographical boundaries where noninstrument wayfinding was traditionally practiced. To prepare, the navigators researched extensively into the currents, weather systems, wave patterns, stars, and wildlife they would potentially see along the way. (See the resources section for more information on Polynesian noninstrument navigation.)

Foreword

THE WORLDWIDE VOYAGE OF MĀLAMA HONUA is a testimony to the human spirit—that human beings can be so courageous, that human beings can be so inventive that they are ready to sail around the world to share the message of the peace of sustainable living. It is a voyage of respect for each other, for our whole planet, and for all who live on it. The message is that we must care for each other and for all life on Earth, for it is only then that Earth can take care of us and our future generations.

A great navigator must be deeply committed in order to take the risk, to enter into the unknown to seek a better future—sometimes with only a vision of one's destination. It takes faith to stay the course and weather the journey ahead. And despite challenges, one must dance, laugh, and find joy along the way. This mission of the navigators on the *Hōkūleʻa* speaks to all of us.

In Hawaiʻi, they call it "Aloha." In South Africa, we say "*Ubuntu*." When you live this quality, you are known for your generosity. *Ubuntu* means that you recognise that you can't exist in isolation. It speaks to our interconnectedness, to our common spirit as humans on our one shared planet Earth. This is the destination that the great navigators have envisioned as they have connected with their brothers and sisters around the world.

We think of ourselves far too frequently as individuals, separated from one another, divided by country, by race, by vast oceans. But it is the universal water that connects us and makes us aware that each thing we do ripples out and affects the whole world. When we do good, it spreads out; it is for the whole of humankind. When we do good for the planet, we do good for all mankind.

Our Polynesian brothers and sisters sailing aboard this vessel, the *Hōkūleʻa*, have witnessed the magnanimity of the human spirit—the *Ubuntu* in all our hearts—that yearns to change the course of our planet.

This voyage of hope is an invitation to connect to our primal roots, as one people, living in peace on Mother Earth.

May the mission of *Hōkūleʻa* continue to swell from the hearts of those with whom she has connected and continue to inspire for many voyages to come.

- Archbishop Emeritus Desmond Tutu
Hermanus, South Africa

Introduction: *Mānaiakalani*, Bite the Hook

"Sometimes the Gods will send down a hook. And when you see it, bite it. Bite that hook as hard as you can so it will set, and you will find yourself being pulled up and then be amazed at what you will see..."

SO, WHERE DO I START? At the beginning, I suppose.

Forty years ago this past July, I boarded *Hōkūleʻa* for the first time. I was in my twenties, a Vietnam combat veteran, and a college student earning a living playing music nightly in a trio.

Then one summer day in 1975, I found myself at Hōnaunau on the island of Hawaiʻi. And, anchored in the bay just off of Hale o Keawe, at the City of Refuge, was the voyaging canoe *Hōkūleʻa*—together with its surroundings the canoe created a living mural from the past.

On the day that the canoe was to depart, *Hōkūleʻa*'s crew came to the shoreline—many dressed in *malo*, and wearing *lei* of maile and ti-leaf—the scene added to the visual that recalled another time, when we were "we."

I was standing on the rocky shoreline watching them with my friend Andrew, who paddled for the then newly formed Keōua Canoe Club, when *Hōkūleʻa*'s captain, whose name I later learned was Herb Kāne, approached and asked if we would help take the crew out.

"Shoot, of course," we said, and commenced to shuttle the crew from shore to vessel.

When all were aboard, including two *kūpuna* from the area, Aunty Clara Manisse and Papa Moses, they formed a circle at the stern, and bowed their heads as Aunty started to pray. Out of respect Andrew and I waited in our koa outrigger racer until they finished before heading back to shore.

"Amene ..."

At one point during their *pule*, a crewmember looked down at me from *Hōkūleʻa*'s deck as we sat alongside in the outrigger. When the prayer ended, he jumped down into the hull of the large canoe and said, "I think you belong on this boat."

Confused at first, I asked, "What?" And he held his hand out as if to invite me aboard and said again, "I think you belong on this boat."

I grasped his hand, he pulled me aboard, and I entered a whole new world of responsibility, enlightenment, and change. There occurred at that moment for me, a shift in the axis of time, and it was from that point on that I have existed in two worlds, with one foot planted in the past, and the other in the present.

An elder I know named Hale Makua, who has since passed, but who I continue to respect and admire, once said, "Sometimes the Gods will send down a hook. And

Billy Richards (at right above) has been involved with Hawai'i's voyaging community since 1975 (at left above) and has voyaged aboard Hōkūle'a, Hawai'iloa, Makali'i, *and* Hōkūalaka'i *throughout the Pacific. He is the president of The Friends of* Hōkūle'a *and* Hawai'iloa *and serves as cochair of* 'Ohana Wa'a, *a round-table collaborative of voyaging organizations from all of the Hawaiian Islands. Billy is also the director of communications for Partners in Development Foundation, a public not-for-profit company that serves the Native Hawaiian community through social and educational programs.*

when you see it, bite it. Bite that hook as hard as you can so it will set, and you will find yourself being pulled up and then be amazed at what you will see...."

Out of Africa

IT IS FORTY YEARS later, and my cell phone buzzes. I check the caller ID to see who it is—Nainoa Thompson. I smile a bit, because you can never reach Nainoa on his cell, but he can always reach you. I answer, "Hello?"

"Hey Billy, this is Nainoa. You wanna go to Africa?"

So I go, along with the other members of the Leg 15 crew, aboard a Hawaiian Airlines plane called *Heiheionākeiki*, the Hawaiian name for the constellation Orion. We are making our way to the island nation of Mauritius to rendezvous with *Hōkūle'a*—something that more than a few of us have been doing for three or four decades.

The crew consists of long-time veterans, next-generation voyagers, and a first-timer. They are both male and female, of all ages, from different backgrounds and locations, and all walks of life. But they have one thing in common. They all bit the hook.

– Billy Kahalepuna Richards

GALLERY I
Hawai'i to Aotearoa

Title page: *Hōkūle'a* departs O'ahu's North Shore for Kaua'i, Hawai'i.

Opposite: *Pwo* Navigator Nainoa Thompson remains *maka'ala*, ever alert, as the canoe sails through the reefs, shoals, and cays of the Great Barrier Reef, Australia.

Pages 14-15: Taievau Maraetaata drapes *lei* over the bow of *Hikianalia*—*Hōkūle'a*'s escort vessel for the first segments of the voyage—as part of the blessing ceremonies before leaving Hilo, Hawai'i.

Pages 16-17: It takes six miles of rope to lash *Hōkūle'a* together—*'iako* to hull, deck to *'iako*, *'iako* to braces.

Page 18: Kahua Mersberg, O'ahu, Hawai'i.

Page 19: Māori warrior at the *pōwhiri*, arrival ceremony, in Waitangi, Aotearoa.

Pages 20-21: Situated near the International Date Line, American Sāmoa is the last place where the sun sets each day, Tutuila, Sāmoa.

Pages 22-23: Oceanographer Kelley Anderson Tagarino carefully removes the highly poisonous crown-of-thorns starfish, which eat live coral tissue. The species thrive when there is a nutrient deficiency—most often due to warmer water temperatures and abundant pollution, Tutuila, Sāmoa.

Pages 24-25: The *hoe uli*, at twenty-two feet long and two hundred pounds, is equal to the task of executing the navigator's intentions.

Pages 26-27: Mount Taranaki, an active stratovolcano, rises above the clouds on the west coast of the North Island of Aotearoa.

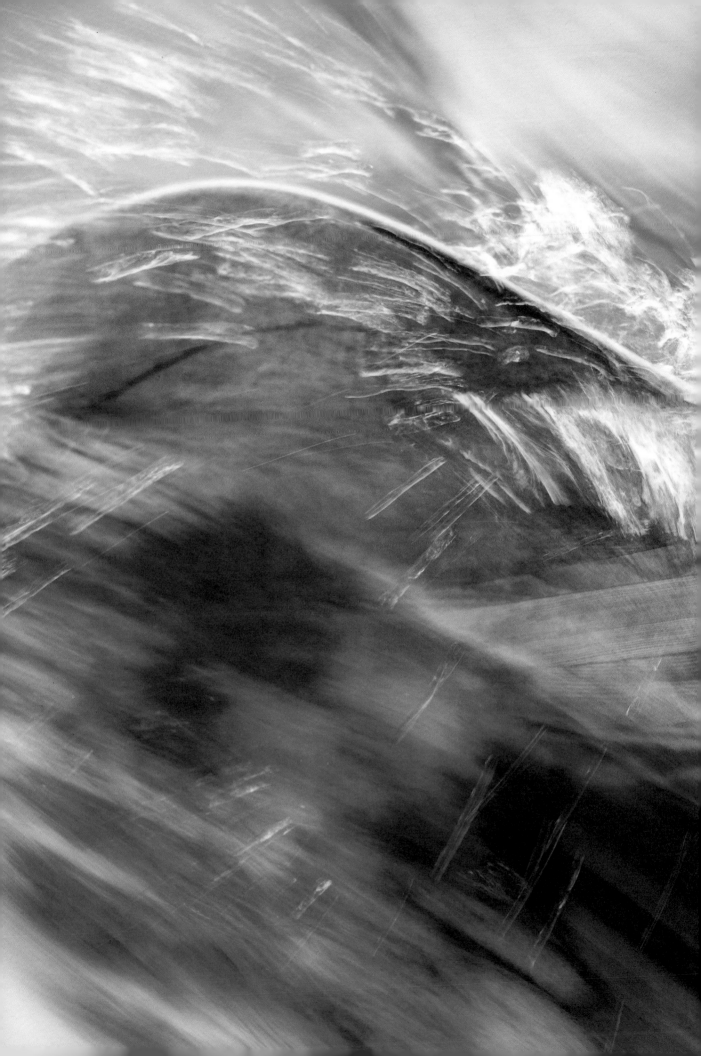

"On this voyage, Mālama Honua,
we recognize that this isn't just our cause.
This is everybody's cause—to take care
of planet Earth."

Bruce Mealoha Blankenfeld
Pwo Navigator and Captain

HAWAI'I

CHAPTER 1

E ola mau ʻo Hōkūleʻa
—
Long live *Hōkūleʻa*

THE WIND IS QUIET. THE WATERS, STILL. THE ONLY RIPPLES ARE those following children on paddleboards, making large, awestruck circles around the double-hulled sailing canoe, *Hōkūleʻa*. Lei maile drape the hulls. Ti-leaf garlands hang on the bow. Sails are wrapped and tied around the masts. In full wind, those sails will billow into a fifty-foot spray of crimson, the color of a Hawaiian king's feathered cloak.

Hōkūleʻa has been harbored here in Palekai, a spring-fed cove near Hilo for nearly a week now. Merchant ships, cargo containers, and petroleum tanks surround this lava-rock girded bay. *Hōkūleʻa* seems like an island unto herself, undaunted, anchored, awaiting the winds to sail.

It has been a big-sun day, with a sharp horizon, and no sight of clouds. Her captain is barefoot in blue jeans, adjusting the lines that swing the boom. His name is Charles Nainoa Thompson. He is known as Nainoa. Nainoa has been navigating *Hōkūleʻa* for thirty-five years now, more than half his lifetime.

"You do not tell the winds what to do," Nainoa has told his crew. "The winds tell you what to do."

Right now, the winds say, wait.

The wait has allowed many things. It has allowed locals to stream into Palekai, dawn to dusk, with offerings. Busloads of school children have come, gifting lei, candied ginger, and poi for the crew. Paddlers have come by outrigger, just to have a look, all sharing the venerable greeting of *honi* with captain and crew, touching forehead to forehead, nose to nose, breathing in the same breath, sharing *hā*, sharing spirit. A pastor presented a hand-sewn silk flag that reads, *Hae O Ke Aloha*—His Love Is The Banner Over Us—to wave alongside the flag of Hawaiʻi on the mast.

The Hawaiian flag has yet to be raised. It, too, awaits the winds.

The wait is teaching patience. Patience is key when you are about to launch on a three-year global voyage. First stop—Tahiti, two wind systems and 2,500 nautical miles away. In sailing to Tahiti, Nainoa will trace the same path Polynesians sailed centuries ago when they explored and settled the Hawiian Islands. Like his forefathers, Nainoa will rely on the wind, moon, swells, birds, fish, and stars as guides.

Using these traditional wayfinding skills, *Hōkūleʻa* will be sailed through and eventually beyond Polynesia, crossing the Indian and the Atlantic Oceans before returning home to the Pacific. Across the globe, the crew will connect with communities who protect our shared island, Earth. The mission is called Mālama Honua—to Care for the Earth.

Opposite: A *Hōkūleʻa* crewmember holds a *lei* of blessing, Hilo.

"Caring for the Earth is in the traditions of Hawaiian ancestors for the world to use," Nainoa says of his homelands. "*Hōkūleʻa* is the needle that collects the flowers that get sewn into a *lei* by Hawaiʻi and gives it to the Earth as an act of peace."

This act of peace continues to pour into Palekai even as the sun lowers over the mountains. The limping man with the koa-branch cane, the mother with the baby on her hip wrapped in a sarong, the fisherman steaming oysters, the farmer offering fresh kalo, the woman giving *lomilomi* massages ... they continue to come, paying respects to *Hōkūleʻa*, the *mana*, the spirit of the Islands. *Hōkūleʻa* is the Hawaiian name for Arcturus, the star that sits at the zenith above Hawaiʻi.

The fisherman opens the oysters and places them onto a tablecloth-covered card table. It is dinnertime, and another captain, this one named Bruce Mealoha Blankenfeld, has just now stepped ashore. Bruce shares *hā* with the fisherman before diving in, dousing his oysters with chili-lime sauce. He smiles, nods, eats. Island-born and ocean-bred, Bruce has the broad build of a long-distance paddler and the steady gaze of a man who has studied miles of horizons. His palms are wide, worn, and strong from years of building and restoring *Hōkūleʻa*. From the hulls to decks, crossbeams to booms, his hands have worked and sanded and seamed her into a watertight vessel.

Bruce will captain and navigate *Hikianalia*—just behind *Hōkūleʻa*—to Tahiti. *Hiki* is a hybrid canoe, half-tradition/half-modern, sailed in the ancient navigational way but with sixteen solar panels that can power motors. Hikianalia is the Hawaiian name for Spica, the star that rises alongside *Hōkūleʻa* in the Hawaiian skies.

In the low-lying sun, *Hikianalia* glides into Palekai. The crew is returning after practicing safety drills through the afternoon. Bruce watches as a crewmember tosses a line to Nainoa and his crew aboard *Hōkūleʻa*. They bind the canoes, side-by-side, like sisters together for the night.

There will be a *hilo*—a new moon—tonight. The skies will be dark, the stars, bright.

The wind remains unchangingly still.

"We just need a little bit of wind," Bruce says, with a knowing smile. "A bit of wind to give us a good push."

IF YOU ARE LOOKING for the Southern Cross, just ask Nainoa. North Star, Hōkūpaʻa; Sirius, ʻAʻā; or Procyon, Puana: all you have to do is ask. Nainoa can show you where these stars and hundreds more rest in the nighttime sky. He can show you how he measures their movements, using his palm like a sextant along the horizon. He has been "calibrating" his hand for many seasons now, long before he was married and the father of five-year-old twins, Naʻinoa and Puana. "I am old," he says. But he hardly seems so, with an agile grace that allows him to walk hands-free along the narrow safety rails, the *palekana*, of the canoe. For Nainoa, wayfinding has become a journey into his ancestral past.

"We must now sail in the wake of our ancestors—to find ourselves," Nainoa says, of the crossing to Tahiti.

Hōkūleʻa was originally built with the clear desire to help Hawaiians find their path. By the 1970s, the culture of sailing canoes had "been asleep," as Bruce likes to say, for over six hundred years.

But in 1973, three men founded the Polynesian Voyaging Society—artist and historian Herb Kawainui Kāne, expert waterman Tommy Holmes, and anthropologist Ben Finney. They wanted to prove that Polynesians were once master ocean navigators who purposely found and settled the Hawaiian Islands. They wanted to dispel the myth that Polynesians had happened onto Hawai'i by drifting aimlessly along currents. They wanted to resurrect navigational knowledge and to revive the culture that had been diluted by colonization. Hula was forbidden. Songs of the sea had been translated to suit tourists in Waikīkī. The native language was a whisper. When people lose their dance, songs, and language, they risk losing their history and narratives—a part of their collective soul. The Polynesian Voyaging Society wanted to help Hawaiians rediscover their strength, wisdom, and spirit.

The plan was to build a replica of a voyaging canoe and sail her across the trades to Tahiti. They researched the massive double-hulled sailing canoes of Eastern Polynesia, designed to transport several thousand pounds of people and goods. They looked to oral, written, and drawn historical records in Hawai'i—including petroglyphs—to study the shape of the canoe and its sails. From this, they built *Hōkūle'a*, a sixty-two-foot long *wa'a kaulua,* double-hulled voyaging canoe, using plywood, fiberglass, and resin, with twin masts, claw sails, no motor, a sweep as a rudder, and a twenty-foot broad deck, all held together by eight cross beams and five miles of lashings. But to make the passage authentic, they needed to sail without modern navigational instruments. They needed someone to lead them, someone who could, as Bruce explains, "pull us through the curtain of time" so that Hawaiians could relearn what had been known centuries ago.

Opening that curtain of time meant traveling to the coral atoll Satawal, in the Central Caroline Islands of Micronesia. There lived Pius 'Mau' Piailug, a master

Above: An outrigger takes supplies out to the *Hōkūle'a*
before the voyage to Tahiti in 1976.

navigator known as a *Pwo*. Only a handful of Micronesians still knew the art of way-finding, and none, other than Mau, were willing to share it outside their community.

Mau knew a navigational system that modern sailors had never before seen. It was something that Nainoa, then a twenty-three-year-old crewman, yearned to understand.

"If you can read the ocean," Mau would say, "you will never be lost."

Mau could read and discern eight separate patterns of ocean swells. Lying inside the hull, feeling the various waves hitting it, he could determine the direction of the winds and the direction to steer the canoe. At dawn, he would study the horizon and predict the weather for the day to come. At dusk, he would predict the weather for dawn. And in the midst of a gale-swept, stormy night, days away from any safe harbor or land, Mau could steady the mind of any novice navigator—he could look the man in the eye, and with an unflinching gaze, tell him, "You are the light, you have the light within you to guide your family home."

Some called it magic.

Bruce calls it being *maka'ala*—vigilant, observant, awake.

In May of 1976, Mau safely guided *Hōkūle'a* to Tahiti in thirty-one days. Upon entering the bay of Pape'ete, the canoe was greeted by more than 17,000 Tahitians, over half the population, welcoming her and her crew ... home.

Two years later, *Hōkūle'a* embarked on another voyage to Tahiti—but without Mau. Both Bruce and Nainoa were on board when she capsized in thirty-foot swells, only hours after her launch out of Ala Wai Harbor in Honolulu. Without an escort boat, the crew sat on upturned hulls from midnight to sunset the following day, lighting flares in hopes that ship or airplane captains might see them. One

Above: A photo of Eddie Aikau presides over the opening ceremony of the Eddie Aikau Big Wave Invitational contest at Waimea Bay, O'ahu.

crewmember, the legendary big-wave rider and lifeguard at Waimea Bay, Eddie Aikau, convinced Captain Dave Lyman to allow him to paddle on a surfboard to find help on Lāna'i, some fifteen nautical miles away. Nainoa can still see Eddie taking off his life vest in order to freely paddle into a wind so fierce that the salt from the waves was blinding.

The crew was eventually rescued. Eddie was never found.

Nainoa understood why Eddie wanted to voyage to Tahiti. Eddie's passion was not for his own glory but rather a reflection of his reverence for the past and his hope for the future. "Eddie had wanted to go to the land of his ancestors, to educate new generations, to bring dignity back to our *kūpuna*, our ancestors," Nainoa remembers.

Eddie's legacy is why the Polynesian Voyaging Society continues to sail today. Eddie is why Bruce volunteered to help rebuild the severely damaged canoe. Eddie is why Nainoa went to Satawal to ask Mau to teach him wayfinding.

Until a Hawaiian could sail *Hōkūle'a*, the quest would not be fulfilled. Nainoa needed to learn the ancient skills of Oceania and then share this knowledge with future generations.

Mau knew that a *Pwo* must pass the wisdom on. He also knew that wayfinding was on the verge of disappearing in his own islands. Mau then asked his own teacher, his grandfather, for permission to share these lessons. His grandfather agreed, reminding Mau that the Hawaiians were, after all, part of the Polynesian family.

Positioning stones, shells, and palm fronds in the sand, Mau recreated a star compass for Nainoa. Mau taught him how to identify the stars as they rose up out of the ocean and then dove back in. Mau showed him how to decipher wind systems, how to understand sea birds flying to and away from land, how to interpret clouds. Mau taught him how to study the shape of the ocean and read the "character" in the waves. Mau taught him how to distinguish the varying widths and hues of the sun's path along the waves. Mau was teaching him the language of the navigator—what Mau called the "talk of the sea."

Just as the Hawaiian god Māui is said to have fished the Hawaiian Islands out of the ocean, Nainoa would now need to pull Tahiti out of the sea.

In *An Ocean in Mind*, author Will Kyselka renders the multilayered teachings of Mau and their limitless affect on his student, Nainoa.

"Can you point out the way to Tahiti?" Mau asked Nainoa during the last lesson of his two years of study.

The teacher and student were observing the sky at Lāna'i lookout, a coastal perch on the southeastern shore of O'ahu. Nainoa pointed to the direction of Tahiti.

Then Mau asked another question, one that required a deeper knowing.

"Can you see the island?"

Nainoa could not literally see the island but he could, he told his teacher, see "an image of the island in my mind."

"Good. Keep the island in your mind," Mau told him, "otherwise you will be lost."

"See the vision of the island rising from the sea," Mau would often remind Nainoa. "If you don't have a vision, you will be lost."

In 1980, with Mau on board, Nainoa safely navigated *Hōkūle'a* to Tahiti. In doing so, Nainoa became the first Hawaiian to make a noninstrument passage from Hawai'i to Tahiti since the fourteenth century.

Since then, *Hōkūle'a* has become the heart of the Hawaiian renaissance and, in the last forty years, she has sailed over 140,000 nautical miles across the vast Pacific, igniting a revival of sailing canoes throughout Polynesia, and igniting a voyaging revival that now includes twenty-eight *wa'a kaulua*, voyaging canoes.

None of this would have been possible without the guidance of Mau. As a gesture of gratitude, Nā Kālai Wa'a, the group responsible for Hawaiian Island voyaging, built him a deep-sea voyaging canoe, launched in 2007. Mau named his canoe *Alingano Maisu. Alingano maisu* is the wind that blows the breadfruit out of the tree, providing an offering the people can freely enjoy. Otherwise, people are only allowed to eat the fruit under the sole permission of the island chief. Mau named the canoe this, because he saw the *wa'a* as a blessing bestowed upon all the people of Satawal. With crews from Hawai'i, Nainoa and Bruce traded navigating *Hōkūle'a*, and Chad Kālepa Baybayan and Chadd 'Ōnohi Paishon navigated *Maisu*, both *wa'a* sailing together to Satawal. Mau then honored them with a ceremony inducting five Hawaiians into the *Pwo*. The five Hawaiian *Pwo* are Nainoa, Bruce, Kālepa, 'Ōnohi, and Shorty Bertelmann.

"*Pwo* is a model for living," says Kālepa. "It is not only about wayfinding at sea, it is also about being a leader and a steward within a community." To be *Pwo* is to be deeply connected to all living things—birds, animals, fish, oceans, air, earth, and all mankind. "Mau's greatest lesson," Kālepa says, "is that we are a single people," realizing the global *'ohana*—global family—is a key element in the Worldwide Voyage. Kālepa has been sailing *Hōkūle'a* since he was nineteen years old. He's now passing the knowledge on to his daughter, Kalā, a crewmember aboard *Hikianalia* for the voyage to Tahiti.

"*Pwo* is a way to take care of the Earth," Kālepa explains.

Taking care of the Earth is why Kālepa has committed his life to this canoe, and why you can find him on her decks at Palekai, teaching the next generation of navigators how to listen to the talk of the sea.

THE CLOUDS HAVE COME, lowering the sky. With them, a soft breeze blows, like a whisper over a bare shoulder.

Today was the day the canoes were scheduled to launch out of Hilo. But that date was set by man many moons ago.

Nainoa has let everyone here know that the canoes will not be sailing today, or tomorrow, or the day after.

When someone suggests that the winds are "bad" for sailing, Nainoa is quick to correct. "The winds are never bad," he says. "The winds are allowing us time." The time to "deepen your understanding of why [you are] going on this voyage," Nainoa explains. "The winds are allowing *you* that time."

When Nainoa says *you*, you feel he means everyone gathered here at Palekai is being allowed this time to deepen the understanding. Bruce has echoed this to the hundreds who have come to bear witness to the sacred blessings of crew and canoes.

The ritual began in the starlit dawn, with the crew wading in the warm, shallow waters of Moku Ola, a small, sheltered island known as the "healing island" where King Kamehameha would go to be cleansed, strengthened, and healed before and after his battles. There, the crew shared and drank the medicinal *'awa*.

The crew marked their bodies with turmeric and octopus ink. They listened to the complete genealogy of *Hōkūle'a*, an incantation of all the places she has ever sailed. They then sailed to Palekai where they received a procession of the Royal Order of King Kamehameha I, Native Hawaiians, with royal red velvet capes, who sang a hallowed song as they bowed, offering garlands for protection to the *Pwo*.

"Now is the time, ultimately, to be very clear about who you serve," Nainoa explains.

His wife, Kathy, and their children, Na'inoa and Puana, wait nearby. It is clear they all know what is coming—the embrace that will become the beginnings of a

long farewell. Now that the rituals are complete, these are the last moments before the crew and canoes enter *kapu*, when the crew withdraws into a more meditative state in preparation for departure.

For crewmember Noelani Kamalu, *kapu* will be reflecting on the first time she saw *Hōkūle'a*, when she was just in middle school, and how she knew, even then, that she wanted to someday sail the canoe. For her crewmate Kaleo Wong, *kapu* will involve collecting water from Lake Waiau, atop Mauna Kea, to eventually share with the equator, *Ka Piko o Wākea*. For Nainoa, *kapu* is "a time to be with those who matter the most—primarily, family. You need to take that time. If you don't, you're foolish as a leader."

"I am by nature a very private person," he says. "*Kapu* is my final preparation to rebuild strength that was taken away by all the things we had to do to get here today."

When Nainoa says "we," he means everyone who has helped the voyage prepare for this day. To get here today involved hundreds of hands, hearts, and minds committed to the Worldwide Voyage. There were those who sailed *Hōkūle'a* and *Hikianalia* 12,000 nautical miles among all the Hawaiian Islands and the Pacific; those who trained and tested crewmembers; those who worked on land to help to raise over a million dollars to fund the voyage; those who worked in the dry-dock— sanding, lashing, and varnishing *Hōkūle'a*; those who masterminded a viable sail

Above left: *Pwo* Navigator Bruce Blankenfeld receives *makana* from the Royal Order of King Kamehameha I before beginning the Worldwide Voyage, Hilo.

Above right: *Keiki hānau o ka 'āina*, a native son, pauses on the bow of a paddling canoe, Hilo.

plan that will connect environmentalists around the globe; and those who reached out to ocean communities in the many ports that will warmly welcome the *wa'a*. In his own humble way, Nainoa feels a deep responsibility to all these people who have served and helped prepare *Hōkūle'a* for this day.

"I cannot find that strength unless I go to places that I trust, places that allow me to find who I am," Nainoa explains. "In doing so, that's how you get strong—and that's how you lead." That place of trust comes in the time he shares alone with his family.

Last winter, he told his wife that he was not sure if he should leave his family to sail to Tahiti. He thought his wife would be pleased with his decision, after all, he was choosing his family over *Hōkūle'a*. But her reaction was far from what he had expected.

"Are you kidding? You have to go!" she told him. "The crew needs you!"

"Nainoa is an ocean man, a fisherman, a teacher, a navigator, a captain," she says. "All the planning for this voyage has kept him on land."

One of his favorite places on land is Mauna Kea. And so, during *kapu*, Nainoa took his family there.

"Mauna Kea and Mauna Loa are dear to Nainoa," Kathy explains of the two volcanic mountains that shape the Island of Hawai'i. "They are the first things he sees when he is sailing home from Tahiti."

"It is such a sacred place, so peaceful, so raw," she says. It was their children's first time to the volcano. The walk was long. Puana rode on her father's shoulders as they hiked past steam vents in the lava-bedded earth.

Reaching a high plateau, they could see the ocean below. Nainoa stretched out his palm to show his children the way of "measuring the heavens."

"I think for a little while we were in heaven," Kathy says of the family's time together that day, so private, so uninterrupted, so *kapu*.

Seeing him with their children reminded her of when their children were babies. They were restless sleepers, and Nainoa would carry them outside and calm them by reading them the stars across the nighttime sky.

Puana is named after a star. She can show you which one is hers in the sky. Puana, the star, rises just ahead of the sun. You can see Puana at dawn off of Cape Kumukahi, the first place Hawaiians welcome the sunrise, the last spot of land *Hōkūle'a* will see when she launches to Tahiti. The voyage needs to begin from a place that symbolizes light, Nainoa has said, and this light will help find the way.

"Finding a way" is one of his son's favorite expressions. When young Na'inoa meets a problem, a maze, a puzzle, he is patient to find its solution and often talks about "finding a way."

Kathy says Na'inoa is much like his father. She once found Na'inoa in the backyard, staring up at the sky or maybe the trees or maybe even the clouds.

When she asked him, "What are you looking at, Na'inoa?" he replied, "The wind."

THE FLAG OF HAWAI'I has been raised on the mast. The winds are here, sending waves through the flag, and shivers across the waters of Palekai.

The rains have passed. The sun is breaking through the clouds.

Opposite top: The hot spot that created the Hawaiian chain is still active at Kīlauea.

Opposite middle: The Royal Order of King Kamehameha I honors the legacy of King Kamehameha, who united the Hawaiian islands, Hilo.

Opposite bottom: Tava Kahalioumi bears witness to both his future and his past, Hilo.

A conch shell is blown, calling all to come, come now. Sol Aikau, Eddie's brother, has come. All *Pwo* have come. All families have come, too.

It is time.

Hundreds line the rocks of the bay and, even more, the shores, where crates of fruits and vegetables are being passed, arm-to-arm, in a long line to the crew making its final load onto the canoes.

"The crew is good," Bruce says to a local reporter. "They've asked all their questions, all their concerns. We told them this is what it's all about. This is an expedition. An adventure. By its very nature, there's supposed to be some unknown around every corner."

"We are just conduits," a crewmember says. She wears a ti-leaf garland, like a halo, around her head. "All of Hawai'i is sailing with us."

On the shore, Nainoa's wife, Kathy, weeps. She cannot help herself. She remembers the first time she saw Nainoa standing on the deck of *Hōkūle'a* and how it was the most beautiful vision she had ever seen. She is overwhelmed, she says, by it all. "The incredible embrace of love from the community for *Hōkūle'a*, *Hikianalia*, Nainoa, and all the crewmembers."

Nearby stands Nainoa's sister, Lita, wiping her eyes. Lita is Bruce's wife. She has organized the purchasing and packing of all the provisions for the long leg ahead.

A small dinghy carries the last of the crew to the canoes.

Someone calls out, "Enjoy the ride!"

Someone else calls, "A *hui hou!*"

IN THE COMING DAYS, *the apprentice navigators will practice, alongside Nainoa and Bruce, guiding the canoes the ancient way.*

The canoes will be hit by relentless squalls.

There will be shouts of "All hands on deck!"

There will be seasickness.

They will learn, as crewmember Noelani says, the things that teach you where you came from, what you're made of, and who you are.

They will speed through the usually stagnant doldrums.

They will drop sails at the equator, Ka Piko o Wākea. *Here, in the place known as* Ka Houpo o Kāne, *the diaphragm of the ocean god Kāne, they will pour the waters of Mauna Kea in an act of reverence and pure gratitude.*

And they will reach Tahiti in record time—just seventeen days.

But none can see this far into the future. Not even Pwo.

As *Hikianalia* heads out of Palekai, Nainoa gathers the crew into a circle on *Hōkūle'a's* deck. All hold hands.

On the shore, his wife pulls their children close.

"Take them with you, take your family with you," Nainoa begins in an open prayer. "Take everybody with you. Be strong!"

Nainoa motions the crew to begin moving the sweep to turn the canoe away from shore.

The *pū* are blown, the sound is steady and strong. You can hear them long after the canoes have left the bay, long after you can no longer see *Hōkūle'a*, only her sails, unfurled, freed in the breath of the winds.

Opposite: Kimo Piihana watches over the waters bearing *Hōkūle'a*, Hilo.

——

Local Voices
Kawika Lewis
Organic Farmer

In the days before the launch of Hōkūleʻa, you could find Kawika Lewis wading in the waters of Palekai. Kawika was offering produce from his farm for the upcoming leg to Tahiti. His farm is a modest one: a nine-acre slip of land carved through a former sugar plantation in the Pāhoehoe Valley near Hilo. Kawika is living what Hawaiians call ke ala pono—*the right path. It's the path of Mālama Honua, and the longer you spend in Hilo, the more you see the depth of this path running through those who live close to the land. Kawika hopes that his farm will someday be an educational facility where kids can learn the "simple Hawaiian life," how to farm in a more sustainable, Hawaiian way. Navigators listen to the "talk of the sea." Farmers listen to the "talk of the land." Kawika is one great listener.*

In His Own Words

THE NAME OF OUR PLACE IS 'ĀINA UNIVERSITY. 'ĀINA refers to our land. Here, the land teaches you what to do.

I have the Hawaiian blood, and I am putting my spirit in it. Farming is work from inside your soul. If you look at it as hard work, you're off to a bad start. You got to have love. That's why you have to have *aloha 'āina*—love for the land—so that the land can love you back. That's what it's doing right now; it's loving us back.

What happens on land affects the ocean. Whatever happens in the ocean affects the land. We're talking interconnectedness. And there's the spiritual connection, too. It's not two separate entities; it's one—a symbiotic relationship. This is what I am trying to teach the kids.

This is simple, very simple.

Here, come see what we have ...

We have coconut leaves for weaving, for cooking, even for making lashings for a canoe. We have ginger, kalo, black sugar cane, chili pepper, 'awa plant, lemongrass. Lemongrass is good for teas and calming the system. *Mai'a*—bananas—some for cooking, some for snacking, and then the apple banana for dessert. Ti leaves—we use for wrapping and to make *hula* skirts. Wild jasmine, ginger, coconuts, *kukui* nuts—we use them for oils and to mix with salt for shrimp—strawberry guava, tulip, papayas, elephant grass.

In Hawai'i, the plants represent the parents. The stalk is the parents, and the leaves are the kids around the parents. If the parent is good, the kid will be good.

Of course, we had to clear all this land when we got here. You couldn't just plant right into it. We didn't use machines. We used our hands, shovels, and, of course, our pigs. We have two pigs here. One's hiding—Bacon, he's shy. This land was all covered with trees. But the pigs, they broke it down for us. They dug it up for us. We don't need motors or plows or have to spray any pesticide. The pigs do it for us. They like the sugar cane so we just break it off and throw it in their pens. We use recycled products for our pens—the wood is from the trees, and the wires are all recycled.

And we do all our trimmings inside their pens because the pigs like the wood, too. Wood has absorption power and gives shade for them. It minimizes us buying posts too, because we're going to move the fence eventually, once the pigs have cleared through this area. We're minimizing petroleum usage by letting the pigs help us.

Everything we do has a reason here.

And here, this here is the *koa* tree. It's just a sapling. We love koa and its significance of strength. Hawaiians used koa to make voyaging canoes. It's just a sapling now. But maybe one day, it will be my great, great, great grandson's canoe!

In the Hawaiian way, you plant for the future. Whatever you do, it's for the future; it's not for today.

Everything takes a while. It doesn't happen overnight. That's the Hawaiian way too.

Patience. Patience is really a virtue for us, truly. Giving up is not an option.

When our *kūpuna* (ancestors) made the fish hooks, the question was "How is my grandson going to use this when he's ready?"

That's the thinking. It's real generational. It's really about doing things properly.

We call this the simple Hawaiian life. That's what we're doing. We're living the simple Hawaiian life.

Above: The pig named Bacon doing his part on Kawika's farm.

Next spread: Lava on the Big Island where Pele is reclaiming her land.

Charles Nainoa Thompson

Pwo *Navigator*

Nainoa Thompson is the first Native Hawaiian since the fourteenth century to navigate without modern instruments from Hawaiʻi to Tahiti. Inspired by his kūpuna, his teachers, Nainoa has dedicated his life to studying the deep meaning of voyaging. Nainoa is the recipient of numerous awards, including the NOAA National Marine Sanctuary Foundation Lifetime Achievement Award, the National Geographic Society's Hubbard Medal, and the Unsung Hero of Compassion, awarded to him by His Holiness XIV Dalai Lama. He is the president of the Polynesian Voyaging Society, a position his father, Myron 'Pinky' Thompson held before him. Pinky was an educator, a social worker, and a leader in the Hawaiian cultural renaissance. Nainoa reflected on his father's continuing influence on the Worldwide Voyage, while sitting on the porch of his childhood home in Niu Valley where his family has remained rooted for seven generations.

I DON'T KNOW HOW I separate who I am from who my father was. He, of all the people in my life, is my greatest navigator. And so, this voyage that we're taking around the world is all about him and what he stood for and what he believed.

He believed that the well-being of his people depended on the well-being of its culture and its first peoples. He believed that pride and dignity equates to someone feeling good about himself. From that point of view, if you don't feel good about yourself, you're not going to take care of yourself. It's so simple, right?

When you have a race of people that believes, from one generation to the next, that you are second rate and that your identity is not a strong one or one that you should be proud of, then all the negative statistics start to make sense. My dad understood the dilemma of Native Hawaiians in a very deep way.

Readers need to understand that this is not my generation's voyage. There was a generation that had already planned and mapped it out. It had all been laid out. Myron 'Pinky' Thompson and Herb Kāne and Eddie Aikau and Mau Piailug and Lacy Veach, these men set the instructions for us. It was just a matter of us finding the courage to execute them. It's a dangerous thing to do. You need to make sure that the purpose, the reasons for going, outweighs the risk.

So let's go back to when *Hōkūleʻa* was changing everything, changing worldview, changing cultural integrity, changing how we see our history, changing it from being aimless to being the greatest navigators on Earth.

But then, when we lost Eddie, the leadership of the voyaging canoe was crushed. Losing Eddie, when I look back at that, all I see is shame. I was absolutely broken. I would go to the ocean— everything in my life has always been directed there. It was a spiritual place for me. The ocean is its own language. I just wanted to become fluent in that language. I wanted to go to a place that was quiet, that was peaceful, that was private.

At that time, there were suggestions to put the canoe in the Bishop Museum so nobody could get hurt. It was a rough time. It was a time when you needed someone to come in and take all that pain and redirect it into a positive place and drive it in the right direction, and that was my dad.

For the first meeting after we lost Eddie, he pulled all the leadership together in a room in a building at the university. We couldn't even talk to each other. We weren't brothers, we weren't even friends. We were just so traumatized. It's almost as if, *"If I feel so junk about who I am, how in the world can I be a friend to anybody?"*

Above: Nainoa presents Archbishop Emeritus Desmond Tutu with a peace quilt, painted and woven by children of Hawaiʻi.

Hōkūleʻa really was the starlight of hope for our people at the time, but it was becoming so cloudy that you couldn't see the light anymore. Essentially, that was it. You couldn't see the light.

That's when my father stepped in, in front of everybody. He didn't care who was in charge. All he knew was this canoe needs to go to Tahiti. But it needs to go the right way. That's when he first said to us, "You need to earn the voyage."

For him, it was about how many generations are you going to set back the healing of the Hawaiian people because *Hōkūleʻa*'s legacy would be one of tragedy? And that was expected by the larger society because it was Hawaiian—essentially, society expected Hawaiians to fail. So he put all these pieces together, connecting them and centering them on all children. He wanted that child to be able to look up and say, "Wow, there's a star up there that is worth following, there's a light up there that is of goodness, and I'm part of that light."

In his mind, *Hōkūleʻa* was that light, and *Hōkūleʻa* had to sail again.

My father was so masterful. He knew that you had to have a clear vision. You had to have a purpose. You had to have a set of values—goodness and caring—to navigate by. You had to have the community behind you and give them something worthwhile to follow. You have to train for success. You just don't take off and go.

He said 95 percent of the success of this voyage is going to be done in the training. He said, "You guys get together and you train, and you give me the training schedule and I'm going to hold you to that schedule. Don't talk about departure dates. You need to earn it."

You had to earn your right to go and that permission was in the training. But *not going* was *not* an option.

After the meeting, my father mapped out our homework. He figured it all out. All those things he talked about, we use today. The values, the principles, and the way that we conduct ourselves are reflected in how we train the crews today. If the attitude of the crews was not respectful and they didn't ask permission, this voyage wouldn't work.

So Mālama Honua, at the bottom line, could be defined as a whole set of values of caring, caring for each other and caring for the Earth. To me, it's about taking responsibility. It's about being a responsible citizen. It's about acting. When are you going to act?

Taking action is an honor. It's a privilege that you can do something for the Earth. It's a joyous responsibility. If we make any difference, if we make any impact on Hawaiʻi and the Earth, that is the kind of joy that I seek in my life.

The question is this. The question is whether you're willing to go.

Now if you ask my teachers, Would Mau go? Yeah. Would Eddie go? Yeah. Would Herb Kāne support the decision? Absolutely. And would my father be there to make sure we would do it right? Yes. Because he is. He's with this voyage all the way.

Opposite: Nainoa steering the *waʻa*.

"One piece of insight that I gained on the voyage was the idea that navigating is not always about steering the canoe in a particular direction. Sometimes, it's just keeping track of where she'll take you. I would attribute the record speed of the voyage from Hilo to Tahiti to the fact that we spent very little time steering on the sweep and just tried to keep *Hōkūleʻa* pointing as high into the wind as we could. Regardless of our own desires to point higher, *Hōkūleʻa* was only going to do so much. Navigating was, to a large degree, simply keeping track of what the canoe was doing and the track that she was taking us on."

Noelani Kamalu
Apprentice Navigator

AMERICAN SĀMOA

Sā'ili matagi

—

Seeking a better future through voyaging

THE SUN HAS BROKEN THROUGH THE EVER-CHANGING CLOUDS. Some offer shade, others, rain.

Sun and clouds drift in and out as gracefully as the words do here on the island of Tutuila, where Sāmoan flows into English in one fluid breath. Few speak as fluidly as the young crewmember who stands, children gathered around his feet, listening to how he was a child, just like them, when he first learned about *Hōkūle'a*.

"I was just a young boy who had a vision," Rex Lokeni explains to the grade-school children. "This voyage has connected me back to my roots, and my calling, as a Sāmoan boy."

Alongside Rex stand his crewmates. Teachers lean in the doorway, listening. An elder has also come to listen.

Rex says this vision was stirred by a story once shared with him by those who were here when *Hōkūle'a* first ventured into these waters a generation ago, those who paddled their canoes out to *Hōkūle'a* and escorted the *wa'a* carefully through the shallow, reef-filled cove to the shore.

"All the village folks were incredibly happy to see *Hōkūle'a*," Rex says, greeting her as if she were a distant relative who had traveled thousands of miles and was now safely home.

After hearing the story, Rex had a dream that he would someday sail *Hōkūle'a* and learn the ancient way of navigating to share it with the people of Sāmoa.

"Maybe one day you, too, will sail on *Hōkūle'a*," he tells the children. The children listen, attentive and still, a few with knees held tight to their chests.

Like many here, Rex grew up living *fa'asāmoa*—the Sāmoan way—in an extended family of aunts and uncles, grandmothers and grandfathers. Often, the village elders helped teach the children the time-honored ways of living. Rex recalls the elder who carved canoes, the man who intimately knew the shape and depth of the reefs, the patterns in the currents, the way the tides were linked to cycles of the moon. This was the man who only caught what was needed, never taking more, Rex says, the man was responsible for watching over the fishing practices of the entire village. If an area was depleted, he could declare it *sā*—sacred—and off limits. To Rex, sustainability is not a modern concept. It is a traditional Sāmoan practice.

When Sāmoans first settled these islands, their main source of food came from the ocean. But Rex says this connection has been lost. Many Sāmoan children do not even know how to swim. Living on an island, surrounded by water, the fear of drowning can be engulfing. Rex tells of his own fear when he first learned to

Opposite: The village of 'Amanave is nestled between the rain forest and the Pacific Ocean on the island of Tutuila.

swim—his uncle taking him on a long paddle beyond the reefs and forcing young Rex to jump out of the canoe. The uncle then paddled ashore and left Rex treading water; the lesson being, swim or sink. That day, Rex says, he learned to "relax," to float and drift with the waves. It was then that he "became one with the ocean."

"We are all connected to the ocean," Rex reminds us, "wherever you go in the world, you are still connected by this ocean."

A prime task of Mālama Honua is precisely what Rex is doing now: inspiring and educating the future stewards of our planet. Rex is an integral part of a crew that has been journeying throughout Sāmoa for over a month now. In a few days, a new team will come in to sail toward the Kingdom of Tonga. His final days as crew are committed to reaching as many children as possible.

The Sāmoan voyaging word for ocean is *vasa*—sacred space—*vā*, meaning a space, and *sā*, meaning sacred. The ocean is viewed as a holy entity that joins all the Pacific Islands and Pacific Islanders. It is from this understanding that Mālama Honua speaks to the children here.

Some are just now learning that plastic is not biodegradable, that plastics tossed in the rainforest eventually end up in the ocean and then in the fish and finally in us. Others are learning that there is no shame in picking up someone else's trash. Yet others are learning that caring for the Earth begins with caring for your own self. Not littering your body with junk food is a way of taking care of yourself, a crewmember explains.

The logic evolves from there. If you can take care of you, you can take care of others, like your family, your home, your ocean, and your Earth.

"The same values we have on land are the same values we take on the *wa'a*," Rex explains to the children.

"One *'ohana*, one *'āina*," he explains in Hawaiian.

The Hawaiian and Sāmoan languages are so similar, he needn't provide the children with the translation. But after a pause, he does, as if to emphasize the connectedness of the languages of the Pacific.

"One family, one Earth."

Rex pauses to allow it all to sink in. Soon, hands shoot up. The questions come in waves.

"How do you go to the bathroom on the canoe?" one child asks.

"How do you find your way without a compass?" another one asks.

"Where do you sleep?" someone else wants to know.

Rex slept in the hulls, he says. At night, he felt like *Hōkūle'a* was his mother, rocking him to sleep. He slept so peacefully on *Hōkūle'a*. Once home, on land, he couldn't sleep.

"*Hōkūle'a* is like our mother, she takes care of us," he says. "We need to take care of her, too. *Hōkūle'a* is like our Mother Earth."

Life on the canoe is much like life on land. While at sea the canoe is home, providing shelter and resources for living. Each crewmember must abide by the canoe's limited reserves. Like the canoe, the Earth provides for us, too. If anyone is slack in their commitment to caring for our environment or is greedy in their desire to take more than they need, the Earth, and its people, will suffer. In this way, life on *Hōkūle'a* teaches the need to take care of each other, and the world around us. The

Opposite: Water jugs ready to be stowed aboard *Hiki-analia* and *Hōkūle'a*. Each crewmember is allowed one gallon per day for all their needs, Pago Pago Harbor.

Mālama Honua Voyage is based on these truths—that we need to live like we are sailing on one canoe together.

A rooster crows. The clouds shift in. The rain resumes.

It is time to sing a song of thanks. Singing is a clear way to express your gratitude in Sāmoa. The children stand and sway as they sing a thank-you song. The crew is clearly moved, and then they hold hands to sing a song of gratitude in Hawaiian.

Hōkūleʻa will be sailing for another three years, until 2017, a crewmember tells the kids.

"How old will you be in 2017?" Rex asks, before leaving to visit another school. "Who will be willing to carry on the message of Mālama Honua?"

IN SĀMOAN, *MĀLAMA HONUA*, to care for the Earth, can be expressed as *mālamalama e fanua*, to understand the Earth. Sāmoans believe that in order to care for the Earth, you must first understand your land, and from this understanding comes compassion, empathy, and love. This belief unites the entire archipelago of Sāmoa—American Sāmoa, including five islands and two coral atolls, and the Independent State of Sāmoa which includes two islands. Situated on the Pacific Ring of Fire, where tectonic plates converge, these volcanic islands rose up from the ocean floor over a million years ago. By the late nineteenth century, American Sāmoa and Sāmoa were divided politically by colonial actions. The two countries are also separated by the International Date Line—making Sāmoa the first place where the sun rises, and American Sāmoa the last place where the sun sets each day on Earth.

The American Sāmoan island of Tutuila is covered by a lush, healthy rainforest. Trees and plants and ferns have thrived here for hundreds of thousands of years. A third of this vegetation is found only in Sāmoa. Most plants arrived in the wind or on ocean currents or in the stomach of birds. The call of the white-collared kingfisher, a bird whose song foretells the coming of rain, can be heard throughout the rainforest.

One-level homes prevail throughout the coastal valleys and lowlands. Village *fales*, open-air gathering platforms with domed leaf-thatched roofs, seem designed to endure all possible acts of nature—earthquakes, cyclones, hurricanes, and tsunamis. But in 2009, an 8.1 earthquake shook here. The ensuing series of tsunamis upturned an oil rig, spit out villages, leveled palm trees, tossed cars into Pago Pago Harbor, and left over a hundred dead across both the Independent State of Sāmoa and American Sāmoa. Since then, tsunami-zone warning signs have been mounted and are prominent along the coastline where the only escape route may very well be a steep climb up a mountain's basaltic slope.

More than 90 percent of the land here is communally owned and governed by the indigenous *faʻamatai* system. The *faʻamatai* head large, extended descent tribes and act as a trustee for the communally held lands. In this system you build and live where your ancestors once did and where they now rest. Your grandparents and great-grandparents are buried in the front yard; their headstones are placed prominently, greeting visitors at the doorstep. This allows your ancestor to watch over you and the familial land. At birth, your umbilical cord is buried in the backyard, so that even if you move away, you will be forever bound to this soil.

"Our land is probably the most valuable asset of our people," explains American Sāmoa Park Ranger Pua Tuaua. Along with a team of rangers and marine biologists,

Pua is responsible for overseeing and managing 2,500 acres of rainforest and 1,200 acres of beach, ocean, and coral ecosystems across American Sāmoa. No small task.

The park is the only US National Park south of the equator. In American Sāmoa the United States leases the parkland from the village *matai*. Back in 1993, when the US government tried to buy the land, the *matai* said, "Our land is not for sale." Since Sāmoan custom forbids the selling of land, the final decision to lease the land was based on a collective vote by the village council. The rental income is then distributed to all the constituents of the village. The National Park Service is fully committed to preserve and protect this valuable asset.

You can see the efforts of the National Park Service and the Environmental Protection Agency along the rocky, winding shoreline where hand-painted signs read:

STOP LITTERING
REPORT VIOLATORS TO THE
AMERICAN SĀMOA EPA
KEEP AMERICAN SĀMOA BEAUTIFUL

"Littering is one of our main problems right now," Pua says. "Litter. It's a major, major, major concern right now."

Pua is beginning his day in the park ranger's office in downtown Pago Pago. Pua's office overlooks Pago Pago Harbor, a deeply protected bay with a shoreline that winds and wraps five miles into the center of the island. On one side of the harbor, you can find the governor's mansion, on the other, Mauga Pioa (Rainmaker Mountain). Along the docks, you will find crowds of fishing boats: Pago Pago is the most valuable commercial fishing port in the South Pacific bearing the US flag.

"In the old days, we didn't have plastics," Pua says. "Now, plastics are everywhere."

Plastic is the prime invasive species throughout the harbor and the thoroughfares of this island. A soda bottle on the side of the street, a plastic bag wrapping your ankle in a swim, a cup on your hike through the community college medicinal garden. You need only drive away from the busier roadways to see how trash pickup is a daily Sāmoan practice in the family grounds. In more remote areas, away from the center of Pago Pago, you can see how the rainforest, lowlands, and beaches still flourish, untouched, and seemingly unreal.

"We understand it's a bit arduous to change the habits of the people, but we will never give up," says Rex's sister, Tumau Lokeni, who works within the EPA. "We will continue to tell them that this land is God's gift to us, and we have to take care of it. There's nobody else we can depend on to take care of it but us. That's our job. That's our responsibility."

People used to weave a *laufola*, a bowl, out of leaves or fashion a cup out of a coconut shell. You could take these anywhere, to the beach or to the forest, and leave them on the land or in the sea, as they would naturally biodegrade.

"But it's plastic now," Pua says, that folks just toss out, not realizing it will never biodegrade.

Plastic, aluminum, Styrofoam—it all comes in through the harbor's main shipping yard. Ship containers, ten stories deep and four stories high, are stacked in the yard. An estimated 1,000 containers come into this harbor every month, providing the island with 90 percent of its food and supplies. This is a concern to a man who grew up as a fisherman, a hunter, and a farmer who harvested taro, bananas, and breadfruit. This is a man who used to spearfish in the harbor, but who now has to venture out of the harbor and to the outer reefs to find any fish at all. This is a man who used to hunt wild pig in the rainforest. This is a man who in the mere fifty-year span of his life has witnessed the shift from a relatively independent sustainable existence to a highly dependent unsustainable lifestyle.

"My family was poor," Pua explains. "We didn't have a refrigerator, so we would only fish for what we could eat now." Fishing and hunting and farming are survival skills no longer required of children. "Today, everybody's going shopping at the store."

"The rainforest, that's where the Sāmoans used to turn to a long, long time ago," he tells me. "Now, today, McDonald's is here."

The McDonald's golden arches drive-thru sign is written in Sāmoan. *Talofa*, it reads, welcome.

"All the kids say, McDonald's! I want to go to McDonald's!" but Pua offers another option. "Let's go in the forest. Let's go back to the land."

To guide children back to the land, Pua wants to teach them how to pick a coconut, how to weave a basket, how to catch a fish. Pua is hoping to teach them how to be independent of imported goods. He's encouraging them to pick up trash, even if that means you need to walk a few blocks with the trash in your hands until you find the nearest trashcan.

No recycling yet exists on this island. If you want to recycle, you need to find a way to use it another way. Many use empty laundry detergent bottles to form a makeshift barrier around their property. It's one way to keep the many stray dogs out. It's also another way of making use of something twice. Reuse, renew.

Small lessons. Large gains.

"I'm trying to teach kids to think ten years from now, five years from now, what's going to happen if we keep doing this? It's not going to be good. It's not going to be good for the environment, and it won't be good for us, the people."

In 2012, the EPA banned plastic bags. Those who do not comply are fined. The EPA distributes alternatives called Bio Bags, made from corn, with a set expiration date, as they will naturally biodegrade in 180 days. But even these must be imported.

"What's going to happen if those ships stop coming in? What are we going to do?" Pua often asks the children. "Will you still be able to pick a coconut? Will you know how to catch a fish? What are you going to do when the boats stop coming?"

Pua shakes his head. Puts on his ranger hat. Time to get to work.

"This is what really scares me. I'm afraid. I'm afraid to see where the culture will be fifty years from now."

Pua speaks of *mana*, a word that is also used in Hawaiian. When crewmembers speak of *Hōkūleʻa*, they often invoke her *mana*, her spirit to empower people to carry on for the good, a *mana* that can join all people toward a common good.

"If I had so much *mana* I would make everybody go back to the rainforest," he tells me. "Go to the rainforest. Get a peace of mind."

PURSE SEINERS, LONG LINERS, and massive rust-eaten tuna boats are parked, single file, like taxis, along the berth beside the Sāmoa Starkist tuna cannery and the former, now shutdown, Chicken of the Sea factory in Pago Pago Harbor.

Opposite: Trash is a common sight in the waters of Pago Pago Harbor, a bay with a shoreline that wraps five miles into the center of the island.

Eleven million pounds of yellow fin, albacore, and big eye tuna are brought into this harbor each year. Blue marlin, swordfish, and mahimahi are exported from this port too. Large industrial countries conduct most of the fishing for tuna on our planet. These countries then use ports like American Sāmoa to process and can these products. There are no US import tariffs here, making this a lucrative spot for international fishing enterprises.

"When I see these fishing nets over here, it really, really hurts me inside," says crewmember Kawai Warren, while looking at the nets on the purse seiners just across the water from *Hōkūle'a*.

It is nearing sundown. An overflow of clouds rolls down from Mauga Pioa.

Soon, Kawai will return home to Kaua'i. It is nice to have a last few moments with *Hōkūle'a*, he says. Back home, Kawai is a fire chief. On the canoe, he is a safety officer and rescue swimmer. He is also responsible for carrying the *ko'i*, an adze with a milo-wood handle and a fierce thousand-year-old basaltic stone, lashed together with cordage from Satawal—Mau's birthplace.

The *ko'i* was given to him by *Hōkūle'a*'s Captain, Kālepa Baybayan, to carry from place to place, island to island, school to school on this leg of the voyage. The *ko'i* has been on the voyage since the launch out of Hilo and will be passed from crewmember to crewmember throughout the Worldwide Voyage. When the *ko'i* is given to you, you carry it with you everywhere, with honor. To the crew, the *ko'i* represents strength and fortitude of the people; it has its own *mana*, spirit, Kawai explains.

Kawai has sailed on *Hōkūle'a* for nearly twenty years—including one epic voyage from Rapa Nui (Easter Island) to Tahiti in 1999. Born and bred on the Big Island, Kawai has found his time in Sāmoa, visiting the school children, deeply moving. Sāmoan children still speak their native language and sing their native songs, keeping them connected to their roots and a deep sense of who they are as Pacific Islanders. For hundreds of years, Sāmoa's central location in the Pacific made it a key navigational post for those exploring Polynesia.

While Kawai speaks, the slamming of steel at the cannery across the harbor interrupts his words. At times, he pauses, as if jolted by the sounds, and takes a look over his shoulder at the activity.

In all his years sailing, Kawai says, the magnitude of these tuna facilities is beyond anything he has ever before witnessed.

"I've never seen boats like that," he says. "Never."

The handful of boats is just a sampling of the fleets that patrol the Western and Central Pacific waters.

Kawai grew up learning to fish when he was only three years old, long before the word "sustainable" had become an ecological catch phrase. Sustainable fishing has been a tradition throughout the Pacific island states for centuries.

In Sāmoa, villages still control the rights to fishing near their shores and fishermen abide by the rules on when and where to fish. There are restrictions on fishing within each community—in most, no fishing is allowed on Sundays. The *tautai*, or master fisherman, determines when and where fishing is allowed in order to sustain the marine life for this generation and for generations to come. It is the same philosophy Kawai grew with up in Hawai'i.

Opposite: Kālepa Baybayan watches a ferry boat surf through a closed-out harbor entrance.

"I was always taught you take what you need, you share," Kawai says. Kawai learned that you give your first catch to your elders because they cannot fish anymore. "You teach the next generation to fish so that when you are too old to do so, they can fish for you."

"Being aware of the needs of the community, you learn these values on this canoe," Kawai says.

"On the *wa'a*, you can learn how quickly you can run out of important resources. What if your water is contaminated? What happens if that's the only water you have to drink? What if that's the only water you have to live on? The canoe can wake people up really quick."

Water jugs are lined up on the dock alongside *Hōkūle'a*. Once the next crew comes in, the bottles will be refilled. Each crewmember will be allowed one gallon a day for drinking, washing, and cooking.

Conservation is a continual practice.

As he spoke, another international fishing company, Tri Marine, was in its final stage of remodeling the old Chicken of the Sea plant. The new $70 million facility is predicted to have the ability to process a million cans of tuna daily.

When Kawai learns that soon there will be more boats, with more nets, he shakes his head and asks, "Is there enough tuna out there for another one?"

A STRAW FLOATS BY, then an empty bottle of dish soap, next comes a plastic cap. All are floating by along the current, swift as a river, to the greater waters beyond.

It's a misty Sunday morning at Nu'uuli Uta, Coconut Point, a cape on the southern end of the island bordering an extensive, shallow reef. Along the rocky shore, a couple of locals are pulling on wetsuits, preparing to venture to the reef to extract the most destructive species to coral life here, the crown-of-thorns starfish, or COTS. They eat live coral tissue. COTS increase when there is a nutrient deficiency. The starfish bury themselves in the deepest part of the coral and grow until they cover the top of the coral heads, some barely submerged beneath the water's surface. Touching one of their poisonous spines causes instant paralysis that can last for several days.

The locals are all students—a couple are in college, one in high school—all are guided by their mentor, oceanographer Kelley Anderson Tagarino. One has the flu, another has a cough, but still they all have come, eager to *mālamalama e vasa*—understand the ocean.

As a native of Florida, Kelley fully understands the insidious ways invasive species destroy an environment. Kelley is currently working within the University of Hawai'i Sea Grant program at the American Sāmoa Community College, promoting stewardship of coastal and marine resources. She also teaches students how to manage the aquaculture and aquaponics systems on campus, offering viable solutions for sustainable island living.

"American Sāmoa's reefs are famous for being very thermally resilient," Kelley says, meaning the reefs are able to endure high temperatures without much detriment. But it's impossible to be resilient to invasive species.

"A lot of [the COTS invasion] is probably due to land-based pollution," says Tim Clark of the National Park Service. "Land-based pollution and a disturbance in the equilibrium of the ocean—like that which occurs from a tsunami or an El Niño are the greatest supporters of COTS."

COTS were first noticed in the 1970s here, growing in the reef systems on this side of the island where all the major waste pipes drain into the ocean. In the late 1980s, COTS were even thriving in the nearby National Marine Sanctuary of American Sāmoa. More recently, Tim has noticed an influx of the crown-of-thorns along the northern shores of the island too. In the last two years, Tim and his divers have killed an estimated fifteen thousand COTS throughout American Sāmoa.

There are two common ways to terminate COTS. In both cases, you need a specialized gun, similar to the ones used to inoculate cattle, to inject directly into the starfish. The first option, which takes a couple of rounds, is injection with sodium bisulphate. The second option, an injection of ox bile, takes only a single shot. The COTS will then form lesions and their tissue will begin to disintegrate. Within forty-eight hours, you're left with a pile of spines. All without harming nearby marine life.

Kelley and her crew plan to be here for several hours. She straps an empty bucket onto the paddleboard. Each student has a three-pronged spear. Together, they mount the boards and begin the paddle out to the reef.

For hours, you can see them; working, bobbing, like seabirds, all along the horizon.

SĀMOANS ONCE BELIEVED THAT the horizon was the meeting place between heaven and earth. It is there where the navigator measures the rise and fall of the stars. But for the children of Sāmoa, the horizon is neither a spiritual construct nor a navigational guide. The horizon is the future. The horizon is now.

This becomes ever more clear in the closing minutes of the crew's last school visit. An entire school has gathered under an open-air tent, rippling in steady, wind-blown showers.

"Why do you sail?" a student wants to know.

A few crewmembers offer answers, but these answers do not seem to satisfy. She is thirteen years old. She yearns for more.

Crewmember Mary Anna Enriquez steps forward, offers another answer, and then it is time to go. As Mary Anna and her crewmates walk across the muddy parking lot, a floodtide of students follows them.

"They wanted more. They wanted a piece of it," Mary Anna explains of the kids asking for hugs, pictures, and email addresses. "There was this energy, the momentum of what was happening."

Mary Anna is a middle-school teacher on Maui. She grew up in New Mexico and was a grade-school student who asked so many questions that she was sent to sit outside the classroom for her insatiable curiosity. She remembers being the age of these kids here and seeing a *National Geographic* article about a man sailing the world and knowing right then that that was what she wanted to do. She had never been on a boat and had no idea that once she did sail, she would be relentlessly seasick. But that didn't stop her from sailing the entire Western coast of the mainland United States to Baja and then Hawai'i and then here to Pago Pago. That was over twenty-six years ago.

When she learned she would sail on *Hikianalia* to Pago Pago, she was somewhat hesitant. The last time she was here, the harbor was grossly polluted. So much plastic covered the ocean harbor floor that it was hard to set the anchor. A rainbow-like oil

slick covered the waters. But coming here now, she was pleased to see that much of the harbor was in far better condition than it once was. She was even more pleased to see that the children seemed ripe to carry on the task of *mālamalama e fanua*.

Now, as Mary Anna begins to climb into the back of a pickup, she feels a familiar presence behind her.

She turns around and it's the same girl, asking her, "Mary Anna, but why do you sail? You're not telling me that you sail to give a message around the world about picking up litter."

This isn't a challenge. It's a need to fully understand the scope of Mālama Honua.

"Well, yes," Mary Anna tells her, "we do want to give that message, that message is very important to take care of the Earth."

The girl is determined. "But why do you sail?"

Mary Anna could see that this was "an old soul," a soul that was just now beginning to "wake up."

Mary Anna places her hands on the girl's shoulders. She meets her in the eyes and tells her firmly, "I sail because I want to meet people like you that are going to make changes!"

"She melted," Mary Anna later recalls. "It was a rite of passage right before me. I saw a child go from somebody that is just going along with the world to somebody that knows and believes she is going to be able to make a change in the world."

For all the work that still needed to be done in American Sāmoa, the wake-up call had indeed been heard.

"We can look at the young ones because they are the ones being awakened," Mary Anna says. "These will be your activists!"

As the clouds continue to stir, a sea of children remain standing in the rain-filled wake of the pickup truck, saying good-bye, waving hello to the new path ahead.

Opposite top: Crewmembers enlist a student in the sharing of stories learned onboard the canoe.

Opposite bottom: Children are forever entertained by the logistics of how the crew uses the bathroom on the canoe.

Local Voices
Tiara Drabble
Ocean Environmentalist

On a rainy Sunday morning, Tiara Drabble was pulling on a wetsuit to venture into the waters of Nuʻuuli Uta, Coconut Point. The seventeen-year old National Honors Student was beginning a research project that would earn her first place in the American Sāmoa High School Science Symposium. Tiara often credits the many who have helped her with this scientific inquiry—Kelley Anderson Tagarino, Johann Vollrath, Dr. Timothy Clark, Dr. Ian Gurr, Dr. Mark Schmaedick, and Dr. Ndeme Atibalentja. But as an aspiring environmentalist, she knows that solutions require more than heartfelt passion. Real solutions demand knowledge. Breakthroughs. For this, she intends to continue her studies of marine science in university—seeking ways to further understand and heal our oceans.

In Her Own Words

GROWING UP, I WOULD ALWAYS HEAR ABOUT ALAMEA— the crown-of-thorns sea star. They looked like a big, red starfish. They were hurting our coral reefs, and they were dangerous to humans. These were the basic facts everyone knew growing up in the islands. Talking with Kelley [Anderson Tagarino], and seeing her passion for our marine life, motivated me to look more deeply into the issue.

I found out that *alamea* does so much more than just "hurt" our coral reefs here in American Sāmoa. It is damaging coral reefs all over the world. Aside from global warming, *alamea* is the single largest factor in the demolition of coral reefs worldwide.

There was an *alamea* outbreak in the 1970s that really affected us here in American Sāmoa. It resulted in the destruction of over 70 percent of our islands' coral reef ecosystem. Seventy percent! The current outbreak has the same devastating potential.

To kill them, we use commercial products—ox bile and sodium bisulfate—that we inject into the *alamea*. It doesn't disturb the marine life or the coral. But being on an island, it's costly to get these chemicals here. So I have been thinking about natural alternatives that are inexpensive and local, so that we wouldn't have to rely on imported commercial products anymore.

I completed a project last year, in microbiology, testing local plants as sources for antibiotics. That gave me an idea for finding something local and organic that could kill *alamea*. I asked family and friends for plants used locally, ancient methods, for fish poisoning here.

Here's what I found: I tested extracts of two plants— *futu* and *ʻava niukini*. These have toxins that would hopefully kill *alamea* without affecting other marine life around them. With the help of Kelley and Dr. Tim Clark, we gathered several samples of live *alamea* and took them to the lab for testing. The *futu* extract killed *alamea* the fastest—at an average of eight hours. The *ʻava niukini* took ten hours. The sodium bisulfate took ten and a half hours.

But unfortunately, we found that these plant extracts could harm other marine life, so further research is needed to derive a method of using them to safely kill and eradicate *alamea* on a large scale.

I still believe this project was an extreme success. Not only did it explore new avenues for *alamea* eradication, but more importantly, it educated many people on exactly how destructive *alamea* are, instigating what I feel to be a push in the movement to rid our community of *alamea*. If people understand how it is killing their coral reefs and endangering marine life, they will have a personal incentive to help save our reefs.

I believe that the protection and management of our natural resources in the marine environment is a responsibility of every resident on Earth. I also believe that a lot of people, the youth especially, do not fully understand why it is so important to take care of our ocean.

Marine life contributes to the amount of oxygen in our atmosphere, ranging between 25 and 80 percent. This oxygen supports life on Earth. All life here is interconnected and our ocean is the central component linking us all together.

Local Solutions
Manuʻa Islands Microgrid

THE PACIFIC ISLANDS ARE ON THE FRONT LINES OF climate change. Rising tides, erosion, coral bleaching, and superstorms are some of the environmental insults felt throughout the Pacific. In recent years, two Category 5 cyclones have blown through Polynesia: Vanuatu in 2015 and Fiji in 2016. NASA recorded the warmest year ever worldwide in 2016. Climate scientists widely believe that the primary cause of global warming is the excessive burning of fossil fuels.

For the past century, small islands have remained dependent on shipments of outside resources such as food and fuel. On many islands diesel generators are the main source of power. With diesel, there is always the risk of an oil spill in shipping, and shipments are often delayed due to weather and ocean conditions leaving communities stranded without energy. Blackouts and power outages are common, creating an unpredictable, unsustainable way of life.

Located six miles away from the main island and some four thousand miles away from the West Coast of the United States, the island of Taʻū was once fully dependent on diesel to supply its energy. On an island measuring just more than seventeen square miles with a population of six hundred people, electricity generated from fossil fuels used to consume 110,000 gallons of diesel a year. But in 2016, Taʻū turned away from fossil fuels and toward solar energy instead. Now, an advanced solar microgrid is able to supply the island with nearly 100 percent of its energy needs.

Designed by SolarCity, the grid is built to withstand winds measuring a Category 5 cyclone. Covering over seven acres of land, the $6 million structure took a year to install. The solar-power and battery-storage advanced micro grid provides 1.4 kilowatts of solar generation capacity from 5,328 solar panels and 6,000 megawatt hours of battery storage from sixty Tesla Powerpacks. A Powerpack is a massive lithium-based rechargeable battery; this network is made up of sixteen individual battery pods, with a built-in heating and cooling system. Powerpacks store solar energy at night, allowing energy to be drawn upon twenty-four hours a day. The entire unit fully recharges in seven hours of sunlight and, once fully charged, the island can remain powered for three complete days without sunlight. Operated by three groups—the American Sāmoa Power Authority, the Environmental Protection Agency, and the Department of the Interior—this grid provides a cleaner, safer, more reliable, more affordable energy alternative.

Taʻū is part of a group of three islands collectively known as the Manuʻa Islands in American Sāmoa. Situated some sixty-eight miles east of Tutuila, Taʻū is the largest island of the three, with the other two islands, Ofu and Olosega, connected by a bridge. A year after the Taʻū facility was completed, a similar solar structure opened on Earth Day on Ofu. The Ofu Solar Park is currently capable of powering 80 percent of Ofu and Olosega. Built by the American Sāmoa Power Authority and Honolulu-based Pacific Solar Innovations, it relies on a battery made of salt water. The battery is nonflammable, nonexplosive, and 100 percent recyclable at the end of its lifespan.

By 2018, the three islands of Manuʻa will be entirely powered by 100 percent renewable energy. These are strong steps toward American Sāmoa's plan to have all its islands free from the dependence on diesel and powered by 100 percent renewable energy by the year 2040.

Opposite: Taʻū's solar array provides 100 percent of the island's electricity needs.

Next spread: Keeping the tradition alive. Dolan Manaiaisiva Iaulualo performs a Sāmoan fire dance.

CREW STORY

Ka'iulani Moanike'ala Murphy

Apprentice Navigator

Ka'iulani Murphy has studied under Nainoa since she was nineteen. She currently teaches Ho'okele, Hawaiian navigation, at the University of Hawai'i and, like Nainoa, still humbly refers to herself as a student of navigation. Sitting along the quiet shores of Kualoa and Hakipu'u where Hōkūle'a was initially launched in 1975, Ka'iulani reflected on her experience of navigating to the island of Nihoa in 2004. Less than one-half square mile in size, Nihoa is the tallest of the ten uninhabited Northwestern Hawaiian Islands, known as Papahānaumokuākea. Ka'iulani was Hōkūle'a's first student navigator to successfully pull Nihoa up from the sea.

WHEN WE PLANNED TO sail to Nihoa, it was May, and we were delayed for two weeks in Hanalei because of weather. With this extra time I thought, *Oh, good, I have more time to get myself ready to go.* I spent most of my time helping get *Hōkūle'a* ready, so I appreciated the additional time mād quiet space to go over our sail plan, and study the sun, moon, and stars.

Sailing to Nihoa is a condensed version of a long voyage. You still need to know everything you would for a long voyage, just for thirty hours instead of thirty days. Knowing what stars will be visible is helpful for telling direction, latitude, and time. Keeping track of time is important to calculate how far we've sailed, but also for something as simple as calling watch changes. The crew works in four-hour shifts: 6-10, 10-2, 2-6. It's good to know what ten o'clock and two o'clock look like in the stars. More importantly, you need to know what stars are going to be available to guide you along your course. But stars are only visible half the time, if it's clear! Being able to read the ocean swells is key—sometimes swells are the only clues you have.

The plan was to leave out of Hanalei and try to sail to an imaginary line from the island of Ni'ihau to Nihoa. We line up the edge of the tallest cliff on Ni'ihau, Pānī'au, behind us to know we're on the right course.

That imaginary line is our reference course that we plot on a nautical chart. You picture that line in your head while you're out there and keep track of where you are relative to that line. At sunrise and sunset we ask ourselves, "How far along our course line are we? Are we east or west of it?" You need to get that course *pa'a*, memorized, in your head before you sail.

Even with the extra time to study, I never really felt confident enough to say, "OK, I'm ready to go!"

When we left Hanalei, the winds died just outside of Nāpali, and we couldn't get to our Pānī'au line. I could see the course in my mind, the line that I needed to get onto, but we weren't going to make it there. We didn't have the wind to do it. That did a number on my head.

Nainoa talked me through it, "OK, so, we can't get to that line. What is our heading now? Where is Nihoa from here?" It was helpful to have that voice telling me, "Think about what our new course will look like." You can plan and study for months, but you can only do what Mother Nature allows. It's important to always know where the island is in your mind.

I think about Nainoa's last lesson with Papa Mau. Mau told him as long as you have a vision of the island in your mind, you will never be lost. In my mind, I had to see that Nihoa should be right there. So, I pictured a new course line to get there.

Navigation involves a lot of brainwork, making decisions on direction, and tracking speed over time to calculate distance sailed. But once you get out of your head, you can get to a deeper sense of knowing—not having to think about it and just letting yourself feel it. But in that trip to Nihoa, I was just too nervous to get out of my own head. I felt so much pressure that I never got to a place where I could release. I think fear of failure, of not finding the island, was getting in the way of being able to get to the place I needed to get to.

I stayed awake the whole time. More than twenty-four hours. Once we saw the island, I finally felt, OK, now I can sleep.

As much as we prepare, I do feel that *Hōkūle'a* has this *mana* about her—she's leading us. She's older than her years. She's designed after our *kūpuna wa'a* and, being on her deck, you just feel this sense of going back in time. My *kūpuna* came here on a canoe like this. This is the same ocean my *kūpuna* sailed on. These are the same stars they looked at. You really feel that you're sailing in their wake.

CREW STORY

Kaniela Hōkūwelowelo Lyman-Mersereau

Watch Captain

Kaniela Hōkūwelowelo Lyman-Mersereau grew up in a family of seasoned sailors. His uncle Dave sailed as first mate on Hōkūleʻa in 1976, and later was captain in 1978. His mother, Marion, was also onboard in 1978 and was again a crewmember when Nainoa made his original trek to Tahiti as traditional navigator. Kaniela's father, Art, sailed with Mau in Micronesia long before Mau came to Hawaiʻi. Kaniela's kuleana, responsibility, has been as safety officer and rescue swimmer for several legs of the Worldwide Voyage. When he is not voyaging, he teaches Physical Education to middle school students at Punahou School. Overlooking the Haleʻiwa harbor, Kaniela talked about his childhood and his journey to serve his greatest teacher of all, Hōkūleʻa.

MY MOM, SHE'S A HERO. She was there at the dry dock every day with all those guys in the 1970s. My dad was there from the beginning too. He was a professional sailor. He had this modern, mono-hulled, kauri wood, double-mast schooner that scientists would charter, and he'd take them all around Micronesia. My dad needed Mau's help navigating through the channels. Back then they were doing instrumental navigation, but they didn't know the reefs and the waves, so Mau would help them. My dad speaks so highly of Mau and his traditional navigational knowledge. The Micronesians were so in tune with the boat and their environment. That was their family, those canoes and vessels—*He wa'a, he moku, he moku, he wa'a.* The canoe is an island, the island is a canoe.

Growing up, I wasn't a sailor; I just wanted to surf. Even with my dad, when we'd go sailing, I was looking for waves. But Uncle Dave was always pushing the seamanship and the sailing. Uncle Dave would come over, "Hey, Kaniela, you got to get into sailing and go to Cal Maritime!" He'd be pressing those college recruitment letters on me all of the time in my high school days. Dave was a gnarly 'ole sea dog kind of guy. He died right after I graduated in an unexpected boating accident while working. That's how he would have wanted to go, ingloriously at sea with his boots on. Now, in the last ten years, I've been asking my dad to teach me to sail. Uncle Dave's probably looking down, laughing, now.

I never thought that I'd be sailing on *Hōkūle'a.* I was twenty-two, maybe twenty-three, when I first started going to the dry dock. I was happy to go down there—sanding hulls—I just wanted to help. Uncle Bruce invited me on a night sail. I was super lucky. It was one of the most beautiful things I'd ever done—sailing through the night. When you first get onboard, you start thinking about those who came before you, and how amazing humans are, especially the Polynesians, who created this technology, the *wa'a.*

I was blown away when I was chosen to sail on this voyage. I had a full-on panic attack. I said to Uncle Bruce, "Uncle Bruce, you sure I'm supposed to be here?" I was super intimidated being around all these really experienced people. But everyone was so kind to me. It brought me out of my shell.

Hōkūle'a is a *kumu,* a teacher. Absolutely. She's the number one *kumu.* Once you step aboard, you have to give yourself away. You have to. And this is why it doesn't work out for some. They don't give themselves away. If you're in it for yourself, you're fired. Once you step aboard, you're completely at the service of the canoe, the captain, the navigator, the crew. That's hard for a lot of people to do.

She's a microcosm for people having to get along—this vessel—and travel from point A to point B safely. You can't get away from the other humans onboard. There's all these things that come into play—you get tired—and even the best people aren't always in the best mood. You really got to put out the right energy at all times, no matter if you're awake or sleeping.

You step onboard this canoe—with twelve, thirteen, fourteen individuals—and go out to sea. Take your business friends out to sea, spend a week together, see how it works out, and come back and tell me. Let me know who's still onboard! Take a human out of their comfort zone—and see what they care about.

What do you care about? Why are you here? What are you doing?

Those who are very close to her refer to her as Māmā *Hōkūle'a.* She brings a lot of hope to people. Not just here, but wherever she goes. No matter where you are, there's an energy that she brings to that place. She brings people from all sorts of backgrounds together.

When you look at the human odyssey, every culture has something they could call their *kumu,* their ultimate teacher, who shows them where they came from, shows them where they are, and gives them an idea of where to go. Some of the best teachers, they'll tell you the best way to learn is by doing, then failing, and then succeeding. *Hōkūle'a* is just that.

"Mālama Honua is a new voyage, but it's linked to deeper values and movements that have been around for a long time. It's part of our long genealogy of caring for the land—not just an environmental caring but also a spiritual caring for and connection with the land. Sometimes it's picking up rubbish and those sorts of acts of *mālama*. But sometimes it's going to the place and singing the song for the place so that the place can hear the words. That's what *mālama* means."

Maya Kawailanaokeawaiki Saffery
Cultural Liaison

AOTEAROA

CHAPTER 3

Kia mau ki ngā taonga ā ōu tātou tūpuna

—

Hold fast to the treasures of our ancestors

IF YOU LISTEN CLOSELY, YOU CAN HEAR THE CALLS OF SEABIRDS. You can hear the waters lapping the shore. You can hear the chant of Māori paddlers. These are the sounds surrounding *Ngātokimatawhaorua*, the largest ceremonial war canoe in New Zealand. Nearly ninety feet long, with enough seats to fit eighty paddlers, she is a sacred treasure to the Māori nation, and remains, ever ready, in the sheltered shade of the canoe house atop a grassy slope in the Waitangi Treaty Grounds. The most revered listener is here today, pausing on the seat of his walker, studying the majesty of the canoe. It is something he has done since he was a child.

His name is Hekenukumai Ngaiwi Puhipi. He is known as Uncle Hector. Uncle Hector has carved twenty-six single-hulled canoes, including two double-hulled voyaging canoes that have sailed over 30,000 nautical miles throughout Polynesia. Hector is *Pwo*, a master navigator who was trained by Mau Piailug. Hector is known as the man most responsible for reviving the canoe culture and traditional voyaging in Aotearoa, the Māori name for New Zealand, "the land of the long white cloud." Today, Hector will direct the proper way to launch this massive canoe into Waitangi Bay—an act reserved for only the most hallowed ceremonies. Tomorrow, *Ngātokimatawhaorua* will greet *Hōkūleʻa* and escort her ashore.

"We are waiting for the tide to rise a bit," Hector tells the broad-shouldered paddlers who have come to help. No easy task. The canoe weighs six tons, dry. She is propped up on three keel blocks. There are two-wheeled carts and a sand-covered, railroad-like track beneath her. Her prow is a fierce figurehead, facing the water a couple of hundred yards away. "Best to wait a bit," Hector says, and everyone agrees.

Hector speaks in the slow, measured voice of a man who has passed his eighty-third year working these lands. As a child, he grew up on a farm with eleven siblings to help care for, rising before the sun to tend to the forty family cows, each one milked by hand in those days. As a teenager, he poured cement and dug gum fields—digging and cutting through fields and swamps and tree roots to unearth "gum," a once highly prized export used for making varnishes and linoleum. As a man, he built bridges, over 200 in all, throughout the North Island.

When someone asks what time is high tide, Hector does not offer up an answer. To a *Pwo*, time is not measured by the numbers on a clock dial. Time is reflected

Opposite: Tāne Mahuta, "The Lord of the Forest," is the largest living kauri tree in New Zealand. Standing 165 feet high, with a girth of 45 feet, this tree has presided over Waipoua Forest for what is estimated to be more than 2,000 years.

in the natural world around you. Right now, time is gauged by the slow afternoon climb of the tide, bringing the water closer to the *waka*, the canoe.

Ngātokimatawhaorua appears immoveable. She was carved out of kauri, the giant rainforest trees most revered by the Māori. Kauri wood is prized for its strength and durability, and able to withstand deep-sea voyages. Two were felled for the hull; another for the gunnels, stern, and prow. Te remnant of one of the trees chosen for *Ngātokimatawhaorua* is on display. The axed remains of its trunk lay on its side—six feet wide—its inner core fully exposed like an artery severed from the earth.

Ngātokimatawhaorua was built to mark the centennial celebration of the signing of the Waitangi Treaty. In 1840, the Waitangi Treaty served as an agreement between Māori tribal groups and the British Crown. The contract was designed to protect Māori interests while allowing the Crown to govern the country. Part of the promise permitted the Māori to retain possession of all things *taonga*—treasured—be it ancestral lands, sacred sites, fauna, trees, native language, the ocean. But what is deemed *taonga* has led to years of debate between the Māori and the British; these debates continue to this day in tribunal meetings throughout the country. In 1990, Queen Elizabeth arrived by barge to visit the people of Waitangi, an offering of apology for the trespasses of the treaty. The war canoe was paddled out into the bay to greet the queen, and the queen renamed the canoe, *Her Majesty's Ship*. But locals will not refer to the *waka* this way.

The last time *Hōkūleʻa* arrived here was during the 1985 Voyage of Rediscovery, a voyage intended to sail the migratory path that led people to islands across the Pacific Ocean. To prepare to navigate through the star system south of the equator, Nainoa Thompson travelled to the North Island, where he first met Hector and his wife, Ngahiraka (Hilda). Nainoa stayed with Hector and Hilda for weeks, studying star patterns so he could successfully guide the canoe to this southernmost point in the Polynesian triangle. Nainoa found that while the canoe culture had fallen aside long ago, the Māori still spoke their native language.

"We have lost our pride and the dignity of our traditions," Hector then told Nainoa. "If you are going to bring *Hōkūleʻa* here, that will help bring it back."

Nainoa soon began to view Hector not as Uncle Hector but rather as his "Father in the South."

When *Hōkūleʻa* arrived in Waitangi, Sir James Henare, an elected Parliamentary Māori representative, was so inspired by the canoe that he inducted the Hawaiians as the honorary sixth tribe of the Tai Tokerau, the northernmost land of New Zealand. When Sir James passed away in 1989, Hector vowed to fulfill his chief's vision to reawaken the voyaging culture here by carving a canoe that would sail by traditional wayfaring means throughout Polynesia.

In keeping his vow to Sir James, after the funeral Hector went immediately to the forest. With the help of *Hōkūleʻa* crewmembers, Hector felled two kauris that would become the hulls of the voyaging canoe, *Te Aurere*.

Te Aurere was sailed from New Zealand to Rarotonga in 1992 with *Pwo* Mau Piailug as navigator. In 2012, another canoe, *Ngahiraka Mai Tawhiti*, named for his Hilda, sailed from Aotearoa to Rapa Nui—Easter Island—reaching the easternmost corner of Polynesia.

Opposite: Hekenukumai Ngaiwi Puhipi, known as "Uncle Hector," directs the proper launching of the ceremonial war canoe, *Ngātokimatawhaorua*, Waitangi Treaty Grounds.

Hector's sail to Rapa Nui is rendered in his whale tooth necklace. The delicately carved necklace reveals a migratory bird, her tail in Aotearoa, her beak in Rapa Nui, her long elegant spine, a long waving wake.

Now, in returning to Waitangi, Nainoa seeks permission and also a blessing from Hector before voyaging beyond the Pacific into the Tasman Sea, Coral Sea, and across the Indian Ocean. The permission is to sail within New Zealand waters. The blessing is a chant, a *karakia*, invoking spiritual guidance for the long voyage ahead. Uncle Hector knows the *karakia* to calm the winds and quell the seas. He knows the *karakia* to fell a tree and carve a canoe. These *karakia* are sacred and reserved to be heard only by those who sail on *Hōkūle'a*.

As the afternoon draws on, a crowd of tourists has collected around the canoe. Tourists wonder aloud, how do you get six tons of canoe off its racks and onto a track?

Someone suggests maybe a crane. Someone else suggests a tow truck.

Slowly, more barrel-built barefoot men begin to arrive. Each one gives Hector the revered greeting of *hongi*—touching nose to nose, meeting eye to eye, breathing breath to breath. Then, each man places a hand on the rail or the prow or the stern. For the Māori, the canoe represents your tribal identity. Every tribe has its own migrational canoe. The tribe's canoe is viewed as a link to their voyaging bloodline—and the sacrifice, courage, and wisdom their forefathers showed in safely forging across thousands of miles of open ocean to reach this distant frontier of the South Pacific.

"It is time," Hector says. Time to place the wood plank seats. "The seats are numbered, and all you have to do is follow the numbers," Hector says, guiding them, sometimes in English, sometimes in Māori.

Once the seats are in place, the men now need to drive a wedge of wood on top of the carts to raise her off the blocks.

The paddlers line her gunwales, awaiting Uncle Hector's cue. Hector directs them to drive another piece of wood in—and it works; it is enough to lift her and allow her to rest on the carts. The blocks are moved out of the way.

The men now manage her on a slow, easy glide. But once she reaches the tilt of the sloping grass, someone gives out a loud shout. They try to hold her back, like a racehorse at the gate. Their legs are her brakes, their arms, her guide, as she makes her way down the gentle slope to the water's edge. When Hector gives the call, they release their grip.

You can hear the sigh, all around, as she slides in with barely a splash, embraced by the waters.

OUR WATER IS NOT FOR SALE
NO DEEP SEA OIL DRILLING

THESE ARE SIGNS ALONG the roadsides of the North Island where the national Māori flag waves high. The flag was created as an act of sovereignty, its design symbolizing the creation of sky and earth and light. Nature is the physical constitution of the Māori kingdom. You will often see the flag beside environmental protest signs.

"A large area of land has been taken by the government," says Chief Kingi Taurua, standing on the grass grounds of the Te Tiriti o Waitangi. The chief gestures to the

---

Opposite top: The six-ton *Ngātokimatawhaorua* moves inexorably into its home water's embrace, Waitangi Treaty Grounds.

Opposite bottom: *Ngātokimatawhaorua* escorts *Hōkūle'a* into Waitangi.

bay where *Hōkūleʻa* and *Hikianalia* are now anchored—the Māori and Hawaiian flags flying on both *waʻa*. "We can only control the sea out there."

Earlier today, the chief had been pacing as he waited for the arrival of the Hawaiians. He wanted to make sure everything was in order for the greeting of the sixth tribe. He closely watched as *Ngātokimatawhaorua* escorted *Hōkūleʻa* into the bay, the paddlers jumping into the water to lift and carry captains and crew on their shoulders to the shore. He then witnessed the fierce *haka*, and listened intently to Nainoa as he thanked all the Māori elders, including Kingi and Uncle Hector.

The chief has now stopped pacing, but his speech remains swift. When asked if he will be here tomorrow, he makes a swirling gesture to the sky, explaining that he is all over, everywhere, continually.

Like the cosmos?

"Yes," the chief laughs, "I'm like the bloody cosmos!"

Ask him the extent of his domain, and he will tell you he is chief as far as you can see—east, north, south, and west. A *tā moko*—tattoo—has been chiseled into his broad face. The intricately laid design tells the stories of his family and his path throughout his long life.

"The environment is very dear to us," the chief says. "The environment is all rubbish now. Rubbish has floated into our sea here so we can't eat our fish. The farmers have polluted it. We have no control, but we're having an argument with the government to clean it up. And stop it."

The Waitangi River flows like a vein flushing farmland waste into the bay that feeds into the ocean. The river is a nursery for the sacred *tuna*, the name of an eel in the Māori language, that will migrate to the ocean and all the way north to Tonga before returning home. As of late, the eel population has been low—an indication of a suffering river system. When the rivers suffer, the ocean suffers too. The Māori believe that the ocean is a *marae*—a gathering place—of their ancestors. The destruction of this space is a spiritual trespass.

According to a report in *New Zealand Geographic*, New Zealand is home to one of the largest ocean territories on the planet with a marine estate over twenty-one times the size of its total land mass. This marine estate includes the New Zealand Exclusive Economic Zone as well as the Extended Continental Shelf approved by the United Nations. To scientists, these waters hold a rich biodiversity of whales, dolphins, and seabirds. To others, these waters also hold the rich promise of fossil fuels. Permits to explore for oil, gas, and minerals have already been issued for over two billion square miles of this area. Only fifty-three million square miles are currently sheltered in marine reserves.

"We are trying to actually stop deep-sea oil exploration—with hope that they'll listen," Kingi says. "They" being the government.

The Māori have a history of fighting against deep-sea oil exploration. In 2012, the tribe Te Whānau a Apanui led a forty-two-day protest off the East Cape against the government's permit to allow the Brazilian-based Petrobras oil company to perform seismic testing. Soon after, Petrobras abandoned all deep-sea oil drilling plans for the region.

Oil seeps were first noticed on the beaches off the west coast of the North Island in the 1860s. A hundred years passed before international oil companies came in,

exploring and developing oil fields both onshore and along the sea coast, around the volcanic mountain the region is named after—Taranaki. By the early 1970s, this area was considered one of the largest oceanic oil beds in the world, widely known as the Māui gas field. And just like the sea god Māui is said to have fished New Zealand out of the ocean, oil companies have been drilling oil out of the ocean floor off the western coast of the North Island for nearly forty years.

But here, in Kingi's northern territory, the ocean has only recently been threatened.

In 2013, the Norwegian oil company Statoil was given a fifteen-year permit to explore and drill for oil off the west coast of the Northland—covering nearly 6,210 square miles of seabed. In late 2016, Statoil started using seismic surveys— sonar explosions to penetrate the seabed to determine the prospect of oil and gas. Whales, dolphins, and giant squid are some of the marine life affected by these underwater bombings—noise pollution marine biologists refer to as "acoustic smog."

"The environmental ethic is never far away from debates about what ought to be the narrative for our country," says Shane Jones, a former Labour Party MP. A Northland-born Māori with English, Welsh, and Croatian roots, Jones was on hand when *Hōkūle'a* first landed here in 1985. And he is here today—to greet them again. Dressed in a grey blazer with a crisp collared shirt, Jones is the ambassador for Pacific Economic Development for New Zealand. It's a position the government created specifically for him to develop economic opportunities in the Pacific.

"The Kiwis are very proud of our clean, green country, probably to the point of hobbling development opportunities," Jones says. "The environmental ethic eclipses everything else."

Above: Oil refining in Taranaki, the center of the nation's oil and gas production fields.

This environmental ethic stopped the French from performing nuclear testing in the ocean here in 1972 and created a standard of awareness that has filtered down to the next generation. Grammar-school children ask crewmembers how much plastic they've seen en route from Tonga. The children are concerned about how the crew disposes of their trash at sea. These are children who will write city officials about rubbish seen in a nearby waterfront. These are, in the words of one *Hōkūleʻa* crewmember, the face of the future of Mālama Honua—"children learning to be global citizens." It's an ethic that is surely alive and thriving, but children do not run the government or the gas and oil industry.

"New Zealand, for many years, has had a gas and oil industry off the west coast in Taranaki, but off the north, there's never been a tradition of mining oil and gas," Jones says. "There is some prospect activity going on but it's very, very modest. It's being carried out by Statoil. They themselves are treating it as a long shot. But then again, oil and gas prospecting is a long shot."

"It's not a resource that's easily found in this part of the country," he adds. "And to be fair, there's a lot of apprehension that it could ruin our environment. So there's a big hurdle in terms of people's anxieties in the community."

The anxiety is real. Two months before *Hōkūleʻa*'s arrival, a *hīkoi*, peace march, interrupted the Statoil conference in downtown Auckland. The reality being that oil is a great contributor to global warming, and the prospecting of oil has led to more than a few environmental disasters. In 2010, the Gulf of Mexico oil spill occurred while drilling in 4,900 feet of water. The Statoil oil permit allows for drilling down to depths of 6,500 feet.

Jones mentions the fracking going on in the United States, the oil platforms lining the Pacific horizon off of the towns of Santa Barbara and Huntington Beach in California.

"In my lifetime, that kind of stuff will never happen in the north," Jones says before excusing himself to speak to another journalist here.

"We will never hand over these lands to you, or we will be like the seabirds whose rock is covered by the tide and who have no resting place," a Māori leader stated way back in 1859. His words still resonate today.

And as Kingi resumes pacing the grounds, it seems there is no rest for those devoted to the care of the oceans.

WHEN THE MĀORI FIRST settled here a thousand years ago, the North Island was a rich forest of kauri trees, spreading across four million acres of land. Since then, logging and farming and the invasive "dieback" disease has shaved the kauri down to eighteen thousand acres. The bulk of the remaining trees grow in the Waipoua Forest where Te Roronga, a local Māori tribal group, works with the National Forest Restoration Trust to protect the endangered kauri. You can no longer cut down a kauri—even those on privately owned land are protected under New Zealand law. Kauri timber can no longer be sold for profit. It can only be gifted. Uncle Hector gave a block of kauri to Nainoa to place on the deck of *Hōkūleʻa* as a way to connect the *mana* of the tree with the *mana* of *Hōkūleʻa*.

On a morning after the gifting, Captain Bruce brings his crew to the Waipoua Forest to pay their respects to the largest living tree in this sanctuary, *Tāne Mahuta*— Lord of the Forest. Believed to be two thousand years old, *Tāne Mahuta* stands nearly 200 feet high. Its trunk is more than twice the width of *Hōkūleʻa*'s deck. The giant tree has fragile roots. Just a step on these roots can cause damage. Invasive dirt on hiking boots is believed to be the cause of kauri dieback disease—a fungus-like condition that leads to the progressive decay of roots, branches, and twigs. Microscopic spores in the soil first infect the roots and then damage its tissues and prevent nutrients from reaching other parts of the tree. Nearly all kauri infected with this disease will die. Visitors are asked to walk along the wood planks elevated above the roots. A railing prevents those who are curious from touching its bark.

Crewmember Matt Kanemoto has brought an offering in a long bamboo stalk. It holds water collected from the lake at the top of Mauna Kea. On behalf of all the crew, Matt pours the water around the base of the tree while another crewmember, Pomai Bertelmann, leads the crew in a chant of reverence. Pomai, whose name implies "blessed," is the bearer of song and chants on this leg of the voyage, her guidance providing a continual wake-up call to remain connected to the soul of the Earth.

"In one breath, we are reminded that we are *kanaka honua*, men of the land," Pomai will later reflect. "And that there is a point after our time on the ocean when we must return home."

When asked how the songs and chants help keep the ancient Hawaiian culture alive, Pomai pauses, then clarifies, "The Earth IS our culture."

The same could be said of the Māori who have chants for felling a kauri—an act reserved solely for the carving of a canoe. Like the Hawaiians, the Māori relied on the strongest wood to build their voyaging canoes. Bruce says the kauri reminds him of the Hawaiian koa tree.

In the afternoon, Te Roroa, the tribal owner of the Waipoua Forest land, invites the crew to share songs, prayers, and lunch on an open lawn in the heart of the forest. Bruce stands, thanking the leaders, and then begins his story of the koa.

Back in 1989, when the Polynesian Voyaging Society wanted to build *Hawai'iloa*, a fifty-seven-foot voyaging canoe, using only traditional native materials, they visited the forests near the Hawai'i Volcanoes National Park on the Big Island to select prime koa trees. But what they found was devastating. The majority of the koa had been stripped by logging or for cattle grazing.

"It became clear to us how degraded our forests were," he says. "Our koa trees are like your kauri trees—sacred."

"The Forest Service was planting pine trees in its place. They were altering the whole landscape," he says. "They weren't just taking away trees. They were removing a habitat."

When Bruce talks, he does so with a smile—even when what he is discussing is something as discouraging as deforestation. Bruce brings the intention of *Pwo*—to bring light—into every place he steps, speaks, and sails.

"In that whole web, they were displacing and removing a habitat," he continues. "There's that sense of taking something in exchange for money, but [they were] altering the land forever."

A Māori host replies, *kia ora*—meaning amen, and sometimes, also, aloha.

There are birds that have become extinct, and others endangered, due to the loss of the kauri.

Pomai's husband, *Pwo* Chadd 'Ōnohi Paishon, picks up his guitar and begins strumming "Ka Pilina," a song devoted to the birds of the islands and those whose calls can be heard deep in the forest.

The melody has a wandering charm, and soon, a young Hawaiian girl named Kuʻulei, who is part of ʻŌiwi TV, a Hawaiian documentary team filming *Hōkūleʻa*, stands. She begins a slow, barefoot, blue-jeaned hula. Her eyes follow her hands. Her hands offer her heart. She sways with the rolling winds, offering a graceful bow to the blessings of the forest.

A LATE WINTER STORM has begun to stir. The canoes were scheduled to depart today, but Uncle Hector has advised against it. Everyone heeds Uncle's warnings.

Hōkūleʻa and *Hikianalia* are docked side by side in the Opua Marina, a short sail away from Waitangi. The driving rain offers a fine opportunity to practice raising the sails. It takes eight people, hand over hand, to raise the wet sails.

Student navigator Kaʻiulani Murphy is overseeing a practice drill of changing the sails. Kaʻiulani exudes a warm, laid-back poise, a reflection perhaps on her years of experience with *Hōkūleʻa*. In 1997, she was just finishing high school when she went to work to repair *Hōkūleʻa* in dry dock. From the first moment she put her hand on the *waʻa*, she feels like she stepped into a current that has guided her along ever since. Kaʻiulani conavigated *Hōkūleʻa* from Sāmoa to Tonga to Aotearoa.

Her first deep-sea voyage was from Tahiti to Hawaiʻi in 2000, and in 2004, she sailed from Kauaʻi to Papahānaumokuākea. For that journey, one of her *kuleana*, responsibilities, was to find the island of Nihoa. Nihoa, more than a day's sail away from Kauaʻi, has an extremely low profile on the horizon. There aren't any lights to mark it by night, and by dawn, the only way to spot it is from the sun rising directly behind it. Finding Nihoa is the only deep-sea navigational test possible within the Hawaiian archipelago. Kaʻiulani was the first student navigator to pass this test on her own. Still, she considers herself a "student" of navigation.

In 2007, she crewed on *Hōkūleʻa* from Hawaiʻi to Micronesia and then onto Japan. As a crewmember for nearly twenty years, she is fully adept with the on-deck tasks such as raising and changing sails in all conditions—through shifting winds, squalls, and currents.

Kaʻiulani knows that a "master navigator" is also an exceptional leader. She recently witnessed this in Captain Bruce while navigating to Tonga.

On the night before landing in Tongatapu, the boom broke. "It felt terrible to see *Hōkūleʻa* like that," Kaʻiulani says, going on to explain the series of events that led to the break.

"We were doing the watch change, coming off the 10:00 pm to 2:00 am shift."

Navigators can work in pairs in four-hour shifts. Her partner was fellow student of navigation Kaleo Wong.

Both had finished briefing the next watch captain and navigating team on the wind and sailing direction. *Pwo* navigator Bruce was on the deck, resting. Kaʻiulani had to step off the deck to the *lua*, the loo—over the back of the canoe. Then Kaleo had to answer a radio call at the electrical call box. In this brief moment, the canoe turned. It felt as though the wind had suddenly changed course. The sails were back-winded, the boom hit a shroud and broke into two pieces.

"It was a bit of a hairy situation—to see the boom like that," Kaʻiulani says. "There were lines still connecting the boom to the sail and to the spar."

Opposite: Māori tribesmen perform the *haka* before the *pōwhiri*, the welcoming ceremony, of *Hōkūleʻa*, Waitangi.

"The way it was handled was an awakening for everybody," Kaleo would later say. "Uncle Bruce, as captain, made sure that everybody knew what needed to be done in a very calm way."

Bruce guided the crew as they closed the sail, lowered the boom, and put up a new sail.

"His leadership style was awesome," Kaleo said. "It showed us how to handle a situation that was potentially chaotic out there in the middle of the ocean at two in the morning," Kaleo said.

Kaleo's full name is Kaleomanuiwa, which means "the voice of the ʻiwa bird." A soft-spoken leader in the Worldwide Voyage, Kaleo is fluent in Hawaiian. His speech is as fluid as a song—as one elder noted—like that of the native Hawaiian ʻiwa bird from which his name derives.

"*He waʻa he moku, he moku he waʻa,*" he says, incanting the proverb. "The canoe is an island, the island is a canoe."

"Everybody came together and did what we needed to do to take care of our *honua* [world]—which was the *waʻa*—in the middle of the ocean," he says.

"The *waʻa* is a perfect microcosm [of our planet]," Kaʻiulani says, alluding to the fact that we will all need to come together—as islands, nations, continents—to take care of our Earth.

Once in Tongatapu, everyone came together to repair the boom. Local carvers allowed *Hikianalia*'s Captain, Bob Perkins, to use their shop and offered him a selection of wood and materials to get the job done. Bob chose a clean piece of fir and fashioned a sturdy scarf joint that would allow her to sail "rough and ready" to Aotearoa.

"She's fully recovered now," Kaʻiulani says, looking up at the boom, noting where it was broken, seamed, sanded, and now joined.

Above: *Pwo navigators Bruce Blankenfeld, Nainoa Thompson, and Kālepa Baybayan participate in a Māori welcoming ceremony.*

Many of the young sailors come and go, says veteran sailor Mel Paoa, who has been sailing *Hōkūleʻa* since 1977. Over the years, he says, there's a continual flow of new sailors coming and going, but only one has remained a constant. "Kaʻiulani," Mel says. "Kaʻiulani, she's always here."

Mel is eating clam chowder at the dockside café on the outside porch. A sideways rain licks his bare ankles. Sailors run into the café, huddling inside for the dry warmth. Mel prefers it out here. He still has his straw sun hat on.

Mel was on board the night the boom broke. "The boom breaking was no big deal," he says. It was a highly trained crew that sailed from Sāmoa to Tonga to New Zealand. "Six of us are captains," he explains. "We work well under pressure."

Pressures will mount as *Hōkūleʻa* approaches the Indian Ocean. Cyclones, shallow waters, rogue waves that can flip over container ships: these conditions seem to rattle Mel as much as a long-winded yawn. Back home on Molokaʻi, he's a paramedic. Here, on the voyage, he's interested in what *Hōkūleʻa* will teach you.

"Patience," he says, that day. "*Hōkūleʻa* will teach you patience." But only if you are patient enough to listen.

"I talk to the younger crewmembers," Mel says. "Once we reach port, I ask them, 'What did you learn when you sailed?' They'll tell me, 'Oh, I learned about the stars.'"

"The other part—the inside," he says, urging them to look a little deeper. He points to his heart, "Here," he says. "What did you learn here?"

"OUR *WAKA* IS OF PEACE, the paddle raised, a wellspring of love. We who have traveled here as ever, ensure the path of kinship is never too distant or lost."

This is a traditional Māori song of welcome. It can also be the song for farewell. A tall, lissome woman named Hinekaa Mako sang this to the Hawaiians when they arrived days ago. Hinekaa is here on this morning of departure, seated in a small skiff waiting to help give *Hōkūleʻa*, held to the dock by the wind, a bit of pull out of the bay toward the open waters.

In this day of farewell, you can feel a sense of returning. *Hikianalia* will soon separate from *Hōkūleʻa* and return to Hawaiʻi where she will continue sharing the lessons of Mālama Honua.

Uncle Hector has returned home to resume work on the Kupe Waka Centre, an educational facility that intends to keep the art of canoe carving and traditional voyaging alive. Hector brought the stone Nainoa gave him from his family's farmland in Niu Valley to anchor the center. The stone will be an energetic connection between the earth of Hawaiʻi and the island of Aotearoa. It will also bind Hector and Nainoa's shared vision to sustain Polynesian wisdom.

"We all come from a place that we call home, a place that means something to us," says ʻŌnohi, on the decks of *Hōkūleʻa*, as the crew prepares to sail.

"Whether it's California, Hawaiʻi—wherever that place is—you have some place that is special to you," ʻŌnohi says. "And whatever you need to do to *mālama*—take care of this place—you do it."

"This is our home, our place," he says of the vast Pacific empire that connects Māori to Tongans, Sāmoans to Tahitians, Cook Islanders to Hawaiians, all those places *Hōkūleʻa* has so far ventured on Mālama Honua. "If you're listening, if you're connected to your home, your place, it will speak volumes to you," says ʻŌnohi.

'Ōnohi offers up barrel hugs to those coming to say farewell, including a young boy who says he plans to someday sail on *Hōkūleʻa*. 'Ōnohi leads as Papa Mau taught him many years ago—with an open heart and an open hand.

"That's what Mau always taught us, 'Don't make like this,'" 'Ōnohi says, making a closed fist. "'Make like this,'" he says, opening his hand.

"Mau helped us to wake back up. Mau told us that these things aren't ever lost. You just forget to pay attention to them."

'Ōnohi remembers when *Hōkūleʻa* was about to sail to Satawal to honor Mau, back in 1996. The canoes were loaded, just like they are now, and ready to go when they received a radio call from Mau. Mau said, "Don't come."

Mau had been observing "storm stars," stars that rise just before the sun. These stars can reveal nature's calendar. Those whose lives depend on the ocean rely on these stars as signs—indicating a time to sail, a time to remain on land, a time to sow, a time to plant. Mau relied on them to predict the coming weather.

"Mau looked at the storm stars," 'Ōnohi says, "He said it was going to be bad, don't come."

This was around the time the National Oceanic and Atmospheric Administration first started publicly reporting big shifts in climate change—sea levels rising, typhoons, cyclones, hurricanes, irregularities in the patterns of El Niño and La Niña. Mau could see far beyond the horizon—farther than his people could see, says 'Ōnohi.

"Everything is changing," Mau told them. "Everything is changing. Something is not good."

"Back then, he noticed it, global shifts, from this tiny little island," 'Ōnohi says. "Mau was listening."

'Ōnohi takes off his hat and runs his hand through his thick gray mohawk.

A stream of birds flies by. Not a cloud in the sky.

"If you listen, it will tell you a lot," says 'Ōnohi. "If you listen, it will tell you everything that you want to know."

Opposite: The *Whanau Moana*, built by Uncle Hector, is a *waka tete* in which both males and females can paddle.

Local Voices
Mike Smith
Member of the Ngāpuhi People

Mike Smith's family history goes back to the signing of the Treaty of Waitangi. On his father's side, his great-great-grandfather was the chief who helped craft Te Tiriti o Waitangi. On his mother's side, his great-great-grandfather was the secretary who transcribed the treaty. These two men sat across the table at the signing of the document and said to each other, "He iwi kotahi tātou," We are now one people. As an environmental activist, Mike works amongst many tribes throughout Aotearoa. Mike is also the producer of the 2009 documentary He Ao Wera: Climate Change in Aotearou. He shared his thoughts from the driver's seat of his motor home parked at the Waitangi marae.

In His Own Words

In the matrix of Māori laws, the highest form of law is nature. Caring about the environment is part of our culture. There's a customary Māori practice—your first fish caught is always returned to the ocean. If you catch another, that one is for you. It's a practice in sustainability. It's a practice in not being selfish.

Our ancestors lived close in harmony with nature because they had to. You had to respect those things and not abuse them. It had a spiritual element to it, but it wasn't just that. It was a very pragmatic choice. If you polluted your water, you died. If you ate all the fish in your ocean, you died. If you cut down all the trees, you died.

You can't do anything that is inconsistent with nature. The environment is the framework in which we live, and unless that framework is healthy and correct, then all our other issues, social or otherwise, are almost meaningless.

Along the East Coast here, Māori have a deep relationship with whales. Paikea, an early explorer, was said to have come here on the back of a whale. When whales migrate from Rarotonga, they swim along the Kermadec Trench—one of the longest underwater volcanic arcs on the planet and the deepest trench in the Pacific. Follow that and you pop out here. It's the same path *Hōkūle'a* sailed to get here. When you follow that, we call it, "riding the whale trail." When the whales migrate here each year, you can see them coming, like a herd on the horizon.

Our ancestors had intimate relationships with whales. We see them as our cousins. Anything that would guide you across the Pacific to another country, to another land, you considered your *kaitiaki*—your guardian, guiding you and protecting you. And if you honor it, it will look after you and get you to where you need to go. In a sense, this creature is protecting you from being lost.

With deep-sea oil exploration, they use seismic testing to explore the potential in that area. The oil companies say this testing doesn't bother you in your home. But what about the whales in their home? Seismic testing is invasive. It's a hundred times louder than a jet engine. It's so loud it can penetrate 3,000 meters of sea, then go another four kilometers through the seabed and bounce back up and be collected by hydrophones. It can deafen whales. It interferes with their ability to navigate and communicate with each other. To escape the sound, they'll surface immediately, and get the bends and die. Or they'll distance themselves from the sound. The whales move to shallow water, to escape the noise and run ashore.

The government is talking about opening up more deep-sea permit areas. They have divided the marine area into blocks and made it available to all companies to tender for permits. Right now, the government has allocated two areas for exploration—the Caledonia basin and the West Coast basin. The whales' migration path is right in the area and at the exact time when they plan to begin seismic testing next month.

Before they begin seismic testing, they are supposed to do a baseline survey to establish if any marine mammals are in the area. If there are, under New Zealand Marine Regulations, you are not allowed to do any testing. There are supposed to be marine mammal observers on board to make sure this doesn't happen, but who knows?

We're a people surrounded by water. It's our home. That's why we're here for *Hōkūle'a*. She's reviving the traditions of our ancestors. She's reviving the depth of knowledge we had about the ocean, the environment, and the ancient navigational wisdom. My hope is for people to live simpler lives. We need to get back to the state of grace that all of our people had at one time. Not just native peoples. Everybody.

Local Solutions
From the Wind

In 2013, New Zealand experienced its warmest winter in recorded history—1.8 degrees Fahrenheit higher than average. Many viewed this as a clear indication of climate change. Two years later, the bipartisan government announced a promise to reduce greenhouse gas emissions to 30 percent below 2005 levels by 2030 within the United Nations Framework Convention on Climate Change. The government has also targeted 90 percent of its energy to be generated with renewable resources by 2025.

Increasing renewable resources will mean moving away from dependency on fossil fuels. But oil and gas remain important economic industries for New Zealand. In 2010, crude oil was the fourth largest export, bringing in $2.3 billion. Lawmakers may find themselves caught between the lure of oil and gas export profit and the pledge to move toward a lower carbon economy.

Wind power can be one viable way the country fulfills its promise toward a cleaner, more sustainable source of energy. New Zealand has the potential to generate consistent, reliable, year-round wind energy. The two islands are in the path of the "Roaring Forties"—a strong westerly wind that blows between the latitudes of forty and fifty degrees in the Southern Hemisphere. These winds travel for miles across the oceans unblocked by any major landmass. Sailors are well aware of this swift, persistent flow—with speeds averaging from fifteen to twenty-four knots. New Zealand's capacity for wind-power output is believed to be more than double the international average.

Wind energy emits zero emissions. It does not require fuel. It uses minimal water. There are no toxic substances used or created in its transition from wind to energy. According to the National Renewable Energy Laboratory, it takes less than six months for a wind farm to produce more energy than it will consume in its entire lifetime.

Bird mortality is the single most negative side effect of wind energy. Flocks of birds can fly into the massive turbines. But newer models are being designed to reduce this danger. Some turbines have bonnet-like flags around the perimeter of the turbine to wave the birds away from the blades. Others use noisemaking devices and UV lamps to divert the birds. Some farms will shut down the turbines entirely during migration season.

In the United States, 214,000 to 368,000 birds die annually due to turbines. But turbines injure relatively few birds compared to other man-made structures such as power lines, communication towers, and automobiles. There are 6.8 million fatalities due to cell and radio towers, and 1.4 billion to 3.7 billion due to cats. Even so, many scientists agree that the most serious threat to birds is climate change.

West Wind farm is set on a working sheep farm west of Wellington, the capital of New Zealand. The farm generates enough electricity to power 70,000 homes—that's enough to provide annual electricity to all the homes in Wellington. The sixty-two turbines feed off the sharp winds funneling through the Cook Strait, a strip of water between the mountain ranges of the North and South Islands, where the Tasman Sea and the South Pacific Ocean meet. The wind races through this strait. For nearly half the year, this area averages gusts of over 41 mph. West Wind is widely considered one of the most productive farms on the planet.

In 2015, New Zealand had nineteen wind farms, either operating or under construction, supplying 5 percent (enough electricity for about 300,000 homes) of the country's annual electricity. It is believed that the country's wind resources have the potential to generate over three times New Zealand's current annual electrical demand.

Opposite: Riding the breeze into the future—a wind farm outside Wellington.

Next spread: An awe-inspiring sight: *Ngātokima-tawhaorua*, some eighty paddlers strong, Waitangi.

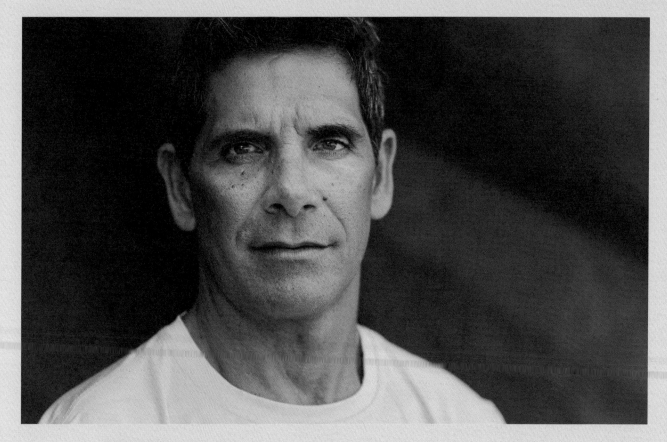

CREW STORY

Manavaroa Kamaki Worthington

Captain

Manavaroa Kamaki Worthington is a fireman for the Honolulu Fire Department at Sunset Beach, Oʻahu. Kamaki's father, Robert, was involved in the Polynesian Voyaging Society from the beginning, and later, as a PVS board member, was instrumental in organizing the Voyage of Rediscovery in 1985, a 16,000-mile passage retracing ancient voyaging routes of the Pacific. His father also served for several years as US Consul to the Cook Islands, Kamaki's mother's homeland. As a respected member of the North Shore community, Kamaki has recently undertaken building a training canoe, Wānana Paoa, that he sees as a child of the Mālama Honua voyage, linked to the ahupuaʻa's fish pond, Loko Ea, and navigational heiau, Kahōkūwelowelo, of Haleʻiwa. Kamaki talked on the beach overlooking Chun's Reef, a place where a flock of the endangered ʻuaʻu kani birds comes nightly to nest. As the sky softened and the stars awakened, Kamaki discussed the virtues of courage—whether stepping into the face of fire or sailing across the vast open ocean.

WHEN I FIRST SAW *HŌKŪLEʻA*, she was sailing into Aotearoa. There were dozens of canoes and hundreds of people welcoming her into Auckland. I was twelve years old at the time and going to boarding school there. I didn't fully understand what I was witnessing. Nobody explained to me that this was a cultural revitalization and was impacting nations across Polynesia. Knowing it was a huge event for so many people made me file it away in my brain and in my *naʻau*, heart; I realized this was something that was going to come up again. I didn't know how or in what context. Then time passed, and I slowly started to piece the story together, and at one point it all came together, and I thought, *All right!*

Back in 1992, I was twenty-two, working at Bank of America as a loan officer. It was never a desire of mine. It was largely driven by pressures from society. "You want to make money? Here's something to make money." No heart in it. No desire. It was just a job. My office was downtown and the office window overlooked the Honolulu Harbor and the ocean. I remember sitting there staring out the window. I could see some waves and surfers. There's people who do a job and go home and don't think about it. And that's fine. But for me, I can't imagine it. I had to leave that job. I have to be connected with what I do.

That change came the first time I stepped on *Hōkūleʻa* and went for a two-hour sail. Finally, when I was on board, I knew that was what I wanted to do. I asked myself, *OK, how can I make this happen?* I started sailing nine years before I became a fireman. Sailing on *Hōkūleʻa* helped prepare me to be a fireman. On *Hōkūleʻa*, you go through a process of understanding your fears—that's what courage is, in my mind. Everybody's afraid. I don't believe anybody who says they're not afraid. It's how they deal with that fear. Some people ignore it. Some forget about it. Some even take substances to bury it.

But then you have this group of people that says, "I acknowledge the fear, and I want to learn more about it, and understand it." You experience the fear to the point where it never goes away, you internalize it, and you face it.

When you begin sailing, you're sampling fear on a small scale. Your teachers say, "Let's go to Diamond Head. Let's try going across the channel." You have these increments of pressure, a slow process of dealing with added levels of fear. The process goes on for years.

Once you're a navigator, the fear ratchets up—now you're responsible for people's lives. Not only are you responsible for eleven lives, but you're also impacting families if something were to happen to those eleven people. There's the fear of getting lost, the fear of failure. You're trying to read wave patterns and clouds going across 2,400 miles of ocean. You're making decisions—sometimes split-second decisions. How do you deal with any uncertainty? And if you consider *Hōkūleʻa* as a symbol, what if you cause that symbol to fail?

How do you have the courage to just know in your gut what is going on, so you're now no longer thinking about it, but feeling it instead? Everybody talks about the gut feeling, that sixth sense, letting go of the intellect and knowing where the land is inside you. It's a process. I definitely have felt it. An island you can't see but you know it's there. Your courage gets a little bit stronger through each of those experiences and this knowledge of how you react when you're facing fear grows.

The greatest lessons have come from watching how my own teachers, Nainoa and Bruce, have reacted as the pressure rises. On my first voyage to Tahiti, I was with Nainoa, and we were just past the doldrums. It was the middle of the night—no stars, no

horizon, no nothing, just black—and he was trying to read the signs. He had everybody on the sails, holding onto the ropes. Nainoa was looking out there, trying to interpret, and he couldn't see anything, but he was still reading whatever signs he could.

He had the crew open and close the sails for an hour or two, just constant opening and closing, and then all at once, he shouted, "Close the sails!" Seconds later, a brick wall—this force from the dark with wind and rain—came right down on us. If we had our sails open, it would have broken our mast. Nainoa knew it was out there, he could feel it. It was up to him to read it coming and remain completely fearless throughout all of it.

The canoe teaches you a lot about the world around you, but it also teaches you about what's inside you. To me, that's maybe the final layer of that fear. Whether you're the captain or the navigator, when all of those risks are weighing on your mind, and you no longer worry, it's a managed fear. You've been in that situation a number of times to be comfortable in that moment, when it's dark and you can't see anything and you're not sure, but you're OK with it. Then, all of a sudden, you have nothing else to face but yourself. *Hōkūleʻa* will impact you and change you. You'll never really realize it until that moment, at least for me, then you realize, OK, this is who I am. Sailing on *Hōkūleʻa* is really a discovery of who you are.

It's a struggle when you sail on *Hōkūleʻa* and you have these experiences and then you come back home and you feel this force of "Let's go!" Society and the regular world beat that down over time. Maybe a year goes by, or maybe a month, and you've lost that momentum. You need to get back on the canoe, and remember, That's right, this is what life's really about. The more society progresses, the more challenging it becomes.

For me, looking back to the first time I saw *Hōkūleʻa*, thirty-four years ago, I see this evolution. You get to a moment, where now, you're looking at yourself, and asking, *Who am I and who have I become? How has this impacted me?*

And that's just me. Imagine how many others *Hōkūleʻa* has touched over the years. How many other places and people and communities has she affected and impacted and changed?

Hōkūleʻa completely changed the direction of my life—not only in my employment, but also my values and priorities. I sat there in that bank office overlooking the ocean believing what I was doing was important, and maybe it was. But I never once stopped to think about the problems of the world or even how to treat people with respect. If you ask me what Mālama Honua means, it means respect. Respecting the Earth starts with respecting each other.

Above: Kamaki voyaging from Cuba to Key West.

CREW STORY
Haunani Hiʻilani Kane
Apprentice Navigator

Haunani Hiʻilani Kane is one of the younger crewmembers on Hōkūleʻa. She is part of a group known as Kapu Nā Keiki, Hold Sacred the Children, *a mission Myron 'Pinky' Thompson initiated, and one that his son, Nainoa, continues to uphold today in mentoring the youngest apprentice navigators. Haunani is currently a graduate student in Geophysics at the University of Hawaiʻi, Mānoa, focusing on how climate change is affecting Pacific Island environments. Early one morning on her way to university, she took a few moments to pause and reflect in Kapiʻolani Park. Under the sway of the coconut palms, she discussed her sense of responsibility for both her future and those who share her native lands.*

WHEN I WAS IN HIGH SCHOOL, I was interested in learning more about the ocean, and then I met Nainoa and joined *Kapu Nā Keiki*. Nainoa is always encouraging us that we can be anything we want to be. Nainoa tells us, "You guys are the next generation, you got to make sure that *Hōkūleʻa* is able to teach all the people who come after you. It's your responsibility. I've given you this knowledge, but it's your responsibility to share it." Nainoa has helped push me to pursue answering questions about our oceans from the perspective of a scientist and of a Hawaiian.

My first vivid memory of seeing *Hōkūleʻa* was during my senior year. We had been paddling around the state with Nainoa in one- and two-man canoes and we had just come back from Molokaʻi, and were in Kailua. I live right up the road from Kailua Beach so it's home to me. Nainoa told us that *Hōkūleʻa* would be sailing into Kailua Bay and that all of the 1976 crewmembers would be onboard. He asked us to paddle one- and two-mans around the canoe to help welcome *Hōkūleʻa* into the bay. I remember paddling our little canoes and looking up at all these people on *Hōkūleʻa* and thinking, *One day I hope to spend time with those people and on the canoe, and to learn what they've experienced.*

Now, each time when I sail on her, I learn so much, not only about sailing and the oceans, but also about myself. Each time I go, it puts into perspective my place on this planet. It makes me question the things that I am doing and really think if I'm making the most of my life.

My name, Haunani Hiʻilani, means "gentle cool breeze from the heavens." I think maybe it was appropriate that I was named after some sort of wind, but my mom says I'm more of a hurricane than a gentle breeze once I get my mind set on something. First and foremost, I'm Hawaiian. I am a person of this ʻāina, this land. I care deeply about this place, about these people, and my family. My goal in life is to make sure that I educate myself through experiences as well as in school so that I can contribute to make this place better for future generations. A lot of this has been instilled in me by my experiences on the *waʻa*, and the people that I've met through those experiences. I think you are the truest form of yourself out on the ocean.

Here in Hawaiʻi, we talk about our *one hānau*, our birth sand. When you're small, you spend most of your time on the beach. It's where you're raised. Your initial introduction to the ocean is by touching these sands. So, before leaving for the leg to Australia, I collected two types of sand from places most special to me. I collected one that's all volcanic—olivine, the green minerals that are exposed when lava cools—and another sand from Kailua Bay, where I grew up. I put them in tiny bottles, and gave them as gifts to those we met along the Great Barrier Reef. This was my way of sharing a little bit of myself.

Looking at the composition of the sand, you can learn about the history of a place and what its people have gone through. Sand is the way I nerd out as a scientist. My doctorate involves assessing the impacts of past, present, and future sea levels on the Pacific Islands. Two to four thousand years ago, an event occurred that was unique to tropical areas mostly near the equator, where sea level rose about one to three meters above the present level, and then it fell. As sea level fell, coastal plains grew, and more land along the coast was seen as habitable. This coincided with the initial migration of Polynesian people.

About two months after we sailed to Tahiti, *Hōkūleʻa* was in Sāmoa at the same time I was there, working on a project where I was trying to reconstruct the sea level history and how the place changed due to prior events of sea level—all by looking at the sand. I was working with an archaeologist from Auckland to unravel the role that past sea level played in the initial occupation and settlement of the Pacific Islands. We were collecting data, digging trenches, and taking cores of sand. Then, through

discussions with Aunties and Uncles on the canoe, and being on the canoe itself, I've been able to imagine what these islands may have looked like, long ago, from the sea. It really brought everything full circle.

I am constantly trying to get my mind around the role climate played in the past in the lives of islanders and then thinking about the modern situation and how climate will continue to impact our lives. My whole study is focused on sea level in the past, and making inferences and discussing what we can learn about those past events to try to move forward. I think a lot of that is a very Hawaiian thing to do—to learn from our past, our *kūpuna*, and using that wisdom to help place it in a modern context.

Nainoa will remind me, "Haunani, you got to succeed. Hawai'i needs you to succeed." It's nice to have that pressure on you. It's nice knowing that what you accomplish isn't going to be just for yourself, but for your *lāhui* (Hawaiian people).

Above: Haunani in her bunk. Anything unsecured may end up in the swamp below your bunk, or lost into the sea.

GALLERY II
Australia to Cuba

"Navigating through the reef mirrors how we'll have to learn to care for our Earth. If we want permission to sail through the reef, we have to observe it, and abide by it, and respect it. It's the same with the planet. If we want to heal our planet, we need to observe it, abide by it, and respect it."

Jenna Ishii
Apprentice Navigator

AUSTRALIA

CHAPTER 4

Nganydji bulmba-barra
Gulu gari nganydjiny-barra
—
We belong to this country
it does not belong to us

Gulu bulmba nyurrbing djanang
Gulu malaway nganydjin
Gulu mundu nganydjin
Nganydji bulmba-barra
Gulu gari nganydjiny-barra
Nganydji bama nguma-barra
Nganydji mugu bulmba-wu maminga-lum
Gulunggu nganydjiny mamingany

This earth and the Great Barrier Reef standing here
Is our reflection
Is our spirit and identity
We belong to this country
It does not belong to us
And we, as the people of tomorrow,
We are responsible to care for our country
For it has looked after us since time immemorial

A STRONG CROSSCURRENT PINS THE STARBOARD HULL OF *HŌKŪLEʻA*
to the tall cement walls of the dock. The tide is low. Flags on the mast are head high
to those standing on the dock, with the deck of *Hōkūleʻa* several feet below.

Only moments ago, *Hōkūleʻa* arrived here in Townsville, maneuvering through
a narrow, murky channel to a dock behind the Reef Aquarium, headquarters to the
Great Barrier Reef Marine Park Authority. Townsville is one of four major ports along
the reef. Its nine berths allow container ships to export fertilizer, sugar, minerals,
and iron ore across the globe. The construction of two new berths and a cruise ship
terminal are currently underway.

While the industrial world continues to press forward, *Hōkūleʻa*, with her simple
design, has been sailing along the Great Barrier Reef without leaving a trace of fuel
or waste. This is her first voyage outside of the Pacific Ocean in her forty-year history. She is midway up the reef in the Coral Sea, en route to Cairns and Cooktown,
and eventually will pass through the Torres Strait—the timing of which will need
to coincide with the full moon, which has an effect on the tides. The full moon will
allow for tidal currents in the optimal direction and an adequate depth of water for
the canoe to pass through safely.

Opposite: Crewmember Jenna Ishii explores the largest
ecosystem on the planet, the Great Barrier Reef.

Full moon or new moon, no map can prepare you for a sail along the Great Barrier Reef. A maze of reefs, shoals, islands, cays, and sand spits; it is a navigational minefield.

At night, the risk of sailing onto a shallow reef is compounded by having to navigate within the shipping lane. Only a beacon at the top of the mast identifies the canoe's presence to freighters and tankers and the many cruise ships, lit up like huge apartment buildings, looming by.

By sunrise, nature adds her own surprises: mangrove-born saltwater crocodiles—"salties," the size of rescue boards—and sea snakes the size of a man's leg chase the hulls; did one just squeeze through a scupper? Ferryboats, dive boats, and family joyride boats zip to and from islands. See that island on the horizon of Townsville? Captain Cook named it "Magnetic," because when he sailed past it hundreds of years ago, the island rendered his compass completely useless.

No worries. There's no compass on *Hōkūleʻa* anyway, only a solid crew, led by Captain Kālepa Baybayan. A former standout linebacker from the Big Island, Kālepa is a *Pwo*, and the lead astronomer at ʻImiloa Astronomy Center in Hawaiʻi. To him, the reef is an oceanic cosmos.

Once the canoe has been bound to the dock, Kālepa gives hugs all around.

Pule, time for a prayer, he says, and the crew forms a circle, holding hands and bowing heads. Kālepa leads the prayer in Hawaiian.

"*Amene*," they say, together.

"Good job," he tells them, and without a single word, each crewmember gets to work, each one knowing his or her own *kuleana*, responsibility, on board.

The *ʻohana waʻa*, canoe family, works together for the common good. Just as it takes all kinds to care for the Earth, it takes all kinds to sail and maintain a canoe. An astronomer, a firefighter, a medic, a Coast Guard officer, a math teacher, a PE teacher, a filmmaker, a painter, a chanter—these have been chosen to sail this leg.

Someone puts on some tunes. Bob Marley's "Redemption Song," a hymn to freedom, adds some ease to the tasks ahead.

Decks are cleaned, supplies organized, cooking utensils stowed. A rope is dropped down from the dock and tied to a bag on the canoe, and from there, the ropes are pulled to lift duffels out of the canoe. Organizing the sails takes more than a few hands.

"Do you think we have enough sails?" someone asks, jokingly.

Plastic bins, the size of large coolers, are packed with sails. Each sail is marked with a name and a number.

JIB #15A is taken down and rinsed with a hose. The winds are picking up. You can see and hear it in the sails, flapping loose. With the tidal currents and the insistent winds, *Hōkūleʻa* will bang into the dock throughout the coming night. So Kālepa ventures to a marine shop to get more buoys to bumper the hulls.

By sundown, the tide has risen and you can step right onto the canoe. The anchor-watch crewmembers do, and take cover inside the hulls, resting for the night.

THE GREAT BARRIER REEF is the largest and oldest living ecosystem on our planet. Situated on Australia's continental shelf, the reef was formed more than 30,000 years ago during the last glacial warming when ice melted and flooded flat

Opposite: *Hōkūleʻa* passes the Sydney Opera House, New South Wales.

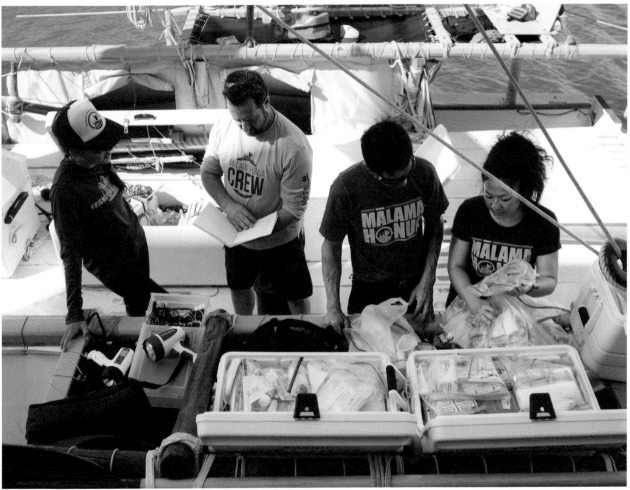

coastal plains. Stretching some 1,400 miles along the Queensland coast—the length of the west coast of the United States—the reef is home to 3,000 coral reefs; 1,050 coral islands; 1,625 species of fish; 133 varieties of sharks and rays; and 30 kinds of dolphins and whales. Two hundred and fifteen species of seabirds, including the white-bellied sea eagle, and endangered green sea turtle and dugong live here, too. Algae, sponges, anemones, worms, crustaceans, and mollusks contribute to making this a highly biodiverse oceanic environment. Some call the Reef the Eighth Wonder of the World. Others call it the rainforest of the oceans. To the original people, it is their homeland, the sea country.

How to navigate the reef and its resources has been a quandary ever since Captain Cook first explored these waters. In 1770, Cook sailed the *HMS Endeavour* to determine the nature of the landscape in a place then known as New Holland. His ship had entered into the southwestern barrier reefs, a landscape of shallow waters, shoals, cays, rocks, and sand. When the hull hit a reef at night, his crew quickly rose and began tossing lead and cannons off the ship in hopes of freeing it from the jagged coral snag. The ship didn't budge.

The following day, the rise of the tide lifted the ship and enabled it to drift to the sandy banks of a nearby river. Cook soon realized that he and his crew would remain stranded there, in summer, repairing a severely damaged hull, in a desolate, unforgiving landscape. This region would someday be named Cooktown.

For 60,000 years, the original people of this area, the Guugu Yimithirr, had been thriving, using *woomera*, *boomerang*, and spears to hunt fowl and catch fish. Cook and his men could only catch small fish—not enough to sustain the crew through the coming summer months. But then a shipmate discovered the enormous green sea turtles—weighing 200-300 pounds each. When Guugu Yimithirr tribesmen came to have a closer look at Cook's ship they discovered nearly a dozen turtles stored on the ship's deck.

Taking without asking. Taking during a "no-take" season. The trespass coincided with the tribe's season when hunting and fishing were off limits to allow the stocks to replenish. Cook's crew had broken the moral and environmental code of the Guugu Yimithirr. The tribe set fire to Cook's campsite in protest. Members of the tribe, carrying spears, approached the ship and tried to take a turtle off the deck, but they were denied. A fight ensued. Cook shot a musket, injuring a clansman.

This is a common storyline in European exploration—the land is "discovered" despite being already occupied by long-established peoples, and with this "discovery" came the belief of entitled ownership. This is where indigenous and European belief systems diverge. In indigenous communities you cannot own the land—you came from the land, belong to the land, and care for the land, so that the land can care for you. You are a servant of and to the land. Colonialists and the eventual Industrial Revolution reversed this philosophy. To industrialists, the land is your servant. Since European settlement, 90 percent of the freshwater wetlands have been removed from around the reef; nutrient inputs have doubled and sediment discharge has increased fourfold.

In 1975, the Great Barrier Reef Marine Park allocated an area of 132,819 square miles—half the size of Texas—that would not be shipped through, fished, or dredged. In 1981, UNESCO designated the reef as a World Heritage Site. While

---

Opposite top: Finding the way through the Great Barrier Reef.

Opposite bottom: Dr. Kawika Zunin and the crew check the medical kits.

the Great Barrier Reef Marine Park Authority has managed the park's area of the reef for over forty years, it also recognizes this is a spellbinding tourist hot spot that generates AU$2 billion for the economy annually. More than two million people visit the reef each year, and more than 500 commercial vessels shuttle tourists to the outer reef daily.

Seaborne trade also has a way of wearing down the reef. The four major reef ports provide service for some 7,000 ships every year. In 2012–2013, these ports handled AU$40 billion in trade, with an average of forty to fifty ships transporting goods through the reef every day.

"Every time a tourist takes away one shell from our beach, they are actually destroying that beach," says Gudju Gudju, founder of Abriculture, a group that teaches tribal ecology to grade-school children. "We get billions of tourists that come here every year," he says. "That's potentially billions of shells a year taken from here to somebody else's mantle because they want a memory. As they do that, the island starts to disappear, the landscape disappears, the reef disappears."

In 2015, UNESCO discussed placing the Great Barrier Reef on its endangered list. The Great Barrier Marine Park Authority and Australian government responded by creating the Reef 2050 Long-Term Sustainability Plan. The plan intends to prohibit dumping of capital dredge, that is, dredging for navigation to create new channels, marinas, and berths within the Marine Park. Sediment runoff is to be reduced by 50 percent below the 2009 levels by 2025, and nitrogen levels reduced by 80 percent. The government has also pledged AU$2.55 billion in an Emissions Reduction Fund—to reduce greenhouses gases—thus trying to protect the reef from the rise in ocean temperatures and the resulting ocean acidification and coral bleaching. For hundreds of thousands of years, the reef has managed to rebuild itself and adapt to the ever-changing global environment. But scientists at the Australian Institute of Marine Science are concerned that the swift shifts in climate change may leave lasting, irreversible damage.

The concern is real, and it is felt throughout the many groups working to protect the reef—from government agencies to Abriculture to school children, like Sophie Traymer, active in the Reef Guardian program in Townsville. Sophie yearns to someday be a marine scientist who can "fix" the problem of climate change. "If we keep going on like this, in a few years, when I have kids, I won't be able to take them out to the reef," she says, quite firmly. "Because there will be no reef left. It will just be all rock."

MAPS OF THE GREAT BARRIER REEF are a colorful, dizzying display of nature's ingenuity and man's attempt to make sense of it.

Great Palm Island, Rattlesnake Island, Dunk Island. Rib Reef, Trunk Reef, Fore and Aft Reef, Dido Rock, Paluma Rock, Cordelia Rocks. These are some of the forms that have remained long after the ice melted and the ocean rose. There are dashed lines indicating areas of species conservation and dotted lines indicating seasonal closure boundaries. Shipping lanes are also designated by dotted lines; northbound left lane, and southbound right lane. The higher you travel up the reef, the slimmer the pass; the closer the lane is to the shore, the shallower the water. Just a few things to consider when you are navigating the reef.

Opposite: Traditional Land Owner Joyce Henderson works as a ranger at Yuku Baja Muliku, Archer Point.

Charts of the reef are spread out across several tables on the porch of the Yongala Lodge in Townsville. The lodge is named after the *SS Yongala,* a passenger ship that steamed into a cyclone and hit a submerged rock, leaving no survivors of the 122 people on board. That was back in 1911. A seven-day search found no trace of the vessel or even a single life raft. Fifty years later, the ship's sunken skeleton was found, teaming with the life of the reef. You can read all about it on the walls of the lobby in the lodge.

Moments ago, Nainoa arrived here, gathering the crew on the porch for a meeting. Just off twenty-two hours of travel and a twenty-one-hour time shift, Nainoa seems immune to jet lag and immediately attuned to the wet tropics heat. To some, it can be confusing to experience winter in June. To Nainoa, it is simply now. This moment. It is how he remains ever present to every detail set before him.

"Today is a rest day," Nainoa tells the crew, with a slight pause. The air is thick and still, providing a shelf for his every word to seemingly rest on. "But we all know there are no rest days."

Captain Steve, who seems to never rest, is also here. Steve Kornberg is the captain of the *Hōkūleʻa* safety vessel, *Gershon II,* a twenty-five-year-old, fifty-foot-long, fourteen-foot-wide, thirty-ton steel sailboat. Steve named the boat after his grandfather and only later learned that "Gershon" is Hebrew for "Traveler in a foreign land to be welcomed as family." That translation suits him well, he says. As a traveler approaching his fifth decade of sailing, Steve listens with a pencil in hand and seems even cheerful about the coming pressures of traveling up the reef.

"You need to prepare not for the sunny days," Nainoa tells the crew, "but prepare for the days when things go really bad."

Nainoa doesn't need to elaborate about how things can go really bad. Everyone is fully aware of the risks of this voyage as it enters into unfamiliar currents, tides, winds, and seas. The safety officer is aware of these risks. His name is Kaniela Lyman-Mersereau. His uncle, David Lyman, and his mother, Marion, were on board *Hōkūleʻa* when Eddie was lost at sea. As second-generation crew, Kaniela holds a rare space in a hallowed lineup of the few who will sail the entire length of the Reef and through the Torres Strait.

The Torres Strait is a concern. The Strait lies between Australia and New Guinea, a narrow and shallow channel of reefs and islands, connecting two bodies of water with two entirely different mean sea levels. Some consider the Strait the most complex tidal area on the planet. Tides on both sides of the Strait are different, with diurnal tides on the west and semidiurnal to the east.

"Fatigue, sleep deprivation, hallucination," Nainoa says, are some of the risks of long, deep-sea voyages. "When the captain gets tired, he may look at the water, and think, the water looks good, let's take a jump in."

The point being, everybody has to do his or her job. Even more, everybody has to remain alert.

"When you voyage, you get on your feet," he tells them. "When you're on your feet, you work better, think better, you're more alert."

Everyone stands. Nainoa then assigns jobs to make sure everyone knows their *kuleana* for the coming days and nights—medical, cooking, safety, food, and water supplies.

Opposite: An injured green sea turtle recovers at the Yuku Baja Muliku Turtle Rescue and Rehabilitation Centre, Archer Point.

"Get your jobs done," he says, sending them off. "By sunset we will be *pau* (done)," he says.

One last thing, there will be a scuba dive coming up tomorrow but no dives to the *Yongala*. No one asks why. It's an unspoken rule: You don't dive sunken ships.

The crew breaks up into groups and scatters away to do their tasks.

Captains Nainoa, Kālepa, and Steve remain on the porch. They stand, leaning over the spread out maps. As they gather in, their voices become more hushed, and it's as if a curtain has been drawn around them, closing them in, together—one mind, one reef.

THE TIDE OF HISTORY is written within the reef. If you cut into the core of corals, you can find growth bands, like those of a tree trunk, providing an environmental record of the past. Floods, rains, heat, and ice—climate details are deeply embedded in the tissues of corals.

"If we think we're the evolved ones, we're wrong," says Dr. Ruth Gates, director of the University of Hawai'i Institute of Marine Biology. "People will say that we, humans, are the most evolved creatures on the planet. But actually we're the newest. We're still being tested. The coral skeletons that form reefs have been successful for millions of years. That's something we, as humans, have yet to do."

You can see Ruth is the naturalist on board, to help demystify the enormous complexity of the reef. Charles Darwin observed this territory more than a century ago, and along the way, developed his theory of evolution. Many view Ruth as an evolutionary biologist, but Ruth prefers to be known as a coral biologist. English-born and bred, she is endlessly attuned to tropical marine ecosystems, offering a keen perspective on what it means to be a coral on the planet today.

"When you really think about evolution and evolutionary success, you really have to look at the organisms that have been on the planet for hundreds of millions of years. Things like bacteria and sponges and corals—these things have persisted over an extraordinary length of time, and they've learned to adapt to the environment over that time."

If adaptation is the key to survival, then coral could be the Earth's greatest survivor. Corals may appear simple but when you study them, as Ruth does, microscopically, you begin to appreciate the flexibility that allows them to continually adjust to all kinds of environmental change.

"Reefs are like tiny cities, with lots of people living in them, and they all coordinate together when resources seem unlimited, but once resources are limited, the infighting begins."

"The reef is exemplary of the large-scale issues on the planet and the large-scale interactions we see with humans," she says. "Reefs are sentinel systems that are extraordinarily diverse just like human populations are ... they have to get along in a small space. The problem is, like humans, you can only push a human system so far before all hell breaks loose."

While reefs may be resilient, they are not indestructible. Environmental "insults," as Ruth calls them, can undermine even the healthiest reef. Trash, sediment, runoff, fishing, boating, anchoring, dredging—these are all insults.

Opposite, clockwise from top: Nainoa Thompson, Kamaki Worthington, Jenna Ishii, and Pam Omidyar tend to their *kuleana* off the Great Barrier Reef.

To Ruth, dumping coastal dredge directly onto a reef is akin to dropping a war bomb on a food supply and creating widespread famine.

"There is nothing in the resilience of that reef that can actually offset that huge insult. It is a done deal," she says. "There is nothing that will save them."

What is the greatest insult of all? Climate change, according to Ruth. Thirty percent of CO_2 in the atmosphere is absorbed into the ocean. As CO_2 in the ocean increases, the ocean's pH decreases—it becomes more acidic—creating coral bleaching. Some bleached coral *can* recover. But not all do.

Why do some corals recover and others collapse? That is the question Ruth is pursuing in tandem with Madeleine van Oppen at the Australian Institute of Marine Science. Over the next five years, their team will conduct studies at the AIMS facility known as the Sea Simulator. Ruth's project is designed to understand the cumulative impacts of changing water quality and rising sea temperatures on reef health. By creating minor bleaching events, what she refers to as putting coral on a "coral treadmill," she hopes to turn on "the memory" in the corals so they can recover. Stress it out and see how and why it endures. In the Sea Simulator, she will be able to maintain multiple generations of corals over time, and then attempt to plant healthy corals in a reef to help it recuperate. Ruth calls this "coral farming."

While no amount of human engineering could have created this reef, perhaps human engineering can help save the reef.

Ruth has considered the risks of intervention versus the risks of doing nothing. She has considered that this may be viewed as altering the evolution of corals. "But doing nothing," she says, "is not a solution."

"A BIRD HAS AN INTERNAL COMPASS," Kālepa explains. "A bird is never lost."

It's an open-canoe day. While some of the crew is giving canoe tours, others are off planting trees with schoolchildren, and Kālepa is giving a crash course in the navigational system that has guided them to another major port along the reef, Cairns. Kālepa stands in the center of a huge diagram of the Hawaiian Navigational Star Compass on the dockside where a crowd has gathered around him—some older, some younger, many tourists, and a few locals. Kālepa has been sailing on *Hōkūle'a* since he was twenty-two years old. With an inner compass anchored in the Hawaiian spirit, Kālepa is a continual reminder that the Worldwide Voyage is about the connections made. Mālama Honua is to care for the Earth and to also care for those who live upon it. Right now, he is *mālama*-ing the folks of Cairns by sharing his knowledge of ancient Polynesian wayfaring.

"Birds always know directions," he tells the group. "The bird flies in the oceanic environment, and it always has a relationship with the edge of the horizon."

Kālepa holds a miniature woodcarving of *Hōkūle'a* and shows the crowd how the canoe is similar to a bird. The Hawaiian word for bird, *manu*, also means the prow of the canoe.

"The compass is a metaphor for a bird," he explains but some seem slightly confused. Some have their arms crossed in front of their chests; others have their heads tilted.

While Kālepa talks, the ever-present modern reality is all around him—just behind him is the Ferry Fleet Terminal where high-speed catamarans shuttle

Opposite: Saltwater crocodiles, "salties," roam from swamps to rivers to sea, North Queensland.

hundreds of tourists off for all-day dives to the outer reefs. Luxury schooners, charter boats, helicopters, and sea planes are also available for hire—ready to take the many tourists to one of the most popular destinations off of Cairns: Green Island, a rainforest-covered coral cay just sixteen and a half miles away. Here, the smell of diesel fuel is a fundamental part of the environment.

Kālepa breaks it down with simple questions.

"If the head of the bird is pointing in one direction," Kālepa asks, "where does the tail of the bird point?"

"If the right wing is pointing in one direction, where is the left wing pointing?"

The answers come quick and correct. But then, he unintentionally stumps them with this question: "If we cover the bird's eyes, can the bird still figure out where he's going?"

The elements of traditional wayfinding techniques are based on understanding the environmental patterns around you, behind you, before you, above you, and even below you. It requires having a full understanding of the cosmos, so that if you can read the constellations above you, you will know what constellations lie beneath you, on the other side of the planet.

"You can figure out direction by knowing what's behind you, and knowing what's off the right side and the left side," he explains.

And then he pauses and says, quite slowly, "If you want to know where to go, you need to know where you are coming from."

The statement relates not only to a directional perspective but also to a deeper understanding of your ancestral past. This is where Kālepa's Hawaiian wisdom and the local original people's wisdom converge.

For centuries, the original people of the sea country have maintained a deep connection to the reef. "There's still a longing to be out there," admits Gudju Gudju. "But we don't need to be on the reef to know what's happening out there."

Like *Pwo* navigators, original people do not need to rely on modern instruments to understand the natural world around them. They do not use a clock or a calendar to know when it is time to hunt or harvest or sow. They need only to look at nature to know a time to hunt, a time to kill, a time to plant, a time to sow. The navigational compass, GPS, sextant, clocks, and calendars are all modern mental constructs. The original people use "signal plants" to let them know when it's time to fish on the reef and when it's time to leave the reef alone because the reef is spawning, just as Papa Mau used "storm stars" to know when the time was right to sail.

"As scientists, we've drilled down into some minutiae to such a degree that we've lost a sense of those natural rhythms—which is essentially what traditional landowners are tuned in to," Ruth observes, as she intently listens to the captain's lesson. "Everything that we study is set by natural rhythms; everything on the planet is set by circadian rhythms and the circadian rhythm is really driven by life cycles."

There is a natural rhythm of the tides, high tide, low tide; daytime star, the sun, and the nighttime star, the moon. There are two horizons, one that is rising, and the other setting, Kālepa explains, and there are thirty-two houses on the compass—each signifying a different direction. Kālepa teaches the group the names of the houses in Hawaiian.

"It's like a mirror," someone says, and Kālepa smiles, yes, it is. Nature is a big mirror. Look to nature to know where you came from and where you are going.

"If you want to know where to go, you need to know where you are coming from," Kālepa says again. As Kālepa continues, a helicopter churns; a ferryboat blasts its horn.

"Why does the navigator always navigate from the back of the canoe?" Kālepa asks the group.

Someone answers correctly. "Yeah, this is where the steering is—you need to know where you come from," Kālepa reminds them.

There's another reason, he says. But no one can answer it.

"If I stand at the bow of the canoe, I get wet!"

Laughs all around. The laughs quiet when Kālepa begins to explain that this is a several thousand-year-old history of navigation. "We learned this because our teacher was a traditional noninstrument navigator. He would always stand in the same place in the canoe—he always looked off the edges—so we knew he had calibrated his canoe to different angular points. We just kind of expanded on that idea and put the mathematical and scientific components into it. This is only the foundational level. Now, you have to go back and learn all the stars and place the stars in the star compass, and then you start to build upon that. But this is the groundwork; this is the foundation."

An older man has just arrived. He's lean, with a faded cap and sea-swept skin.

"But how did you get here?" the man wants to know. "How did you get from Hawai'i to here?" The man clearly knows something about voyaging with stars and Hawaiians using the Southern Cross as a guide to determine latitude. The man asks, "The Southern Cross is not in the same place down here, is it?"

"You have a black hole that the stars turn around," Kālepa explains to his fellow sailor. "We just have to identify that black spot and use that as our south bird."

The sailor understands; others appear perplexed. A child rubs his eyes and begs for ice cream. Kālepa winds the class down.

Above: Swinging wildlife.

"Just know this," he tells the group, settling any loose ends. "We know that the world is round, right?"

They all nod their heads.

"So we're not going to fall off the edge," he says, with a smile. "We're not going to fall off the edge."

"WE CAN MAKE ALL THE SCHEDULES WE WANT," Nainoa tells the crew. "But Mother Nature dictates when we go."

The winds are blowing at thirty knots—just a few knots short of a gale. Nainoa says it's prudent to wait twenty-four hours after the peak of the winds before setting sail. But it's unclear when the peak will be. It's not worth the risk, Nainoa says at a crew meeting on the eve before the scheduled sail to Cooktown, some ninety-two nautical miles north. That night a torrential, window-shaking, winter-solstice storm pounds Cairns.

The following day, while the crew waits out the storm, the winds are fierce in Cooktown.

There is a mount called Grassy Hill in Cooktown, where Cook climbed to get a sense of the lay of the land and the sea and the reef beyond. Up here, a flagless flagpole is shaped like a mast, hooks clank against the pole in the rhythm of the wind. Nearby, the century-old, rusted corrugated iron lighthouse remains unmanned, a chain blocking its narrow steps. Just beside it, there is a brass-plated instrument, shaped like a sundial, telling you the direction of north to Lizard Island, south to Black Mountain, east to Egret Reef, and west to Lookout Range.

Where you are standing is the center, where all things converge—rainforest and mangroves, granite and sand dunes, lagoons and streams and the sea. No ferries, catamarans, cruise ships, container ships, or helicopters. No distractions from the central intelligence of nature. Near the horizon, where clouds eclipse the sun, lies the reef. You can feel it, even smell it, wafting in and out, pulsing with the tide.

Opposite top: Pwo Navigator Kālepa Baybayan visits a Reef Guardian School, one of 276 schools that teach children to be stewards of the Great Barrier Reef.

Opposite bottom: Crewmember Dan Lin demonstrates the Hawaiian star compass at the Reef Headquarters Aquarium, an education facility of the Great Barrier Reef Marine Park Authority.

Local Voices

Russell Butler

Elder of the Girringun People

Russell Butler sat on a park bench in Townsville overlooking Magnetic Island as the sun slowly set. Russell is an elder of the aboriginal tribal group known as Girringun, nine tribes whose territory extends from the mountains to the sea, Townsville to Caldwell. A measured and thoughtful man, Russell was instrumental in the creation of the pact between the government and Aboriginal and Torres Strait Islanders to protect the Traditional Use of Marine Resources Agreements—TUMRA—in the Great Barrier Reef Marine Park. TUMRA involves seventy traditional peoples groups whose country includes the Great Barrier Reef and is intended to assure that customs and traditions are maintained and respected. As he talked about his tribe's beliefs, the "happy hour" birds had gathered in the sprawling magnolia trees. Russell remained long after the sun set and the sky awakened, illuminating the Southern Cross, like a long-lost guide into the night.

In His Own Words

WE CALL THE GREAT BARRIER REEF—*Julin*—THE land way out East. The reef is our homeland. It's where we lived 18,000 years ago. We lived along the continental shelf and all the waterfalls flowed off the cliffs of the reef. When the ice caps melted and the water rose up and chased us back, we had to move backwards off the water and back to the land, here, in Townsville.

We call the sea, *Bandjin*—that's my tribal name. It means saltwater. I'm an elder—like a chief—what I do is give out information to the younger people. I teach them all the stories. I tell them about the country, where they can go, where they can't go, what fish they can eat, what animals they can eat, what animals they can't eat, all about respect for land and sea country. My mission is to bring back to life all of our stories. Not only to us. But to all people, too.

One time ago, we weren't allowed to talk about it. Oppression. Even today the average person doesn't want to hear it. They want to squeeze us into a category—that we're aboriginal people.

You see, when we look at that land, we look at it differently. When we buy land, we don't buy a bulldozer. We care about it. The land is there to give us things and, in return, we have to look after it.

Our tribe is called *Girringun*—a god who came from the Big Lake, the Gulf of Carpentaria, when Cape York was joined with New Guinea and the Northern Territory was joined to Indonesia. That was the biggest saltwater lake in the Southern Hemisphere. *Girringun* gave us our tribal boundaries and our laws of the food chain and our stories. Our boundaries are thousands of years old. We use the mountain range and river systems and reefs to mark our boundaries. In the old days, a pile of stones meant a lot. It marked our boundaries. It's all passed down through generations. I was the youngest in my family, and when I was little, I was stuck with the old people. You might be playing and you hear them say something, and you think, oh, I'll lock that away. That's where my knowledge comes from.

I've got four sons and one daughter and eleven grandchildren and three great-grandchildren. They hear my stories every day, and even though they don't say anything, I know they are listening. I tell them learning to listen is the key to everything that you do in life. If you learn to listen, you will understand everything.

In summer, I come down here and listen and look. I feel good energy when I'm on the water—anywhere out here. I watch the birds and if I don't see seagulls, I know there's a storm coming. There are telltale signs. Ants tell us when rain is coming. I don't have to look at my phone. I don't have to look at the weather channel to know what's coming.

Our people, we don't fear the sea. We respect the sea. In respecting our sea country, there's no hunting turtle or dugong. It's totally banned. When I first came out of the army, the government was saying that my people were the reason why turtle and dugong were gone. But we hunted them only rarely. We only took what we could eat. So I went out on my boat. I looked around and watched. It was the net fishermen that were doing all the damage. The boat propeller strikes, too. I knew who the harmful people were. So I said, "Well, we'll close it down." No more hunting turtles and dugong from our tribe. In 1990, I did that. Then, we just monitored it. We put the onus back on the government, and they eventually bought all the fishing licenses. There are only a few fishermen in there now. No trawlers allowed.

All those animals are in there now. You can go in a boat and see them. We've got herds, up to the hundreds, of dugongs. Turtles, everywhere. They're beautiful.

We still fish. But with all the animals we hunt, we do the same. We apologize before killing it and after killing it. Our first fish catch, you have a choice, either put it back and continue fishing, or eat that one. But once you catch enough, you go home.

The government used to ask us, "Well, how many fish do you take when you go out here?"

Only enough to eat, I would tell them. And then I had to show them how we eat the fish. We don't eat fish the same as Europeans. When we kill a fish, we eat everything—fin, eyes, head, all the bones. We don't waste anything. You should never waste your food.

My whole family are fishermen. A lot of my grandchildren are named after the islands—great-granddaughters too—Palm Island, Orpheus Island, Phantom Island. Go to the top of the mountain, you can see the reefs and islands.

I'm worried about the Great Barrier Reef and about the marine park. Only a month ago they were saying the Barrier Reef was endangered. Then all of a sudden—I think they're trying to fast track this coal thing at Abbott Point—they're saying the reef is good. But, I know. You can't just tell everyone in the world that it's fine, 'cause it's not.

The reef. I still feel like it's my home. Sometimes I sit and I look at it and think one time ago that's where we lived. I tell my grandchildren, we don't have to go there to feel it, because we can feel it in here—in our hearts.

Local Solutions
Australian Institute of Marine Science

IN 1998 AND 2002, HIGHER THAN USUAL SEA-SURFACE temperatures caused mass coral bleaching along the Great Barrier Reef. After the summer of 2002, the Great Barrier Reef Marine Park Authority initiated the world's most comprehensive survey of coral bleaching. Then, in 2009, extreme temperatures produced high rainfall rates throughout Queensland, leading to increased sediment runoff—flood plumes—contributing to even more bleaching. A year later, the Australian government provided a plan to understand the full extent and breadth of the reef, and soon after, provided the Australian Institute of Marine Science funding to create the National Sea Simulator, Sea Sim.

An AU$35 million facility, the Sea Sim was built to understand the many challenges affecting marine life. The facility simulates marine environments to fully comprehend the cumulative effects of multiple stressors on marine ecosystems. By manipulating light, acidity, sediment, salinity, contaminants, and temperature, scientists can analyze the vulnerability and resiliency of this intricate marine ecosystem. Pumps currently deliver nearly 300,000 gallons of seawater daily from the reef, and a saltwater processing plant allows for long- and short-term experiments. With indoor and outdoor aquariums, scientists are able to sustain multiple generations of corals and other forms of marine life. Some tanks are maintained at present-day conditions; others are altered to replicate what scientists expect to see in fifty to one hundred years from now.

The plan: to determine how dredging, port activities, coastal development, erosion, farming runoff, nutrient flows, flood plumes, and the cumulative effects of agriculture, industrialization, and urbanization all affect the health of the reef.

What is the impact of an oil spill? How does sediment runoff affect the reef? With rising sea-surface temperatures, how much more common will these massive coral bleaching events be? Why do some corals recover and others die? What are the major tipping points affecting the life of the reef? These are just a few of the questions marine scientists seek to answer with ongoing experiments in the Sea Simulator.

The Northwest sea country is valued for its immense biodiversity. But the risk to water quality threatens this biodiversity. Risks are generally attributed to sediment disturbance, transport, and sediment settlement associated with dredging used to facilitate processing and port-development activities.

Sea Sim studies are intended to inform future coastal and marine planning—including government, conservation groups, and all industries that operate in or near the marine environment. The goal is to find the balance between human activity and reef vitality to create a sustainable marine estate. With research focused primarily on Australia's tropical marine environment, from the Great Barrier Reef and Ningaloo Reef and the northwest shelf in Western Australia, scientists intend to share information with marine groups in over thirty countries. These findings hope to inform governments and industries to make sound decisions based on sustainable use and management of marine ecosystems.

Opposite top and bottom: Two ends of the spectrum: healthy coral and bleached-out coral.

Next spread: Crewmember Kaniela Lyman-Mersereau dives deep at the Great Barrier Reef.

CREW STORY
Chad Kālepa Baybayan
Pwo *Navigator*

Chad Kālepa Baybayan first sailed on Hōkūleʻa in 1975 and has sailed on all major Hōkūleʻa voyages since. Kālepa has also served as captain on the voyaging canoes Hawaiʻiloa, Hōkūalakaʻi, and Hikianalia and has been the Director of Honuakai, the Exploration Sciences Division of the ʻAha Pūnana Leo, a group that teaches the Hawaiian language to those who crew aboard Hōkūalakaʻi. Kālepa is currently the Navigator in Residence at the ʻImiloa Astronomy Center of Hawaiʻi, developing wayfinding activities, curriculum materials, and conducting outreach. In 2007, Kālepa was initiated into the Pwo, the 2,000-year-old society of deep-sea navigators. Along with four other Hōkūleʻa navigators, Kālepa was initiated by Mau Piailug on the island of Satawal in Micronesia. Kālepa spoke from the comfort of his hillside home in Kona overlooking fields of lava spilling all the way down to the Pacific.

HŌKŪLEʻA HAS BEEN THE BIGGEST mentor in my life. She helped set the direction of my aspirations of what I hoped to become. When you're a young man, you have desire but the articulation of the desire wasn't that strong for me—I was trying to find the words. I always wanted to learn how to navigate, but not necessarily become a navigator. Saying you want to become a navigator, that's a major step. I just wanted to learn about the art, about the process that it took to navigate.

When I was eighteen years old, I had just returned home to Maui from college on the mainland. I showed up at the same time Hōkūleʻa arrived in June 1975. The first time I saw Hōkūleʻa, I fell in love with her. I used to sit for hours, just watching her at anchor. I felt connected somehow to something that was distantly familiar to me.

Then, I helped build a double-hulled, forty-two-foot-long canoe in Maui, Moʻolele. All my training took place on that smaller canoe. We had one teacher, Leon Sterling. In 1977, when Hōkūleʻa was sailing around the state, Leon was captain and he called me on board.

Before the 1976 voyage to Tahiti, I was part of the ʻawa ceremony—and, being part of the circle, Mau was asked to speak. I was in awe of him. Mau was an oceanic mountaineer, a survivalist, a total 'Islander.' He could make fire by rubbing two sticks together. He could make a rope out of coconut husks. Mau was stepping up as a leader on the canoe, but also as a father figure to all of us. He told the crowd gathered that it was time to leave the things of land behind and come together as a family on the ocean. I thought that was truly profound.

My first experience of sailing with Mau came on the trip to get Hōkūleʻa into position in Hilo for the second trip to Tahiti. There were six of us who took the canoe from Honolulu to Hilo. We got caught in a storm, and almost lost our lives. After we got out of the blow, we changed course and were going to be towed. But it wasn't feasible to tow in that rough water, and Mau said, "No, we got to sail." So, we cast off the tow.

Sailing to Hilo is into the wind. It's an uphill climb. The only way to get there is by tacking the canoe up the coast, and that's when I got my first lesson in navigation from Mau.

I would stand on the railing next to Mau and hear him chanting. He was facing the wind. He didn't have a raincoat on, just bare chested, and every time a wave would crash on the side of the canoe, he'd get totally wet, but he just wiped the salt water off his face and his body, and he'd keep on chanting. He was so determined.

I would ask him, "Hey Mau, what direction is this wave coming from?" He'd tell me, "Oh, this is from the northeast." And I'd ask, "Which direction is this one coming from? What about this one, here?"

We stayed up together all night long, closing and opening the sails, tacking toward the coastline then tacking back out again, twenty-four hours straight of opening and closing sails and tacking back and forth up the coast. I was so tired, but I stood by him and kept asking questions.

I liked the way Mau taught class. It was experiential. It was visual. It was in the elements. I learned from Mau the patience required of the student. There's a whole body of information that you need to know. I recognized that the canoe was a class-room and I was a student. I was always humble and willing to learn. I knew that lessons were always being taught to me anytime I was onboard the canoe. I really wanted to become a good servant to the project.

About thirty years later, in 2007, Mau called us all to Satawal for a Pwo ceremony. There were five of us: Nainoa, Bruce, Chadd Paishon, Shorty Bertelmann, and me. There were eleven other Satawalese who were also bestowed the rank and honor of Pwo. There were two big canoes, two big escort boats, and all these people sailing to this tiny island for the ceremony. It didn't feel right, the amount of people who were showing up, putting a lot of pressure on this island. I really didn't want to go; I really respected the need for that island to continue to sustain itself, but Nainoa was adamant that I attend.

This ceremony has been conducted on the island for thousands of years. They recognize the most skilled oceanic person on their island, and they recognize and honor him, and present him to the community. This is the community's leader and, in return, he's tasked with providing for the island, so he becomes the head fisherman. He is the key for sustaining the island; he's responsible for feeding the community. I understood that. I understood that being *Pwo* is about giving back. It's about being a resource for your community. *Pwo* is about being a light for your community.

I had always wanted to learn about navigation in a traditional setting and I was given that gift the night the ceremony had concluded. It was very late at night, most of the Hawaiian navigators had gone off to bed, and it was just me and Shorty and the eleven Micronesian navigators. Mau was seated on a wooden platform in the canoe house, and these eleven fishermen gathered around him.

There are many islands that surround Satawal, and for every island, there's a course line that you sail to get to that island. There are certain bearings that you hold with a rising and setting star. Mau was chanting these instructions. He was teaching in his language, but I knew what he was talking about because I could recognize the star names and direction names.

These fishermen would stop him, and ask a question, and he'd explain. Then somebody else would jump in and ask a question, and he would explain. Mau looked like he was staring off into space, but it was all inside of him; he was recalling everything. When you think about it, that body of knowledge—that two dozen islands they can sail through, and have recorded the angles you need to hold your canoe to, and the direction of the rising and setting stars along the path—is all laid out mentally. It's a really powerful base of knowledge, and they've been able to retain it for thousands of years. That was the final gift for me before I left the island; to be in that presence, to be in that traditional setting, and to hear Mau recite this knowledge.

In navigating, there are a lot of metaphors for almost anything in life. You need a vessel, you need good training, you need good equipment, and you need a sound navigational plan. Once you have those elements in place, you commit to the vision. You also need to remain flexible. You have to recognize that if something isn't working, you need to change your sail plan. If you take those steps, you can basically adapt to anything—in voyaging or in your own life.

Above: A pet snake greets Kālepa in Cooktown, Australia.

Opposite: Kālepa teaches the star compass with a model canoe.

"I've heard the term Mother Africa before.
I understand it now. I understand.
We feel the *aloha* of this *'āina*, this land.
We are children of this land."

Billy Richards
Captain

SOUTH AFRICA

CHAPTER 5

We are interconnected.
We belong one to another.

—

– Archbishop Desmond Tutu

A TERN SWOOPS BY, CIRCLES ONCE, AND THEN LANDS ON THE TIDAL rocks. Just to pause. Check it all out. Watch the slow-rising yawn of dawn. Golden-brown kelp bulbs sway, hypnotic, like buoys, across the waters of this sheltered bay known as Black Rocks. Here comes a gully shark, patrolling the tide pools. There goes the tern, lifting off. Sit here long enough, you can sense the Earth turning.

This is the Western Cape of South Africa where the cold upwelling of the Benguela Current diverges from the warm Agulhas Current, creating one of the richest marine ecosystems on the planet. Along these shores, humans survived during the Ice Age, living primarily on abalone, mollusks, oysters, and the occasional beached whale. Today, there's a guide, offering up what it may have been like to live here during that time. His name is Craig Foster. Nainoa brought the canoe to this shore, a day short of reaching Cape Town, specifically to experience this thriving seascape with Craig. Nainoa has said that the Worldwide Voyage is a way to find great navigators who are caring for our oceans and lands. Craig is one such man.

A native of the eastern coast of Africa, Craig spent three years studying the hunting and tracking skills of the San Bushmen of the Kalahari, and is now dedicated to tracking human history along the Cape Point shores. Along with co-researcher Ross Frylinck, Craig has created the Sea-Change Project, a multimedia project telling the story of the birth of human consciousness during our earliest relationship with the sea. Together, the two men lead Nainoa and *Hōkūleʻa*'s Indian Ocean safety officer, Archie Kalepa, along the tidal front. As a Hawaiian lifeguard captain, Archie's rescue missions during Hurricane ʻIniki earned him the Eddie Aikau Waterman Award. Today, the master waterman and big wave champion remains a student, ever humble, along the water's edge.

"This is the primal address," Craig explains to the men. "This is the original landscape of the human mind."

Craig grew up east of here in a beach bungalow along the shore, just below the high tide mark. "We had waves washing through our home," he says, "and so on...."

With every "and so on," Craig seems to say, this isn't about me. It's about this place and our need to reconnect with our origins. Craig is hoping this experience will close the gap on what we have forgotten. His hope is to inspire people to commune with nature—wherever they reside on the planet, knowing that that relationship can be deeply healing. His years with the San Bushmen led him to this truth. The San believe that to re-remember our relation to the Earth will afford us a direct "rope to god," and this rope will allow us to heal ourselves, and in doing so, will help us to learn how to heal the Earth.

Opposite: *Hōkūleʻa* sails below the Twelve Apostles en route to Cape Town.

"This is quite a sensitive environment. It's hugely cryptic. It doesn't seem that there's that much out there, but literally thousands of eyes are watching you," Craig says. The marine animals can seem shy at first. Craig tells a story that after three years of coming here, and swimming here daily, the animals began swimming toward him. In time, he's been able to swim alongside the sharks, sometimes even holding the dorsal fin; sometimes resting his hand on the shark's nose to lull the shark into a meditative spell. Another time, he lay on the ocean floor to allow a stingray to rest on his belly. Once, after an otter swam near him and gazed at him, the otter reached out to touch his face.

Archie spots a palm-sized octopus within the rocks. The king of camouflage is kelp brown and mossy green. Craig gently scoops it out from between a narrow slip of rocks.

"It's okay," he whispers, trying to coax it to relax in the palm of his hand. "We're not going to hurt you."

Craig explains that octopi actually have six arms and two legs. This one uses all six arms to cover his head. "See how he's protecting his head?" Craig asks.

This octopus has a yearlong life expectancy, Craig explains, and this one is a teenager. Its lifespan of a year seems so brief, he says; once they lay their eggs, they're gone. He lets this one go. Craig explains that many of these same octopi, mollusks, and limpets were around 75,000 years ago. He talks about 75,000 years ago as if it were yesterday. He refers to humans who lived back then as "the early folk" in an affectionate tone you might reserve for a grandparent. When asked how many "early folk" were living here back then, Craig says, "Maybe two thousand people."

Nainoa walks slowly, hands folded behind his back, head down, as he gently makes his way over the rocks, careful to not step on a limpet. Without looking up, Nainoa stops, says, "Wait, you got to say that again. There were two thousand people? That's it?"

Nainoa's trying to wrap his head around the exponential explosion of our species—how those few thousand who lived along this stretch of coastline so many thousands of years ago eventually migrated and grew to become the seven billion we are today.

Craig explains that there were maybe twenty-five people living in each of the cliffside caves up here—a small enough number to gather food and not deplete the place. If a whale washed up, then maybe another neighbor group would come in to share the feast.

"Just twenty-five people lived in a cave here?" Nainoa asks. He looks up at the cliff to the caves tucked into the rocks and shrubs.

"Our original design was for hunting and gathering," Craig explains. "We were the top predator in that environment. Soon as you change your design, a predator breeding like a prey, you've got a problem."

"Ultimately, it's not going to work," Nainoa says. "Coming here, to one of the richest ecological oceanic zones on the planet, the richest I've ever been to in all my life—and it's good for only twenty-five people?"

"This is one of the last intact ecosystems on Earth. If we could just stop the overfishing and release the pressure on abalone and crayfish stocks, the system would bounce back very quickly," Craig says. Much of the abalone has been poached.

Opposite: Craig Foster and Nainoa Thompson explore marine life in the kelp forest ecology at Cape Point.

Crayfish are down to less than 5 percent of their original numbers. Overfishing removes the big fish predators, disrupting the balance of the entire system.

Craig spots a fishing line tangled in the rocks. A single line can wrap around the neck of a seal and strangle it. Craig unravels it from the rocks and tucks it into his pack. He will find a way to make a second use out of it, maybe even fashion it into a piece of art like the massive sea glass chandelier that hangs in the entry to his home.

A couple of baboons have come down from the cliffs to sit in the milkwood. On a hotter day, they will venture down and take a swim. Today, they're staying back, checking out Craig and his small tribe.

"The early folk had an incredible relationship with hundreds of different species," Craig explains, citing the ways the Kalahari Bushmen hunted and shared the meat with lions. That animal connection has been lost. "We've largely severed all that."

It's time to reconnect. The kelp leaves have now risen, spreading out on the surface of the water, like a canopy, soaking up the ever-widening spray of the mid-day sun. Craig believes we first learned to swim in waters like this, using the kelp ropes as lifelines, twelve-yard-long stalks guiding us to the depths of the ocean floor. Nainoa and Archie are ready to give it a try, hoping to meet up with a shark, a ray, or even an otter.

"When you start making the bonds again with the animals, you just start feeling such a relief," Craig explains. "And you start to remember."

Craig, Nainoa, Ross, and Archie walk their way across the rocks toward the water's edge. Once there, they crouch down and slip in, the kelp rising all around them as, one by one, they slowly submerge, disappearing into the depths of the forest.

CRAB CLAW SAILS SPREAD, *Hōkūle'a* seems to sashay as she makes her way across the South Atlantic toward Cape Town. She's halfway around the world, three oceans, four seas, and eleven time zones away from her Hawaiian home. Entering Cape Town is a turning point; from this port forward, the sail will be a return toward home. But it also feels like another kind of turning point for those awaiting *Hōkūle'a* in the Victoria and Alfred Marina. It is only two weeks before the Climate Change Conference in Paris and you can feel the call for global ecological change. One word is carried in the wind today—*ubuntu*—the African spirit of human kindness, akin to the Hawaiian word, *aloha*.

"*Ubuntu* is the essence of being human," Archbishop Emeritus Desmond Tutu once explained. "It speaks of our interconnectedness. When you do well, it spreads out, it is for the whole of humanity."

It is the same philosophy that has guided this voyage this far. *Ubuntu*, like *aloha*, is a kindness not just to the Earth but also to one another.

"We think of ourselves far too frequently just as individuals," Tutu says, "separated from one another; whereas, you are connected and what you do affects the whole world." Tutu is a navigator of humankind.

Today, the Archbishop is on the dockside to greet the canoe. Dancers have come from Hawai'i to offer hula and song to the African hosts. African drummers, dancers, chanters, a children's brass band, sailors, and dreamers have also come to witness the canoe's arrival. The chanting, whistling, and drumming seem to be

Opposite top: Early man survived on a rich diet of mussels and seafood found in the tide pools, Black Rocks.   **Opposite bottom:** Cape fur seal colony, Haut Bay.

calling the canoe in. Within the weaving of African and Hawaiian rhythms, one question remains: How do we navigate, together, into the future?

"The voyage of *Hōkūle'a* reconnects us to each other on a primal level," Mpho Tutu, Desmond's daughter, tells the crowd. "It harkens back to the starting point of our interconnectedness and our human journey ... and so, I welcome our Polynesian brothers and sisters, who have literally sailed halfway across the world to connect, or rather to reconnect, with us in our gorgeous mother city. Welcome home."

In a country that continues to experience the deep wounds of apartheid, the talk centers on the theme of all people coming together as *One*. Here, where the oldest culture, Africa, meets the youngest culture, Hawai'i, the desire to unite is the common thread. It is rooted in the hearts of those who greet *Hōkūle'a* and those who have sailed on her decks.

"Twelve hundred years ago, a canoe-load of experienced and seasoned sailors and explorers landed on the shores of Hawai'i," Kālepa tells the gathering. "Thus ended the final chapter of the great human odyssey."

As climate change pushes people off of Pacific islands, and political change sends some fleeing homelands, and poverty drives others across borders, the human odyssey continues. Our collective human footprint has created a biological collapse scientists refer to as the Sixth Extinction.

"When we look for peace, it should be that we're way more alike than we're different," Nainoa tells the gathering. "And we need to celebrate that likeness ... and it starts here."

The celebration continues with everyone forming a large circle, holding hands, while the crew sings a song in Hawaiian. Though many here may not know the words to this song, they know the feeling that will linger long after this day has ended. The feeling is united, with one another, in our hope for the future of humans and our Earth.

DRIVING THE GARDEN ROUTE, along the southeastern coast of South Africa, you can glimpse a stretch of breathtaking monoculture. Fields upon hills upon fields have been stripped, sowed, plowed, cut, and rolled. The only variation of the terrain can be found in the packaging of the final harvested product: a haystack—either rolled, or rolled with a thin covering of plastic.

"For 95 percent of our existence on this planet, we lived in nature, lived tightly knit with nature," Dr. Peter Nilssen, an archaeologist at Point of Human Origins explains. People have been around for 200,000 years, but for the past 12,000 years, with the advent of agriculture, people have made a point of living on *top* of nature, as opposed to *with* nature. "Before the advent of farming, our very survival depended on a good, healthy symbiotic relationship with the environment."

As an archaeologist in South Africa, Peter has a perspective on the human journey few others have. He can see how we lived 200,000 years ago, where we are now, and where we need to go in the century ahead. "All humans on our planet are descendants of these early people," Peter explains. "The heritage belongs to all of us, and their knowledge is for us to learn from."

Opposite, top to bottom: A school band welcomes *Hōkūle'a* to Cape Town. Archbishop Emeritus Desmond Tutu dances with a band member. Strong winds envelop a Hawaiian dancer who traveled halfway around the globe for the ceremony.

Stone Age people lived in a functional relationship with nature; Peter says this is part of our "coding" that is still alive in us today. But, for the most part, this coding has somehow been nullified, forgotten. As populations grew, he says, "We began altering nature for what may appear to be our benefit."

Some would consider one of those "benefits" to be agriculture, or even the installation of a golf course. In 2000, a developer wanted to convert a spectacular stretch of sandstone cliffs in Mossel Bay into an eighteen-hole golf course overlooking the Indian Ocean. Before any developments were allowed, an environmental impact study had to be performed. An agreement was made that the developer would protect the delicate area, and soon after, archaeologists moved in.

Archaelogists Peter Nilssen and Jonathan Kaplan were involved in the project that revealed a series of caves containing the oldest evidence of modern human behavior. Within time, the area was deemed a Provincial Heritage Site. Nonetheless, the shrubland was cleared, land leveled, sod installed, villas built, and a two-story clubhouse erected to create the Pinnacle Point Beach and Golf Estate. Today, in order to reach the caves, you must first enter the neatly paved roadways of the resort to join the trail, leading some 200 feet down the cliffs to the most accessible cave, known as 13B.

Cave 13B is a wide, deep berth with wet quartzitic sandstone walls. There are sandbags throughout, protecting areas containing archaeological material, and sediments that have been exposed during excavations. Some sandbags prevent residue from slumping down toward the ocean. Areas of the walls are lined with signs of Ice Age human occupation when Africa was arid. While people had access to terrestrial animals, the main consistent food base was along the shore.

Those who lived here created and used complex stone tools, embedding rocks in bone and wood, and using heat to manipulate stone into tools and weapons. Ochre, a natural earth pigment, was used for cultural and symbolic behavior.

Carbon and oxygen isotopes remain in the dripstone formations in the caves, revealing patterns in sea levels and climate shifts from 400,000 to 30,000 years ago. In studying the cave and archaeological record for over a decade now, Peter has come to understand how Stone Age people looked after their own environment. The caves contain remnants of the Stone Age equivalent of a rubbish dump. Nearby shell middens—alternating layers of sand and shell sediments—are indications that people harvested food from the tidal waters, ate, left, and returned. They seemed aware that overusing a place would not allow it to replenish. They understood how to be sustainable.

"Somehow early people managed to survive very well for a long time," Peter says. "It's only in our recent past that we're not surviving as well as a species and not doing that well in looking after our environment."

While his work here is very specific to the place, his view of our life on this planet is expansive. Peter believes in the Gaia principle, viewing Earth as a single organism, and seeing all the geospheres, oceans, biota, and atmosphere working together for the entire ecosystem of the planet. Peter mentions that the notion of a tipping point need not always indicate a point tipping in the wrong direction. It can also tip in the right direction. While the human species is a large, planet-altering force, it can also alter the planet for the better.

Opposite top: Monoculture has replaced diversity in the rich, food-producing regions of the Garden Route.

Opposite bottom: This sea cave may have been home to the first truly modern humans, their brains fueled by nutrient-rich and plentiful shellfish, Mossel Bay.

"You need less than 1 percent of our species to change in order to make an energetic change in the whole," Peter says. What we have been taught can be altered. That part of our brain is malleable. He seems to suggest that it is not simply a question of rewiring the mind, but also a rewiring of the heart. Each one of us needs to remember, he says, "I'm *not* too small to make a difference."

IF YOU LOST LAND
DUE TO RACIAL ISSUES
CLAIM YOUR LAND RIGHTS!

THIS IS A BILLBOARD along the roadway heading to St. Mary's Primary School in Nyanga. Nyanga was the first township in Cape Town, created back in 1948, as a settlement for "colored" migrant laborers. The city planners had envisioned a white-only Cape Town with highways and valleys and railways as buffers against the workers who would live outside the city in places like Nygana. Nygana and its surrounding area, known as the Cape Flats, are often referred to as "apartheid's dumping ground."

The Cape Flats are just above sea level. The land is primarily sand that has been wind-swept from shorelines miles away. With corrugated tin roofs and patchwork walls, the housing provides an unstable future. Electrical wires extend from rooftops—crossing over several other wires—all connected to a single substation box. When it rains, all electricity stops, and the public toilets are known to overflow into homes. The houses share common walls, so when an electrical fire blows through one, it often takes several with it. The Cape Flats are a part of the landscape the Cape Town tour buses zip past. It's a place none of the crew of *Hōkūleʻa* will ever forget.

Today, the crew has come to St. Mary's to practice *ubuntu*. St. Mary's is a public school with a gate and wrought iron fence topped with barbed wire. A row of tires along the entrance keeps cars off the grass. It is situated in a neighborhood of brick-walled homes, many guarded by barking dogs. The crew has come here to continue the task it began since first making landfall on the eastern shores of South Africa several weeks ago. Working with the Desmond Tutu Legacy Foundation, the crew has been delivering Mālama Honua-inspired lap desks to underprivileged children. So far, they have delivered over one thousand desks. Tutu's foundation goal is to have 20 million desks delivered across sub-Saharan Africa by 2020. Each lap desk has the alphabet, a math table, and a compass printed on it, along with a world map and *Hōkūleʻa*'s route on the Worldwide Voyage.

"Time to Shine" reads a hand-painted sign along the playground walls where some six hundred children have gathered to meet the crew. They send out a cheerful cry when they see the crew has brought some dancers with them today—Hawaiian boys in *malos* and girls in flowered cloth skirts. The children are quieted when they see Billy Richards unveil the lap desks—six hundred in all. Nainoa offers up a quilt made by children in Hawaiʻi, a patchwork of hand-painted drawings of what peace means to each child. Nainoa explains that after the Hawaiian children made the quilt, they were asked whom they wanted to give the quilt to and all the children

Opposite top: Schoolchild with *haku lei*, a gift from one of Kamehameha Schools dancers in Nyanga Township.

Opposite bottom: Austin Kino shares the stoke with a first-time surfer.

chose South Africa. The principal says she will hang it in her office, and soon the singing, drumming, and dancing begins.

Song has the power to take the heart back to another time—and this one clearly does, as the South African children sit, listening to a Hawaiian drummer drum the dancers in. The African girls lean into each other, under the shade of a single tree, watching the Hawaiian girls kneel, and sway, and bow. When it comes time for the African girls to dance, one of them asks if she could use the Hawaiian drum, and she pounds out a fast-paced song. Her friends begin to shake and clap and dance. Once they are done, the two groups join together, boys and girls, laughing, swaying, shaking, dancing, forming a braid of *ubuntu* and *mālama*, united together, in dance, and song.

Nainoa is clearly moved. He is not the only one. He leans into a crewmember and whispers, "Now I know what world peace looks like."

THE RATTLED WINDS OF a long day have settled down. The sun is lowering behind the mountain pass bordering a game reserve within the Western Cape. Shadows soften, and the colors of dusk arise in the rocks and bush—elephant grey, springbok gold, zebra black. Time to gather in, and make the trek home to rest.

You can see the wisdom in the animals, soundlessly congregating, out from where they've been all day—joining with their tribes—zebras, elephants, ostrich, blesbok, springbok, antelopes, rhinos, and giraffes all tracking together to their shelters for the night. Each tribe is so different. Yet all are unified in the same slow, measured, reverent pace.

Unrehearsed. Unfiltered. Un-human.

The original design is here. The light of the day grows dim, and the first star of the evening appears.

Opposite: Hawaiian and South African children share traditional chants and dances before spontaneously dancing together, Nyanga.

Local Voices
Mbali Marais
Member of the Khoi Khoi people

Mbali Marais was born in South Africa and, at age three, moved to London where she was reared and educated. After her mother passed away, she moved to America, but eventually felt called to return to the Mother Land. Once here, she found herself on a journey tracing her ancestral path. From the shores to the mountains to the savannah, she spent over eighteen months tracking her people. She met with chiefs and kings, tribes and clans, and was initiated into the Xhosa tradition as a healer. Her experience allowed her to find a place to call home in South Africa, where she lives today. On the day before Hōkūleʻa was set to sail out of Cape Town, Mbali visited the crew and the canoe. She called all of the ancestors in, Hawaiian and Khoi Khoi, and all of the elements—earth, wind, water, and fire—and asked them to bless the crew and to protect them and Hōkūleʻa as she sailed onward.

In Her Own Words

MY MOTHER WAS A DESCENDENT OF A KHOI KHOI healer. Khoi Khoi means "men of men" and "real people." The Khoi Khoi people were pastoralists who lived by the ocean, lived off the land, and communicated with animals. No separation existed between them and nature, them and animals, them and their plants. They were the plant and the tree. They were the desert and the ocean. They were, and still are, fully connected with nature. One.

The Khoi Khoi lived in Oneness. One family. There wasn't this sense of being separate—this is the Jones family, this is the Smith family. They were one family and they travelled as one family. But then people started to get separated into different clans and tribes, due to intermarrying; many married Bushmen, also known as the San people, hence the name Khoi San. They adopted many of the indigenous people's customs, language, and rituals. With the introduction of agriculture and a different kind of family unit, there was a disconnection. "We" became more "I," and the Oneness disappeared. When it became more about the "I" and the "Self"—my cattle, my sheep, my land—then we had to put up fences. The so-called One Community then became divided.

This notion of separateness—apartheid—was also the first people's separation from the land. When you separate from the land, you're not just taking someone's land away. You're separating from the Great Mother. The wound is very deep. This is the deep wound of South Africa, I think. The removal of the people from their land was actually a removal from the Mother. And then they went to work in mines, and they started abusing their Mother. Unless we heal that connection back to the land, the actual true healing that needs to happen in South Africa will not happen. Unless we restore this connection to the land, there will never be true reconciliation; there will never be true forgiveness.

You see, the Xhosa and the Zulu here, these great nations, they kept their communities. They kept their lands. They're still living on their lands, mostly. But if you take the descendants of the Khoi Khoi people, even the ones who are fairly well off, their sense of self is quite different from everybody else's. They carry a very low self-esteem. There's a deep brokenness that is all Earth-related. It speaks to the profound wounds of this country.

Mother Africa is an entity—we're all from here. I always do a ritual as soon as anyone arrives: I take them out onto the earth and let the ancestors know that these people have come from all around the world, and they need to be kept safe and protected while they are here. Just making that ritual brings them immediately here. Just walking barefoot on the earth brings them firmly here. When I take them to sacred sites, I always do a ritual, a sacred reciprocity. When we enter the water, or walk on the land, or go to a mountain, it is like going into somebody's house, we need to greet our hosts first.

For me, nature is the ultimate altar. And I wouldn't approach an altar without making an offering. And my offering is a very simple gift to that water, to that ocean, to the mountain, to say, "I have arrived and I greet you." Just a simple greeting and a request to please keep me safe and protected while I walk on your land or while I'm in your waters.

You see, the bones of the Earth, the mountains, the rocks, we look at these as great-grandfathers, great-grandmothers. People have been so disconnected from nature, from their creative cosmology, I'm simply assisting them in reconnecting and remembering what it felt like when they first came to the earth. And that has the power to transform. So when you come into the natural world, I always say, "Be prepared to be changed."

When they set foot on this Mother Land, they re-remember the ancient paths of themselves. We all carry this indigenous soul. We are all ancient beings. When we come here, or when we're introduced to this place, that is us re-remembering what we've forgotten.

This is the medicine. This is my divine medicine to return people back to the land so they can remember their own divine medicine. This is the only way we can truly join together—return to the natural world, heal the legacies of our ancestors, and move back to that place of Oneness.

Local Solutions
Mission Blue and Sustainable Seas Trust

In December 2014, the Mission Blue Sylvia Earle Alliance and the Sustainable Seas Trust of South Africa identified six community-based Hope Spots in South Africa. There are fifty-seven Hope Spots around the world. Hope Spots are thriving oceanic ecosystems, rich in biodiversity and critical to the health of the ocean and our planet. Most Hope Spots are in remote deep-ocean areas. Those in South Africa are different. They include coastal areas and involve communities in caring for their local waters. South Africans are now referring to the Hope Spot initiative as *Ikhaya Lethemba*—Home of Hope.

The South African Hope Spots extend from the cold waters of the Western Cape to the warm waters of KwaZulu-Natal and include a diversity of ecosystems.

The Cape Whale Hope Spot is home to three species of whales, the great white shark, the Cape fur seal, the West Coast rock lobster, and abalone. While some of the areas are currently protected, overfishing remains a concern in this area. This, combined with the climate-driven shift in ocean temperatures, has led to a decrease in the numbers of anchovy, leading in turn to a decrease in the rock lobster, a decrease in the sea urchin, and a subsequent decrease in young abalones.

Algoa Bay, in the eastern-most reach of South Africa, is the primary breeding grounds of the endangered African penguin. Over 50 percent of the remaining African penguins congregate here to feed and reproduce. Two rivers of freshwater flow under the bay, creating an oceanic environment rich with pelagic fish—the necessary sustenance to feed and to nourish their young.

Knysna is the only Hope Spot in the world that is focused on an estuary, but also includes the coastline and offshore waters. This region holds the highest biodiversity of any estuary in all of South Africa, including it being the habitat for the Knysna seahorse.

Plettenberg Bay remains untainted by industrial pollution, allowing this bay, in the middle of the Southern Cape Coast, to be frequented by three species of dolphins, as well as the humpback whale. It is a community conservation area between two marine protected areas.

The Aliwal Shoal is considered one of the top shark diving spots on the planet. The reef, located some three miles off the coast of South Africa, has subtropical waters where the ragged-tooth, tiger, black tip, bull, copper, and hammerhead sharks all converge.

False Bay is an area of rich, thriving kelp forest. The thick forest provides a protective space for several species, including worms, crabs, urchins, and abalone. The area is also a nursery for many reef fish, including the Hottentot seabream, which can live for up to twenty-one years.

In South Africa, only 2 percent of the penguins remain, 3.2 percent of the rock lobster, and most tuna species are down below 7 percent of their historical population levels. These numbers are sobering. Protecting Hope Spots is a step toward restoring habitats by bringing the oceanic environment into a state of balance.

In 2016, 12 percent of the land on Earth was secured in conservation programs—either in national parks, reserves, or monuments. Yet less than 3 percent of our ocean is protected in such a way. With these numbers in mind, Mission Blue has set a goal to safeguard 20 percent of the ocean by 2020.

Opposite: Nainoa Thompson, Dr. Craig Foster, and Archie Kalepa examine the many layers of sea life in the tide pools, Black Rocks.

Next spread: Three-month-old baby rhinoceros and her mother graze the family homeland, Aquila Game Reserve.

CREW STORY
Kalā Baybayan Tanaka
Apprentice Navigator

Kalā Baybayan Tanaka is an apprentice navigator with Hui o Waʻa Kaulua, Maui's voyaging society. She teaches children the star compass and the history of voyaging and looks forward to someday sailing with these children on Moʻokiha o Piʻilani, the voyaging canoe of Maui. Kalā is also the daughter of Pwo Navigator Kālepa Baybayan. Just as she is a child of a navigator, Moʻokiha o Piʻilani can be considered the offspring of Hōkūleʻa. Since the initial launch of Hōkūleʻa on Oʻahu, nine voyaging canoes have been built on several Hawaiian islands, creating an ever-growing ʻohana waʻa, canoe family. As the mother of two young boys, Kalā has had to find the balance of being at home while also fulfilling her longing to voyage across the deep seas. Far from the shores of home, Kalā leaned on the railing of a pier overlooking the New York Harbor. She reflected on her own personal journey of wayfinding, and how this journey helped her to better understand her father.

I WAS BORN INTO IT, the *ʻohana waʻa*. Maybe I was even a product of a voyage. I grew up with kids who were around the same age as me, and all our dads voyaged together. Hōkūleʻa was part of our life from the start, like an older sibling who was always there.

My dad, he's a quiet guy. He keeps things to himself. I'm the oldest of three kids, and we didn't fully understand the relationship he had with the canoe. We didn't really know him, and that side of him. The canoe took our dad away. When he went with the canoe, he was gone. He'd go away for months, and when he came back home, he'd have this full beard and long hair and I'd think, *Who is that man? Oh, that's my dad!*

I didn't even recognize him. I didn't really know that side of him and I think that's why I got into voyaging. Those were some of my earliest memories. I was just trying to understand him and what was so special about the canoe that he just had to go.

I was in my twenties when I decided I wanted to learn more about voyaging and navigating. I didn't want to ask my dad myself, so I talked to my grandma, his mom, and she said, "Oh, I'll just call him and ask him." So she called him, and immediately she said to me, "OK, you're going to go with your dad."

My first voyage was on the canoe that he was responsible for building, *Hōkūalaka'i*, in Hilo. We went on a twenty-four-hour sail. My dad's such a great teacher. He's taught so many. When you're out there with him at night, he talks about everything that we see, and what we're feeling, and what it means. My watch was from two to six, and we were in the back of the canoe, early, before morning. It was pitch black under this beautiful blanket of stars. And my dad said, "Listen. You hear that?"

All I could hear was the wind and the ocean, and I said, "No, I don't hear anything." And he said, "You don't hear that? OK, come with me."

He took me to the front of the canoe to listen, and I could hear dolphins breathing. They were riding on the bow wave of the canoe, and I could hear them breathing and I thought, *Oh my god, this is it! I want to do this. I want to be so connected to my environment that I can hear and see all these things, I want to navigate. I want to be the ultimate observer of my environment.*

I got off the canoe and asked him, "OK, so what books do I get?" And he immediately recommended a few books to get me started. I was living with my grandma at the time, and every night I would go out in front of her house and just look at the stars. I had a million questions.

Every time my dad would come visit, we would go outside and talk. He'd give me clues. I was having the hardest time in the beginning. At the start, when I looked at the sky, it just looked like a bunch of unorganized dots. I couldn't see the pictures yet.

He would tell me, "Oh, look, see how grandma's driveway lines up with the North Star?" So every time I would stand in this one spot, the driveway would line up to the North Star. I would always start there first, and then I would look for the stars that were closest to it that I knew, and then I would go farther and farther and farther.

I've learned from voyaging that I can achieve things I never thought I could do. I think sometimes we can be very critical of ourselves about what we don't know. I feel like voyaging on the canoe has really expanded my mind about thinking of different ways to do things. Just to understand that there are things that you can control, and things you can't control—the weather, for example. It is what it is, but you can adjust your sails, you can change your steering so it's not so harsh on you, and you can navigate through it successfully. It's been really empowering. It's as if you had something blocking part of your vision and then you just pull the blinder up and now you can see and experience more because you've taught yourself how to open your senses.

I think that's why I like to teach. I want to equip people with the tools that they need, and then tell them, "Go, just go. Go fish up your island, go and dream your dream, and go and get it!"

CREW STORY
Kaleomanuiwa Wong
Apprentice Navigator

Kaleomanuiwa (Kaleo) Wong is the full-time kahu *(guardian) for the lands of Kūkanono, in Kailua, that surround Kawainui fishpond at the foot of Ulupō, the largest* heiau *on Oʻahu. Kaleo directs cultural education efforts, service learning projects, and land reclamation activities. Kawainui is the biggest wetland in all of Hawaiʻi, and a wildlife sanctuary for numerous endangered Hawaiian water birds. His hope is that through his aloha ʻāina work alongside school groups and community volunteers, Kawainui fishpond will return to the health it once had. Seated, with the rock walls of Ulupō behind him and Kawainui before him, Kaleo spoke of his experience as a student of navigation under his teacher, Pwo Navigator and Captain Bruce Blankenfeld, and the most daunting passage for him so far: navigating across the Atlantic Ocean.*

Opposite: Sunrise and sunset are critical times to observe the conditions along the horizon.

CAPE TOWN TO NAMIBIA is about 700 miles up the coast, and when we departed the coast of Namibia, we took a left turn toward St. Helena. The trip across the Atlantic was unbelievable. We went through conditions that *Hōkūle'a* has never been through: fog. We went through fog so thick we couldn't see the stars, the moon, or even the sun. We couldn't see our escort boat less than a mile away. At one point we could hear the foghorns of ships all around us but we couldn't see them. We were in a major shipping lane with oil tankers around us and had zero visibility.

Usually in times of complete cloud cover we hold our course by observing the swells and the wind. But, while we were going through the fog in the Atlantic, the ocean was completely flat, and the wind was swirling around us. We had no clues about the direction we were steering. We had to rely on faith, and trust that we were being led in the right direction. When the fog would clear a little bit, we'd see a star, and say, "OK, I know that star, and based off its position and the relationship to the *wa'a*, we're still going in generally the right direction."

For noninstrument navigation, the changing conditions were really difficult. We were going mostly downswell and the wind kept moving around. If the swell switches one way or another, and you jibe with your sails moving all the way to the other side, you are now going a different direction—you're zigzagging. And every time you zig or zag, you are going off course. You have to keep track of that in your head.

We were navigating to an island in the Atlantic, 1,900 miles from Cape Town. This little island in the middle of the Atlantic with no other islands around it. It's a tiny island, just forty-seven square miles and 2,600 feet high. A slight error and we would have gone right by and not seen it at all—and we wouldn't even have known it.

I remember a day when the winds were shifting. The sun was directly overhead so we couldn't use it. Nainoa often talks about the feeling of having "brain damage." I know now what he's talking about. I was like, *What direction are we going? I think we're going the right way …* As the navigator, you're the leader, so I just kept my doubt to myself. I didn't want the crew to know I was unsure.

I was frustrated. I felt like we were at a crux, the deciding factor. We made it through all the fog, and who knew if we were still on our course, and now we were having conditions like this. Even with perfect conditions, St. Helena is extremely difficult to find because of its size and isolation. Now, with all these other factors thrown in, maybe we wouldn't find the island at all.

Right at that moment of feeling, *Oh my goodness, what's happening, where are we going?* orcas appeared.

That was a *hō'ailona*, a sign, right there. It wasn't just us out there on this tiny little canoe. But the whole thing is bigger than us—I had to remember the whole spiritual side to it.

Even though we're in the Atlantic, far away from our home in the Pacific, we always have our *kūpuna*, our ancestors, with us on the canoe. The *'aumakua*, the familial guardian, of the canoe is the *koholā*, the humpback whale. Before *Hōkūle'a* goes on a voyage, *kūpuna* put the mana of the whale into the canoe. Those orcas came and lifted everyone's spirits. The *hō'ailona* of the whales appearing told me that we were OK; we were on the right course.

We began to see birds, a sign that we were closing in on our target. The picture in my mind of where the island lay was to the northwest of us; the stars confirmed this. We needed to adjust our course slightly to the north, but the wind was not allowing us to do that. One option was to tack north. Based on the wind direction and our speed, we would be slightly north of the island at sunrise. We could tack again and head straight for the island. I talked it over with Uncle Bruce and we decided this was a good plan.

We made the first tack and headed in a northerly direction. As usual for this leg, right about 11 pm, the wind started backing off and changing direction. We kept on going, and waited for what the morning would bring us. As the sun came up, birds were seen, telling us that we were getting close—within about 100 miles of the island, but still only blue ocean 360 degrees around us. Based on the height of the island, we figured on a perfect day we could see the island about forty miles away.

Since the wind backed off during the night, we didn't get the mileage we had hoped for. *Do we keep on going on this tack? Or do we tack back toward the island as we had originally planned?* I contemplated this decision—a decision that, perhaps, more than any other so far would determine whether we find the island or not. Then, out of a relatively clear sky, lightning struck the ocean right in front of the canoe in the direction we were heading. This significant *hōʻailona* was the sign, was the command. It was time to tack back to the south.

And then, as soon as we tacked, a pod of dolphins was all around us, *aku* were jumping all over the place, and birds appeared by the dozens. Two hours later, Uncle Gary Yuen spotted the island directly between the two *manu*, upturned ends, of the canoe.

How did this happen? Through all those days of fog, all those times when we didn't know exactly what direction we were heading? There was something else guiding the canoe besides us. I asked Uncle Bruce, "Is there always that doubt in your mind that you won't find the island?"

He said, "The doubt is always there. Your job is to just not listen to that doubt. As the navigator, you have the plan in your head, you've been studying it, you know the stars, the movement of the sun, the oceans. You just have to trust yourself, trust your teachings, and trust that all the *kūpuna* and *ʻaumakua* with us are also helping to guide the canoe to the destination. Don't listen to that doubt. Don't listen to anybody else. Just listen to yourself."

Opposite: Bruce Blankenfeld listens as Kaleo addresses the Māori dignitaries in fluent Hawaiian, Waitangi, Aotearoa.

"There's a certain *pilina*, a certain
relationship, between people of the
indigenous cultures of the land.
We celebrate the achievements of our
people with the stories they left behind for us.
We find strength. We find courage.
We find the ability to endure no matter
what countries colonized our nations
because we *are* the first people of the land.
Nobody can take that away from us."

Kālepa Baybayan
Pwo Navigator and Captain

CUBA

CHAPTER 6

We need planes dropping flowers

—

We need all the presidents to speak the same language.
We need weapons buried in the center of the Earth.
We need planes dropping flowers and carrying food and medicine to
those who need it all over the world.

– Ramón Portal
Former Revolutionary Fighter, Current Organic Herbalist

THE FARMER TOSSES SUNFLOWER SEEDS. PIGEONS FLOCK, roosters crow, dogs bark. Toto, the monkey, squawks.

In the shade of his shed, farmer Jesus Llerena is beginning his day as the main caretaker of La Finca de los Chuchitos, a private, rural farm devoted primarily to growing flowers. Freshly cut carnations, gladiolas, marigolds, mariposas, coxcombs, daisies, and sunflowers soak in an old, freestanding porcelain bathtub. Step inside the refrigerated den, and you'll smell the long-lingering fragrance of tuberose.

"Welcome to the farm," Jesus says to the group of Hawaiians who have flown to Cuba to witness the arrival of *Hōkūleʻa* and are here today to string *lei* for the crew.

It is a midspring day, the muddy earth still sticky from last night's downpour. Wearing a rain-worn, sundried straw hat, Jesus guides the group toward his fields. "We keep the farm as my grandfather used to have it," Jesus explains, "as an organic farm."

The farm is a pastoral throwback with horses, oxen, and machete-wielding workers. One crop flows into the next—Queen Anne's lace to chard, banana to mango. A single-seat tractor is parked beneath a palm tree, the machine's current use being a place where a worker can sit, catch some shade under its rusty roof, take a break from the heavy heat of the Caribbean sun.

The worker smiles and nods as the Hawaiians greet him with aloha. Around the world, aloha requires no translation. Those who are greeted this way understand its universal embrace. "Aloha," Jesus repeats, seeming to practice the grace of this word, as he guides the group down the oxen's well-worn path.

"When my grandfather was managing the farm, it was less productive," he explains of the fifty-nine-acre farm that also produces plantains, beans, and lettuce. "Now we have a wider variety of plants and flowers and better productivity."

Productivity is a highly valued asset, especially when there are quotas to fill to sell to the state. If a farm does not produce a consistent viable quota, the land may be taken away. By the same token, the government will grant parcels of land to any able-bodied individual who can consistently produce product. Once food has been produced and distributed to the state, farmers are then allowed to sell surplus to the free market.

Opposite: Farmworker harvesting hand-picked vegetables, La Finca de los Chuchitos farm, Guanábacoa.

The Llerena family has tended this land for three generations, beginning at the turn of the twentieth century. Over time, the farm has survived thirty-three tropical storms, the War of Independence, and three political movements—that is—the dictatorship of Fulgencio Batista, the birth of the Revolution, and, in 1989, the dissolution of the Soviet Union. This last movement may have delivered the biggest punch.

The collapse of the Soviet Union was an era Cubans refer to as El Período Especial, the Special Period,—a euphemism for a stark economic crisis that lasted for nearly ten years. Overnight, 85 percent of Cuba's trade vanished and the agricultural system buckled. The Soviets had been supporting farming and providing seeds, agrochemicals, fertilizer, and tractors and parts, in exchange for sugar at a price well above the global rate. The struggle to survive became critical. Sugar water became a staple of the diet. As one Cuban recalls, "We had nothing but our pride."

"It was bad. Bad," Jesus remembers. "There were no resources. We were working hard and, at the end of the day, we couldn't advance. And when you did earn a little money to buy something, there was nothing to buy."

The solution was to return to the old ways. Jesus looked to his grandparents for the way back to organic farming.

"We needed to start replanting with low resources," Jesus explains. "My grandparents were alive at that time. We used [my grandfather's] knowledge on how to plant according to the seasons. We planted mainly with the moon cycles."

"We keep most of these techniques alive today on the farm," he says of the return to sustainable farming.

At that time, the farm was producing and providing its own seeds. Now the government provides the seeds. It is apparent how politics continues to inform land policy, and how the land informs politics. The talk of politics is especially alive today, just days before the arrival of Barack Obama, the first American president to visit Cuba since Calvin Coolidge in 1928.

As the afternoon unfolds, lei are strung, lunch is served, and talk of the changing climate of politics soon flows into the talk of climate change.

It has been a difficult couple of years on the farm, Jesus admits. This past year, the climate seemed confused, the seasons, flipped. There was a drought during the rainy season and rain during the dry season. Mangoes sprouted in March, not July.

"During the dry season, the rain destroyed many of the crops," Jesus says. He says he is thankful for the river on his property. Jesus motions toward the ravine where the river passes through. The hill above it provides a perch for what appears to be a former sugar factory. A mere mention of sugar returns the conversation to politics. The sugar industry began in the colonial years and later was fully supported by the Soviet Union.

Jesus tells a story of how when he was growing up, the government sponsored schoolchildren to spend a month on state-owned farms to teach them about the care of the land, about communal living, about working together to produce a harvest for the common good. It was, he says, "a collective experience." The school farm visits fell away when the state could no longer support the month-long excursions.

Opposite: Street-art culture is vividly alive in Havana.

"Our nation's greatness and prosperity depend on a healthy and vigorous rural population that loves the land," Fidel Castro once famously stated. Love of the land is a philosophy every Cuban upholds.

Jesus says he is installing solar panels on the farm and looking to build some cottages where schoolkids can come and stay and learn what it means to care for the homeland.

The lei are complete. One is given to Jesus's wife with the embrace of aloha.

Jesus sweeps up the scant leftovers, only petals and stems, gathering them all in a cardboard box that will be mixed into the compost heap. In a country that still practices food rationing, nothing is wasted, nothing is lost.

PRESIDENT OBAMA'S ARRIVAL COINCIDES with a brisk lightning storm. Some view the storm as a blessing; others view it as an omen. All agree the storm evokes change. Change is a constant in the Republic of Cuba. As the largest island in the Caribbean, Cuba is constantly evolving, having endured the colonial rule of a handful of countries, beginning with the invasion of the Spanish in the late 1400s and the extermination of the indigenous people, the Taíno. The whispered remains of the Taíno language reside in the word "Cuba," which means "where fertile lands are abundant."

To the world beyond the island, Cuba was known as the "The Pure Rose of the Caribbean" and the "Pearl of the Antilles." These poetic epithets were a nod to the fertility of the soil that, until the end of the eighteenth century, was able to sustain rich forests of mahogany, ebony, and cedar. But during the next century, many of

Above: *Lei* are woven from local flowers for *Hōkūle'a's* arrival, La Finca de los Chuchitos farm.

these trees were felled to create elaborate cabinets, doors, and ceilings in palaces
in England, Spain, and France. The trees were further destroyed in the widespread
clearing of lands to make room for sugarcane fields, for the building of sugar mills,
and for firewood burned within the mills. By the end of the nineteenth century,
Cuba was the top producer and exporter of sugar in the world.

The remnants of this productivity remain in Old Havana today. When you walk
through Old Havana, you're walking on the discarded ballasts of old sugar ships
from Massachusetts. The brick and stone ballasts kept the empty ships balanced en
route to the island. Prior to loading the ships with sugar, the ballasts were discarded
and Cubans fashioned them into cobblestones.

"So, when you're walking the streets of Old Havana, you're walking on American
soil," architect and city planner Miguel Coyula says, somewhat jokingly. Coyula is
well-versed in the many incarnations of his native land. From 1971 to 1990, he
worked at the Cuban Ministry of Construction, and he has also served as Secretary
for Agricultural and Industrial Development for COMECON, the Council for Mutual
Economic Assistance, an economic assistance organization directed by the Soviet
Union. His responsibilities have allowed him to travel throughout the former Eastern
Bloc and Soviet Union, giving him a sharp perspective on commerce and urban
development within communist countries.

Extensive sugar harvesting continued during the Soviet rule, and by the time of
the Soviet downfall, the harvesting of sugar had stripped the land of its nutrients,
and eventually, even its people. As agriculture became more commercial, machines
replaced workers. This led to an exodus out of the countryside and into the cities,
a shift from agrarian living toward the white-collar opportunities offered at urban
universities. Today, 76 percent of the population is urban. The government is now
encouraging urban dwellers to return to the country in hopes of making Cuba one of
the more independently sustainable countries in the world. "This government has
a plan to bring people back to the country," Coyula explains. "More than 170,000
people said, 'Yes. Yes, we want to go back to the country, if we get land, yes, we want
to go back.'"

"It's good news but it's not enough," he adds, noting that 170,000 people are
a fraction of the eleven million who live in Cuba today. One-fifth of the population
resides in Havana.

In 1959, when Fidel Castro first stepped in as prime minister, the population was 5.5 million and agrarian reform was a major tenet of the Revolution. The
reform involved the state recovering land from rich, often foreign, landowners and
redistributing it to the Cuban people. At the time, 85 percent of the rural farmers
paid rent. Over two hundred thousand peasant families did not own a single acre
of land. The Revolution redistributed rural lands, increased literacy, and provided
statewide medical care. But the redistribution of land did not resolve the issue of
how the land would be used. Subsidized by the Soviet Union, 30 percent of the land
was still used primarily as a monoculture sugar crop.

Once the Soviet Union crashed, amidst the continued US embargo, Cuba was
fully isolated. Food was scarce. The mean daily caloric intake dropped more than
one thousand calories and, in the coming years, the average Cuban lost twelve
pounds. Out of sheer survival, *organoponicos*, small organic farms, began to rise

up within the urban landscape. With the Soviet-designed hydroponic systems no longer in use, locals packed the equipment with compostable sugar waste to grow produce. A system of urban farms grew; low concrete walls could be filled with organic soil and irrigated through a drip system hose. Currently, an average of three buildings crumble a day in Havana. In some of these open spaces where buildings have collapsed, you'll find locals, clearing through the wreckage, to make a space for a garden bed. For those without the luxury of an open city space, the government offers concrete boxes filled with soil and seed. For those with access to stable roofs, they have planted rooftop gardens.

Like Hawai'i, this island nation still relies heavily on imports, with most of its staples, such as rice and wheat, shipped in. Similar to Hawai'i, these resources need to satisfy not only the native people, but also the growing tourism industry that has replaced the sugar industry as the prime source of revenue.

In the first few months of 2016, the number of tourists who visited Cuba rose 13.5 percent. At the time of *Hōkūle'a*'s visit, cruise lines had just begun arriving. When the crew spotted a cruise ship docked in Old Havana, there was an audible sigh, a shared understanding that these tourists demand a standard of comfort seldom afforded to the locals. Miguel shares a story of talking with a captain of a cruise ship who bemoaned that the cruisers were in need of four kinds of lettuce.

"Four? There is only one kind of lettuce," Miguel told the captain. "One lettuce!"

But the captain objected, no, there are *four*.

This developed world sensibility has filtered into the former Spanish colony, creating what is known as "the colonized mind." The colonized mind believes it needs white sugar, white bread, and white rice. All of which are destructive to harvest in large scale on this island. The monthly rice ration is seven pounds per person. With a population of eleven million people, the island cannot produce enough rice to fill this need, so the rice has to be imported, at a high cost, from Vietnam.

"One of the problems today we have in agriculture is this: Who's going to work there?" he asks.

A retired professor, Miguel understands the physical effects of time. "It's not the same to age in an office than it is behind the ox plowing the land," he explains. Today, every fifth person in the city is over sixty years old. The average building in Havana is seventy-five years old. Cuba is aging very fast.

"Today we have farmers who don't have heirs because their sons are now professionals in the city."

"Things are changing, and we need to understand that," Miguel says. "We need to change and not wait until things happen and force us to change."

THE DOCTOR IS IN, and neighborhood folks are arriving to gather some herbs, some tonics, some healing. It is early morning at Organopónico Vivero Alamar, a cooperative farm in the suburbs of Havana. Workers are carrying big bunches of carrots to the street-side marketplace. Others are tenderly spraying the netting over seedlings in the nurseries. The doctor is cutting a mixture of herbs to concoct a tonic for a woman with a severely swollen leg.

The doctor is Ramón Portal, an eighty-four-year-old former revolutionary fighter who fought alongside Ernesto Ché Guevara in the mountains of Sierra Maestra.

Opposite top: The hardest working equipment on the farm—strong backs and tough hands, La Finca de los Chuchitos.

Opposite bottom: Jesus Llerena, owner of La Finca de los Chuchitos.

Dressed in a green khaki jacket, worn jeans, and wire-rimmed glasses, Ramón carries a straight knife in a suede holster on his hip. He oversees the care of more than fifty medicinal plants on the farm.

Created in 1997, Organopónico Vivero Alamar is a cooperative urban farm. Employees own the equipment and share in the earnings of the private market sales. Working seven hours a day, six days a week, the farmers here earn more than the average Cuban. Most employees live in the area, and all have a say in the management of the farm, fully rooted within the community. Self-sufficient, Vivero Alamar is a model of sustainability that inspires communities throughout the island.

The farm itself feels like a tropical oasis surrounded by a maze of Soviet-designed, cement block apartment buildings. Built as housing projects where workers could raise a family in the 1970s, this is where the Cuban hip-hop music scene first took root in the struggling 1990s.

"The farm became organic by default," says Isis Maria Salcines Milla, Vivero Alamar's outreach director. Isis is the daughter of one of the four men who founded the farm. Once an 8,611-square-foot vegetable garden with five workers, the farm has since grown to twenty-five acres with over 160 workers. Of the handful of *Hōkūleʻa* crewmembers visiting here today, some are educators, some conservationists, and all are interested in taking this knowledge home to their own islands.

"There is no outside equipment, tools, chemicals, or fertilizers or seeds," Isis explains of the co-op.

The farm practices biopesticide control, such as lacing marigolds within the basil, green onion, and tomato crops. "With many smells and many colors together," Isis explains, "the insects get confused and leave."

Sunflower is planted amidst the lettuce. Corn planted amidst the basil. The corn serves as an "insect hotel," she says. The insects see the corn and miss the basil. A diversion. Even a blue-colored flag can divert insects away from the crops.

The process works. Cucumbers, cabbage, tomatoes, carrots, green onions, tomatillos, beets, peppers, pak choi, eggplant, okra, lettuce, rice, beans, sprouts, sunflower seeds, and peanuts are all grown here. Tomato puree, guava jam, sauerkraut, and fresh guarapo (sugarcane juice) are also processed here and sold in recycled glass beer bottles, rum bottles, and mason jars.

Vivero Alamar sells to fifty thousand people, planting three million seeds, and harvesting three hundred tons of vegetables annually. Ninety percent of the produce is for the community; 10 percent is for hotels, cafeterias, and restaurants. The mint? It's sold to the tourist-trodden Bodeguita del Medio restaurant bar in Havana to make mojitos.

Along with feeding the community, another goal is to teach the next generation.

"We bring elementary schoolkids here once a week and show them how to produce food in an organic way, how to eat in a healthy way. When you ask the children, what will you do when you grow up? Everybody wants to be a doctor, designer, lawyer, a tourist guide!"

"All the vocations are important, but to produce food is one of the most important. Everybody has to eat," she says. "If nobody wants to produce food, what will happen in this world?"

Opposite: Ramón Portal, a former revolutionary who fought alongside Che Guevara, is now the senior herbalist on the cooperative farm Organopónico Vivero Alamar.

When one of the crewmembers asks about the struggles of the Special Period, Isis sighs, and pauses. "I don't know what's better, to die from hunger or die from cancer," she says. "Now Monsanto, they want to come here. For us, we will continue to produce the organic."

When asked what she would like to see in regards to the more open relations with the United States, she replies, "I don't want Monsanto."

She has a school group coming in shortly, so she hurries the crew to the vermi-composting area where she tenderly lifts the netting off the dark, rich soil to reveal stockpiles of red worms.

"Do you know what these are called?" she asks. "California red worms!" she says, with a spring of enthusiasm. "They work twenty-four hours, don't ask for salary or a vacation, and transform poo-poo into gold!"

The worms create an excellent organic fertilizer, and if treated carefully, with proper pH, shade, and light, the worms can live sixteen years.

Sixteen years is a long time, everyone agrees. Where will Cuba be in sixteen years? The future of Cuba is an ever-flowing question when you live in a place that feels as if it has stood still in time.

Isis has her own questions. "What will we do when he passes on?" she asks, of Ramón, who is now by her side to say good-bye to the crew. The loss of one generation can be the loss of knowledge forever. "No one else knows the herbal remedies," she explains.

When the crew sings her the *Oli Mahalo*, a chant of appreciation and love, she weeps. Her devotion to the care of the land is intimate. To Isis, to serve the land is to serve the people. Seeing her emotions, Ramón provides his own offering, an embrace to one, and a coin to another. The coin is a 1995 *Tres Pesos* with the image of Ché on one side. On the other side is the country's motto, *Patria o Muerte*, Homeland or Death.

OBAMA HAS LEFT THE ISLAND, the Rolling Stones are on their way in, and the crew is paying its respects to a canoe carved out of a single Amazonian tree by the Quechua people of Colombia. Along its bow is the name and profile of Hatuey, the Taíno chief who tried to warn the people of Cuba of the destructive invasion of the Spaniards. For his resistance, the Spaniards burned Hatuey at the stake in 1512. Today, the crew is learning the story of the canoe in the Foundation for Nature and Humanity Museum, the former home of Antonio Núñez Jiménez, a captain in the Revolution, and later, the Minister of Agrarian Reform.

In 1987, Jiménez wanted to heal what he called the "national memory" of the Cuban people. He envisioned building a canoe to retrace the Taíno people's migratory path from South America to Cuba, a passage that took place in 700 CE, some seven hundred years before Christopher Columbus entered the Caribbean. The mission sounds familiar to the crew, especially Captain Kālepa Baybayan, who stands with his arms folded, legs wide and locked, as he listens to one of the men who paddled and then sailed the canoe over ten thousand miles in fourteen months.

Angel Gonzales relates the passage in a somber tone. Tall and lean, wearing a straw fedora, Angel explains that five forty-two-foot-long dugout canoes were carved. Only this one, the *Hatuey* remains on display. The expedition included men

---

Opposite top: *Hōkūleʻa* is steered by moving the end of the *hoe uli*. Here, Eric Co has it lashed to the rail to alleviate the effort required to hold the canoe on course.

Opposite bottom: Noelani Kamalu coils a line to stow it.

from Ecuador, Brazil, Peru, Colombia, Venezuela, Puerto Rico, and Cuba; fifty-five crewmembers in all, including thirty-three scientists, who collected information from indigenous peoples along the way. There were eleven people per canoe, ten paddling and one steering.

"We paddled the Amazon River through Río Negro to the Caribbean Sea," Angel explains. Once in the sea, they outfitted the canoes with outriggers and masts and hand-sewn sails from Trinidad. "And then we started jumping from island to island until we made it to San Salvador in the Bahamas where Columbus arrived in 1492."

"We were able to visit each one of the islands except Puerto Rico because the US embassy wouldn't give visas to the Cubans. They gave visas to everyone except the Cubans," he continues. "So the rest of the members of the expedition said, 'If the Cubans aren't allowed to go to Puerto Rico, then nobody else is going to go there.'"

The expedition returned to St. Kitts Island. The canoes were then tied together for the night. Sometime in the night, the *Hatuey* became loose and drifted into the stream of the sea.

Thirty days after the canoe disappeared, it arrived empty on the shores of Vieques Island off Puerto Rico, then a US military base. When word spread, friends of the Cubans in Puerto Rico reclaimed the canoe.

"They filled it with red flowers and sailed it right into San Juan Bay [on Puerto Rico]," Angel says with a knowing smile. "Then they sailed it to the Dominican Republic to connect with the rest of the expedition and we returned home to Cuba."

The story brings silence, a moment of reflection.

Someone has one last question. It's about the colorful wall mural of a bird painted above the voyage's map. The bird feels familiar, a few here have noted, like the Iwa bird embedded in the center of the Hawaiian star compass.

Skimming the waves of the sea, the bird is silhouetted by the glow of the full moon. Her legs are the mast; her broad tail is the stern; her beak, the bow steering straight into the future.

"There's an Ecuadorian legend that a bird would guide the canoe," Angel explains. A bird would guide them on their route to sail with the guidance of the sun, moon, and stars. The bird became the symbol of the voyage for the Cubans, Angel says.

Nothing more needs to be said. Nor asked. Before leaving, each crewmember has a moment, alone with the *Hatuey*, putting a hand on the roughly carved rail, stricken by the connection of one people to another, the search for understanding the self, a people, its past, and the healing that needs to continue as we sail forth into the streams, straits, and oceans ahead.

Opposite: The *Hatuey* on display in the Foundation for Nature and Humanity Museum, Havana.

—

Local Voices
Miguel Angel Salcines
Organopónico Vivero Alamar

As the president and one of the founding members of Organóponico Vivero Alamar, Miguel has been an integral part of Cuba's journey from industrial to organic farming. Daily, for nearly thirty years now, Miguel has tended to the farm. But on this warm springtime day, Miguel was seated in the cool comfort of his couch in his ground-level apartment, just across the street from the farm and its neighboring Hanoi Park. At age sixty-eight, he was recovering from pacemaker surgery. He spoke, alongside his daughter, Isis, about the birth of his farm and why organic farming needs to be the standard bearer for agriculture around the world.

In His Own Words

I WAS BORN IN A RURAL, SMALL TOWN, IN HOLGUÍN, within the Oriente province. My family had land. We were farmers and I was looking for the possibility of going where the action was, to work directly in agriculture. Remember, Cuba used to produce food for 40 million people—in the form of sugar—so I came to Havana to study agronomics. It was the early 1970s. I was about twenty years old. I started to work as an official in the Ministry of Agriculture. It was a bureaucracy, without a doubt.

Remember, we were the first socialist country in the Western Hemisphere. Socialist countries wanted to give the impression that agriculture in Cuba was highly developed. Germany, Russia, Czechoslovakia, Romania, Albania—all those countries started to send technology to develop our agriculture.

But it was chemicals. The only thing missing was Monsanto. The monoculture became more monoculture and more dependent on exterior powers. Before Russia fell, we received most of our food from Russia, and the prices—they were good prices, very good prices, for sugar, for everything. Fertilizer, free! Pesticides, free! Cereals, free! Oil, free! Petroleum, free! Machinery, free!

But, in 1993, there was the collapse of the Socialist camp, and when this structure collapsed, the Cuban agriculture became like a collage. We lost 85 percent of our exports and our imports. So this brought a dramatic effect on the country. A difficult situation in this country was the electricity. They would only give twelve hours of electricity a day. There were very few buses. They brought over about 2 million bicycles from China. The food was gone. Protein, fats, gone.

Now there's another thing; before the Cuban Revolution, 80 percent of Cubans lived on farmland. But by the 1990s, 80 percent lived in the city. So when this structure collapsed, we could not go back to the way agriculture was before because there was no one there to do it.

In my case, the Ministry told me to go to my municipality and organize this movement to create farms in the city. And of course, I didn't know anything about this. I had no idea. I didn't know how to create a structure for an urban environment or how to organize people. But I tried. And I finally got it. I was the one distributing the land in my municipality. We needed to grow our own nourishment or we would starve to death.

This created a very big social movement. And this movement grew to the entire country. This movement started working with compost, in agriculture, in the production of biopesticides and natural pesticides, entomology. There was a very good intellectual reserve of instruction. It became more than just a reform, it was a transformation that came out of necessity.

A movement started in the city to produce food around the city. People started to work agriculture in the city, with organic methods. For over twenty years, we've been farming this way. At the very beginning, this process was to eat, to eat something. But then through this process we began to learn about the contamination of the water and the soil. This process has helped us understand the dangers of chemicals, the danger of chemicals to humanity.

There is an agriculture that is using "doping" chemicals. "Doping" is not agriculture. Permaculture is agriculture. Sustainability, biodynamic, bio-intensive farming—all that is the real agriculture. Monsanto is not agriculture.

People are intelligent—they see the antibiotics, the chemicals, the genetic modifications, and then the illnesses. It is all connected.

Do you use tobacco? Do you use alcohol? Do you use drugs? Do you eat at McDonald's? If you answered no to all, you're fine, you don't have problems. But if you eat at McDonald's, you'll get sick.

Above all, you have to take care of yourself; you have to make a personal effort to take care of your family and yourself. But there are a lot of hungry people in the world, especially in the Third World, and they are eating pesticides.

There's a saying that 25 percent of what we eat helps us to live. The other 75 percent of the food produces disease.

Look, there is a crisis in the First World. The beef—the antibiotics, the chemicals, the genetic modifications, the illnesses. The farming practices in the First World, which is the largest marketplace, are going to have to lead this transformation. There needs to be a consciousness about how we grow food—and it needs to begin in the First World.

Local Solutions
Agroecology

THE COLLAPSE OF THE SOVIET UNION, COMBINED with the US embargo, created a food crisis in Cuba. The country needed to find a way to create its own food supply. At the time, many rural, small farmers were practicing prerevolutionary traditional methods of farming, such as crop rotation and seed diversification. These methods were successful and sustainable for the farmers to feed their families, and sometimes, even their communities. Cuban small farmers have provisions seldom afforded to small farmers elsewhere in the world—health care, education, and welfare. These provisions helped to sustain the farmers as they led what many have called an agricultural revolution.

Cuba's National Association of Small Farmers, ANAP, was instrumental in providing a network and a solution to the crisis. ANAP encouraged farmers to support one another, meeting in groups in their districts throughout the island. This was known as ANAP's *campesino a campesino*, farmer-to-farmer movement. Originating in the Guatemala Highlands by Mayan farmers, the *campesino a campesino* campaign had already spread throughout Central America before being brought to Cuba by Nicaraguan farmers. With the added assistance of the Cuban government, peasant farmers met with agronomists and soil scientists to create highly functioning, agroecological farming systems—choosing biopesticides over chemical pesticides, crop diversity over monoculture, organic matter over chemical fertilizer. The government further helped by installing ANAP offices throughout the country, and state policies urged small farmers to continue to work together by selling their goods in a collective marketplace. In time, the majority of large state farms were dismantled, and the number of urban farms and rural cooperative farms grew. In a span of only five years, the Cuban *campesino a campesino* network expanded to a quarter of a million people, both urban and rural.

Today, Cuba has an estimated 120,000 rural farmers operating organic agricultural ecosystems. There are an estimated 380,000 urban organic farms, capable of producing 1.5 million tons of vegetables annually. Small farms account for only 25 percent of the agricultural land, yet manage to supply 65 percent of the country's produce. With approximately 15 million acres of level farming land, many believe that Cuba is capable of producing enough food to feed its 11 million people.

Global food prices are predicted to double by 2030. Climate change will continue to create unpredictable weather patterns, leading to increased prices for fertilizer and fuel. All of this will have a negative impact on agriculture, especially commercial systems. Studies show that land farmed sustainably is able to recover more quickly after natural disasters, such as hurricanes, droughts, and floods. The distinction between sustainable farming and organic farming is this: organic crops can be produced on large (unsustainable) industrial farms, but while the product is organic, the way in which the crop is mass-produced may not be ecologically beneficial to the land. Sustainable farms seldom have corporate involvement, always consider animal welfare, and are small farms that do not burn fossil fuels for the transport of produce to the table—the farms are supplying food for those within the community. It's been shown that sustainable farms are able to produce more per acre than industrial corporate farms.

Today, the Republic of Cuba is a prime example of how a nation transformed its food production system. With the recent shifts in US relations, many are watching Cuba—specifically its agricultural state. Cuba's model of agroecology may be affected once the United States begins exporting food supplies as well as large-scale farming systems to the island nation. Still, the ANAP intends to remain a stronghold for the small farmer in Cuba. ANAP is now part of an international peasant movement, *La Via Campesina*, that along with thousands of other NGOs is actively galvanizing grassroots, sustainable, small farming revolutions around the world.

Opposite: Organopónico Vivero Alamar.

Next spread: Urban living in a neighborhood near downtown Havana.

CREW STORY

Jenna Chiyono Ishii

Apprentice Navigator

Jenna Ishii is the education coordinator and an executive assistant to president Nainoa Thompson with the Polynesian Voyaging Society (PVS). Raised in Hawai'i, Jenna earned her bachelor's degree on the mainland, and then moved to Okinawa, Japan, where she taught English from 2006 to 2007. While in Japan, she witnessed the historic arrival of Hōkūle'a into Okinawa, a voyage intended to honor Hawai'i's historic ties with Japanese immigrants who arrived in the islands in the nineteenth and early twentieth centuries. The experience led her to return home to devote herself fully to the mission of Hōkūle'a. Between a surf session and a meeting with leadership at PVS, Jenna talked about her first voyage to Tahiti and her faith in the future of Hawai'i.

I LOVE EVERY SINGLE DEPARTURE. When you let go of the lines, there is this sense of freedom. You see the island get smaller and smaller and smaller and then—you have a new family on board. And it's a whole new experience.

When you get to the true deep sea, all the distractions of your daily life go away. It's so much simpler to be completely present. Your focus is on taking care of the canoe and taking care of your fellow crewmembers. And when you add in learning about wayfinding and seeking answers from nature, then your whole job is to be alert—*maka'ala*.

It can be tough for my generation because we didn't grow up 24/7 observing nature. We're connected all the time with our digital devices—with texts and e-mails, there's so much noise—but then when you get out to the open ocean, all you have around you is the sea. You start hearing things, you start seeing birds you've never seen, you start noticing the way clouds move—and every little bit is important. The ocean brings you to life. It just wakes you up.

But it takes a couple of days for me to get to this place because I get really sea-sick. On the leg out of Hilo, it was the first deep-sea voyage for a lot of crewmembers and about half of the crew was down. We left on a tack upwind, and we were changing the sail rig out of the harbor, and for a couple of days, many of us were very seasick. I would say to my crew, "Whenever you need help, let me know, but otherwise I am just going to lie here!" It was miserable. I think I may have been the sickest one. After day three, I was throwing up a little blood, and my captain Nainoa asked me, "Do you think you can get over this? Do we have to turn around?"

I had to make the best guess. I said, "I think I can do this!" And he said OK. He didn't argue.

I felt so responsible because if I wasn't correct and I couldn't do this, they were going to have to turn around for me.

Then, after day four, we were getting farther south, and we had one of our first heavy-weather situations; we needed to close the sails right away. It was an all-hands-on-deck situation. And, in that moment, everyone just jumped into place. We closed the sails and I think that helped us to know, "We have to do this!"

It's amazing what your body can do when your mind gets out of the way. I think that's a part of being fully aware.

You are your best self the moment you step on the canoe. As days go on and you get tired and you're salty and you're wet and you're cold and sometimes you don't know when you're going to find your destination—that's when you really have to dig down deep. I have had moments where I've had a migraine, I'm seasick, I'm miserable, and I need to be pleasant and helpful, and it's my time to get on watch.

Nainoa always tells us that voyaging will bring you down to your bone. At some point, it's going to take you way down deep, and you're going to have to reach inside yourself to find that strength.

Anytime I'm feeling down and think I don't have strength left, I just think, *What would my grandma do?* My grandma, Oma. I hold her as what I hope my highest self can be. She survived World War II. Her mom, dad, and brother were killed in concentration camps, and she hid out for five years. I once asked her, "How? How did you have hope, and how did you have faith?"

She told me, "I always compare myself to someone who has less than I do, even during the war years." That's how she got through. She said, "There must be someone who needs something more than I do."

Oma's compassion and resiliency inspires me in everything I do, and I think for the rest of my life, no matter what I do, I will be dedicated to making my community better. It's not about money. It's not about what you have. It's about honoring the legacy of those who have come before you, and using your gifts to make this world a more peaceful place.

We are a young group, but I think we can let our teachers know that they don't have to carry all of the burden. Every one of us is looking to our teachers still, and they can be at peace knowing we will follow their instructions. We have the right intention to keep moving forward. They've told us, "It's now your turn, and hopefully we've given you everything we can for you to succeed."

If I look back on *Hōkūleʻa*'s legacy, I have every faith that *Hōkūleʻa* and the people who are connected to her are going to help make Hawaiʻi this brilliant, thriving, healthy place.

Over the past forty-two years, the world has become so connected through *Hōkūleʻa*. Just the act of sailing into places with this voyaging canoe automatically breaks down the walls. No matter whether we're somewhere for a day, a week, or six months, in that first interaction with a new community, it's like you are instantly family. It's like you've come home. Wherever that may be.

I have so much faith in humanity. I think we're on a really good track. There is a movement of people in Hawaiʻi all heading in the same direction. All of our leaders in different parts of society are all coming to the table. It's about asking the right questions and connecting with the right people. *Hōkūleʻa* has opened that door of light, and said, "OK, it's time."

Above: Everybody pitches in with a smile, Jenna is helped by Hye Jung Kim and Tamiko Fernelius, Great Barrier Reef.

CREW STORY
Nāʻālehu Kilohana Palikū Anthony
Captain

Nāʻālehu Anthony was born in 1975, the same year Hōkūleʻa was launched. He considers his childhood a blessed one, having grown up in the Aloha ʻĀina Movement. Nāʻālehu's first deep-sea sail was a voyage from Rapa Nui to Tahiti at the age of twenty-four. Since then, his kuleana, responsibilities, have been multifold, as a crewmember—sometimes a captain—and as the main documentarian on board. For nearly twenty years now, Nāʻālehu has documented the major voyages of Hōkūleʻa, as the chief executive director of ʻŌiwi TV and the principal of Palikū Documentary Films. He has also produced and directed several films, including the PBS documentary Mau Piailug: The Wayfinder. *While sailing, Nāʻālehu writes daily letters to those within the PVS community and sometimes shares them with the larger audience of the Hōkūleʻa website. The following excerpt was written from the deck of Hōkūleʻa as she crossed the Indian Ocean.*

IN THE BLACK OF NIGHT, steering by the stars and counting the miles with the bubbles floating by our speeding canoe, we're reminded of how truly analog this process was for centuries. We call it "art" now, a bundle of sennit to hang on the wall or a woven piece of sail, every weave woven in precise perfection. But long ago, these were not items in isolation; they were all working parts of the canoe. The whole society had the technology and expertise to create all the components needed to build these vessels and then sail, with purpose, to other islands.

Today, one could argue that our society is not as resourceful; the great trees are gone, and the tradesmen and women who built the parts have mostly disappeared, save for the few who cling to their craft. So we sail on a hybrid vessel, a performance accurate replica of what most likely once was. She sails the same speed and points the same way as ancient canoes. By the time they got around to rebuilding this one in the 1970s, they had to use some modern stuff to make it all go: fiberglass, Dacron, and a little plywood to fill the gaps in the missing knowledge. But the intent is still very much the same—using only the clues and observational tools of nature, to raise islands from the sea thousands of miles away.

One thing that has stayed very analog, until very recently, has been the communications structure. In the 1970s, there wasn't much to speak of in terms of communications equipment except for a single sideband radio that would only be used in emergencies. And it stayed that way for more than a generation. The thought was to protect the "experiment" of navigation and stay pure to that purpose. No outside information was allowed, no navigational clues to make the task easier for the ones with the *kuleana* of wayfinding.

Over the years, our mission has shifted a bit. We have proven that the gift of navigation from an unbroken line of masters works. Now we are turning our attention to education and sharing the values that come with visiting ports around the world. And the lessons in port are now starting to sound familiar: native perspective and knowledge have a place in solving some of Earth's most serious problems. Our ancestors shared their stories orally; today we use the tools and technologies available to amplify our stories. The communications job surrounding this worldwide voyage has become more critical than on previous voyages. We are now reaching audiences who want to know immediately what is happening on the *waʻa*, and because of this we are forced to compete in the twenty-four-hour news cycle.

And so, today, even on board this ancient vessel, we have entered into the digital age—begrudgingly, like a wandering monk being forced to carry an iPhone on the journey. As I type this blog on a MacBook Pro and use Inmarsat satellites to move massive amounts of data every day, we are careful to keep the crew in the bubble of the past. Our website is updated daily, and our Facebook and Instagram fans have an insatiable appetite for our content, but the crew doesn't get to see any of the posts or comments until we return home or arrive into port. In order to participate in the lessons that are embedded in this process, we must leave the land stuff on the land and go to sea wholeheartedly. So, for me, the job of media specialist on board *Hōkūleʻa* is bittersweet. Even on a canoe in the middle of the ocean, the long arm of e-mail and interconnectedness has its grasp on me. I have to be careful not to let my mind wander too far to the tasks at home, as being present on board the canoe is paramount to our collective success.

Our escort, the *Gershon II*, always within sight and a VHF call away, has a completely different perspective. They sail patiently behind us, knowing exactly where we are. They have a bunch of cool gadgets that sound even cooler by acronym: AIS, GPS, and DSC for our PLB. They call us to let us know we have a slight edge, a quarter knot more than them, and they are losing ground at 1.85 miles out.

That's the paradigm: Old needs to embrace the new, but new also must ap-

preciate the old. Respect goes both ways. Here's the *nīnau*, the question: Is navigation actually more important today than it was 1,500 years ago when navigators pulled Hawaiki out of the sea for the first time in human history?

The simple answer is no; those voyagers were unleashing the single biggest feat of exploration of their time. But in this age where smart devices are ubiquitous and can pinpoint our exact location with ease, traditional navigation is one of the last places where answers cannot be found on a screen. You just have to look up to the heavens for all the clues to find your way. That tangible connection to the environment and the self are lost to many with this influx of technology. For us, however, here, in this space, we embrace the analog and keep the digital at bay for as long as possible.

As the faint glow of sunrise starts to spread on the horizon, the crew slowly wakes from the sway of *Hōkūle'a* gliding across the Indian Ocean. Another day of sailing in the wake of our ancestors has begun.

Above: As the leader of the 'Ōiwi TV documentary team, Nā'ālehu is a producer, director, photographer, and writer—as well as a captain and crewmember. At the Rapa Nui arrival ceremony, he is both an honored guest and a key content producer.

GALLERY III
New York to Tahiti

This spread: *Hōkūleʻa* and the Washington Monument, two iconic symbols of strength and hope within reach of each other.

Pages 214–215: *Hōkūleʻa* crosses paths with a much larger vessel in New York Harbor.

Pages 216–217: Tamiko Fernelius explores the reef with a local in the Galápagos.

Pages 218–219: As most of the crew are surfers, this was a particularly sweet anchorage in the Galápagos.

Pages 220–221: Wildlife reigns supreme in the Galápagos.

Pages 222–223: *Hōkūleʻa* is welcomed into the bay where Ariki Hotu Matuʻa, the first high chief of Rapa Nui, is believed to have arrived centuries ago, Rapa Nui.

Pages 224–225: The sound of the *pū* announces the arrival of *Hōkūleʻa*, Rapa Nui.

Pages 226–227: Billy Richards carries a *pōhaku* from Hawaiʻi to be given to the *marae* at Taputapuātea, Raʻiātea.

Page 228: The strength of the future is rooted in the traditions of the past, Taputapuātea, Raʻiātea.

Page 229: A regal *tutu*, auntie, at Taputapuātea, Raʻiātea.

Pages 230–231: Marae Hauviri, one of several *marae* at Taputapuātea. The *marae* is a temple honoring the solidarity of the people to each other and to the land itself, Raʻiātea.

Pages 232–233: *Hōkūleʻa* sails toward the setting sun on the way to Raʻiātea.

"Voyaging is a metaphor for life—at its core. That is its greatest value. How do you set your course plan? Do you know where you are going? Once you do, you can figure out what stars you want to follow. If you can just pick out one point of light, then everything else will fall into place. But when I say point of light, I'm not talking about stars. I'm talking about people, family, friends, places, things that will guide you home. … Because once you can do that, you will never be lost."

Celeste Manuia Haʻo
Apprentice Navigator

NEW YORK

CHAPTER 7

Think not of yourself

—

Think not of yourself, oh chiefs. Think of the continuing generations.
Think of our grandchildren and those yet born, those whose faces are
coming up from beneath the ground.

– Onondaga Nation Peacemaker

IN ALL FOUR DIRECTIONS, YOU CAN HEAR HER, CALLING HER SONG across the stormy waters. Cloaked in deerskin, she paddles knowingly, as only a descendant of this river could. It's been four hundred years since her people paddled out of here, chased away by the wars with settlers from the Old World. She is known as *Sagkompanau Mishoon Netooeusqua*, Butterfly Woman I Lead the Canoe, and to her, the river is *Mohicanichtuck*, the river that flows both ways. Each dip of the paddle connects to the past, she will tell you, each stroke creates healing for the future.

Safely ashore, she binds her canoe to *Hōkūleʻa* in a marina below the fog-shrouded towers of Battery Park. This is the spot where Dutch artilleries once defended the first world trade center. Today there are no weapons, only peacemakers. Algonquin, Montauk, Mohegan, Munsee, Shinnecock, Unkechaug, Lenape, Carnesie, Haudenosaunee, and the six-nation Iroquois Confederacy of the Mohawk, Seneca, Cayuga, Onondaga, Oneida, and Tuscarora have come together to greet the Hawaiians who have sailed the globe.

Taking shelter from a looming summer storm, the nations meet under a massive awning to talk story and share song with the Hawaiian guests. There is talk of "spirits circling the tent," of "ancestors swirling around," and the ways the "waters of the world"—rivers, streams, oceans, and even rain—join people, communities, and countries into one. There is talk of the upcoming World Oceans Day, an event that will commit all the United Nations toward caring for the oceans of our Earth.

The rain begins. It pounds on the tent. It sounds as if a lake has torn through the clouds.

Time to begin the giving. The gifts come in many forms. A song for safe arrivals, cedar for protection sailing forward, corn to nourish the body and the spirit, sweet grass for strength and courage, and the sacred wampum—the beaded belt woven entirely of shoreline shells—as a gesture of welcome.

In return, the Hawaiians offer dance and chant, and then the drink of *ʻawa*. When the *ʻawa* ceremony is complete, Butterfly Woman asks to speak. She needs to leave soon as the storm is growing and the river is her pathway home.

"It's a very sacred moment for all of us Indigenous people to be here," she says. "Thank you for allowing us to be here in a peaceful way."

Her song is inspired by *Hōkūleʻa*, she explains. The song is dedicated to everyone—the crew, the nations, and the nonindigenous people—collected here.

Opposite: *Hōkūleʻa's* mast has multiple lines running up it; some to keep the mast vertical, and some to deploy and manage the sails, New York City.

"Together we can move forward in this situation," she says. "This situation" is the climate, the environmental crisis, the caring for the world's waters.

"The song I sing, it means," she explains, "together we move forward."

She takes a moment, and then she begins. She bends her knees as she sings, as if she is digging the words up from the earth to send them out and beyond the breaking clouds above.

When she finishes, drums are beat, the *pū* is blown, whistles fly. Thunder cracks, echoing off the city's forest of steel, concrete, and glass.

She remains unflinching in her resolve to paddle the river back home.

"We're going to paddle home in our waters," she tells the nations, as she makes her way out of the tent, "please pray for us."

SKYSCRAPERS CARVE A NETWORK of canyons throughout the island. Streets are streams. Underground, the trade winds of the subway swirl cyclones of trash. Over six hundred miles of transit track line these catacombs, decorated with hieroglyphic graffiti. Those accustomed to navigating by the sun or the swells or the moon or the stars may be lost in Manhattan.

"I've been navigating for thirty years now—and I'm pretty confident," says Pwo navigator Kālepa Baybayan. "Except when it comes to the subway system in New York."

The Archipelago of New York ranges between thirty and forty-two islands, depending on the rise and fall of the tide. Staten, Ellis, Rikers, Governors, Rat, and Pig are just a few that neighbor Manhattan. Seawalls armor Manhattan, shielding the city from three rivers—the Hudson, the East, and the Harlem. These waterways were once the main Native trading trails of the eastern seaboard. Today, New York Harbor, tucked into the Bay of New York off the Atlantic Ocean, is one of the most active harbors in the world.

In the 1600s, the Dutch "purchased" lower Manhattan from the original Lenape people and soon transfigured the marshes, swamps, and woodlands. Roads were carved over Lenape foot trails. Landfill, dug up from the shoreline, became the earthen anchor for buildings. A wall, dividing New Amsterdam land from Native lands, was built and would later become known as Wall Street.

When the British took ownership of the territory, they determined that the winding pathways of lower Manhattan would not suffice for the rest of the island. Instead, they created a symmetrical grid suitable for the three million people who work on the island today.

Avenues run north and south, streets run east and west; some of these thoroughfares run one-way, others, two. Broadway, a renegade route, winds diagonally through the city from downtown to uptown. Navigating the grid requires a deep understanding of the ways man has chosen to control nature. Living within the grid also requires a certain temperament willing to embrace the many ways man has continued to build and live here to make New York the most densely populated city on Earth.

"By midcentury, 75 percent of us will be living in urban areas," explains Ilona Rayan. Ilona is pausing on a balmy summer day on a pier in the Hudson River Park.

Opposite top: Hawaiian musician Paula Fuga sings at the Manhattan arrival ceremony.

Opposite bottom: A Mālama Honua presentation on World Oceans Day at the United Nations.

Born in Papua New Guinea, Ilona grew up paddling and with an island sensibility. A graduate student of New York University, Ilona based her master's thesis on Indigenous Pacific Islander knowledge and how it can be applied to sustainable development. She works for C40 Cities, a climate leadership group, and commutes from Long Island to her job in New York City, travelling two and a half hours each way by bus and train.

"New York is a highly efficient city," she says, citing Citi Bikes, buses, subways, and trains with the capability to move millions of people through the city and its boroughs each day.

There are 5,700 buses, 13,000 taxis, 8,000 Citi Bikes, 34 train lines, and 469 stations moving people through the city on an average workday. Water taxis and ferries also help commuters get from New Jersey and the boroughs to New York City. Less than 50 percent of those living on the island own a car. Thanks to this massive transit system, Manhattan has the lowest per capita carbon-related transportation footprint in all of the United States.

While she upholds the city's strength in public transport, she knows that the terrain has been stripped of nature. "There's a discord between us and nature," she admits. "We feel that when we develop technologically, we need to leave nature behind. We don't realize that we can't survive without nature. Indigenous people understand that who we are is because of nature."

If the last four hundred years have revealed man's domination of the natural environment in Manhattan, the last thirty has seen an urgency to engineer nature back into the landscape.

Rooftop gardens abound in Manhattan. An abandoned elevated freight rail line has been converted into an elevated park—the High Line—a public parkway of self-seeded perennials, shrubs, and trees that extends over twenty city blocks. The Hudson, once seen as a "dead" river, is gradually becoming a water trail for paddlers. In Brooklyn, the Brooklyn Garage is a two-and-a-half-acre farm on a rooftop, growing 50,000 pounds of organic vegetables a year. Slowly, the idea of sustainability is being woven into the city. But it takes a change of attitude from the colonial mindset that leveled this island into a gridiron terrain.

"If we want to tackle our environmental and sustainability issues, we have to change our way of thinking, our approach to everything," Ilona says. "We have to have a climate OF change—if we want to tackle climate change."

A GIRAFFE, A BABY GRAND PIANO, and a Lincoln Continental: These are just some of the items that have turned up in the Hudson River. For a few hundred years, the river was used as a depository. This perspective had begun as early as the 1600s when the Dutch settlers sought to develop the lower island into a world trade center and transform the river into a commercial waterway.

The Dutch succeeded. Hundreds of piers were built along the waterfront to support the maritime industry. But during the second Industrial Revolution, the majority of the piers were abandoned. By the 1940s, upriver factories were dumping waste, including PCBs, directly into the river. As the water quality grew worse, the Hudson Bay oyster beds became the carrier of typhoid and cholera, and the river was closed to fishing and recreational activities due to health hazards. But in 1972,

Opposite top: Crewmembers Noelani Kamalu and
Jason Patterson survey a very different sea.

Opposite bottom: Times Square in perpetual motion.

the Clean Water Act was created and helped revitalize the Hudson by regulating pollutants and setting wastewater standards. Combined with the Pure Waters Bond Act, the river began the recovery process.

The Hudson is an estuary where freshwater and salt water merge in a waterway that extends 315 miles north of the city. Containing more than 200 species of fish, 19 kinds of birds, and 140 rare plants, the river is also a nursery for striped bass which spawn and grow in the freshwater before leaving for a life in the Atlantic.

In 1986, a marine science field station was set up to monitor wildlife and water quality in the Hudson. Known as The River Project, it is the only organization that

has been monitoring fish and water quality continually for the past thirty years. Their studies helped designate 400 acres of the Hudson River as an Estuarine Park Sanctuary in 2002.

"The river is as healthy as it's been in over a hundred years," says River Project educator Melissa Rex. A biology graduate of Yeshiva University, Melissa hopes to someday earn a doctorate in marine microbiology. For now, she is part of a team of marine scientists who oversees The River Project Wetlab, where students and educators learn about the biodiversity of the tributaries of the Hudson.

The River Project is situated on Pier 40 in the Hudson River Park where pile fields, fragments of former piers, still remain. Once dislodged, these neglected timber pilings can sometimes be seen floating along the river, mistaken for creatures as exotic as alligators, seals, and whales. The still-standing pilings have become homes for a wide range of river life, a testament to nature's ability to continually adapt. Decaying wood provides vertical housing, similar to apartment buildings,

Above: Before standing watch, crewmember Keala Kimura snugs *Hōkūleʻa* tight against the barge that serves as her floating dock, Manhattan.

Opposite: Our effect on the environment is inescapable on the Lower West Side.

with tidal residents taking up space on each floor. Grass shrimp, sea squirts, blue mussels, barnacles, sea lettuce, red algae, boring sponges, and gribbles have found homes in the piles. Birds and mallard ducks use the penthouse posts as lookouts. Naval shipworms reside at midlevel. Blue crabs and pollution-tolerant oyster toadfish prefer the darker, basement, riverbed floor.

"On a clear day, when it hasn't rained, the river is swimmable," Melissa says, noting a handful of kayaks out on the river today. The Clean Water Act set standards, but it did not correct the issue of Combined Sewage Overflows.

"About twenty minutes of medium rain can be enough to cause an overflow," Melissa explains, allowing that an overflow means the river goes from swimmable to toxic. With moderate rain, both the rain and sewage will back up in the combined pipes, causing the flow of six thousand miles of sewage pipes to spill directly into the Hudson, East River, and New York Harbor. Each year, an estimated 27 billion gallons of raw sewage flow out of the 460 combined sewage overflows into New York Harbor. Combined Sewage Overflows are not unique to Manhattan. According to the EPA, over seven hundred US cities still bear this archaic design.

"It happens every time it rains," says Pete Malinowski, PhD, cofounder and director of the Billion Oyster Project, an ecosystem restoration project. "It's a violation of the Clean Water Act. If you couldn't go into Central Park because it was full of human waste, they would clean it up, right? The reality is the majority of New Yorkers don't see the New York Harbor as a natural resource."

As a young environmentalist, Melissa knows that where there is despair, there must also remain hope. She offers up a few more signs that the river is in fact recovering. Oysters are again showing up along the shoreline. Striped bass, once endangered, are now more populous than humans in New York City. The lined seahorse, only able to survive in clean waters, has returned. The seahorse had been absent for over a century.

"This year, we have spotted more seahorses than we ever have," Melissa says. And that, alone, she says, gives hope.

HŌKŪLEʻA IS GLIDING UP the East River, her crimson sails vibrant on a misty day. When she reaches the glass fortress of the United Nations, she drops her sails and becomes a powerful backdrop for those gathered on a pier directly across from the United Nations building in Gantry Park, Long Island City. United Nations Secretary-General Ban Ki-moon is here, along with the President of the Republic of Palau, Butterfly Woman, Tadodaho Sidney Hall, and other dignitaries.

So far, *Hōkūleʻa* has crossed through three oceans—the Pacific, Indian, and Atlantic—and four seas—the Coral, Tasman, Arafura, and Caribbean. She has stopped in sixteen countries and has travelled over 25,000 nautical miles. Though the sail plan sometimes shifted depending on nature's ever-changing cue, never once did the plan waver from reaching the United Nations on World Oceans Day.

The *pū* is blown in all four directions—a signal to mark the beginning of the gathering.

The President of the Republic of Palau is first to speak. "The ocean does not divide us," he says. "It connects all of us together."

Opposite top: Harbor School life jackets on the waterfront outside of Manhattan.

Opposite bottom: Aside from general training in boat handling, the New York Harbor School engages students with numerous other water-based activities, one of which is the Billion Oyster Project.

President Thomas Esang Remengesau Jr. is part of a network of Polynesian leaders who have decided to take control of their home waters. Palau, Papua New Guinea, Tuvalu, Kiribati, Marshall Islands, the Federated States of Micronesia, the Solomon Islands, and Nauru are all a part of the Nauru Agreement, which allows these eight nations to collectively control 25–30 percent of the world's tuna supply. These nations have redefined the developed-world notion of wealth knowing that *wai*, water, in all its forms, is the highest definition of wealth. In Hawaiian, the actual word for wealth is *waiwai*. To Nainoa, these nations have "cracked the code."

Cracking the code is key to keeping the global environmental sail plan on the right course. In September 2014, the International Conference on Small Island Developing States gathered in Apia, Sāmoa. Small island nations were the first to sound the alarm about climate change because they were first to notice the impacts of rising sea levels. Though they contribute to global warming the least, they are affected by it the most.

After that conference, Secretary-General Ban Ki-moon sailed on *Hōkūle‘a* and, before disembarking, made a promise to Nainoa and the crew.

"As you tour the globe, I will work and rally more leaders to our common cause of ushering in a more sustainable future and a life of dignity for all," the Secretary-General wrote in a note. He then tucked the note in a bottle and gave the bottle to Nainoa. The bottle has remained on *Hōkūle‘a* ever since. Nainoa holds that bottle in his hands today.

Above: United Nations Secretary-General Ban Ki-moon points to a message of hope: *Hōkūle‘a*.

When Secretary-General Ban Ki-moon stands to speak, he expresses the need for unity in the world community, from small island states to big island countries, to come together to protect the great oceans.

"Oceans may seem endless but there is a limit as to how we should use them. We are dangerously close to breaking that limit," the Secretary-General says. "The ways we treat our oceans affects their future and biodiversity. On this World Oceans Day, we recommit to using this gift peacefully, equitably, and sustainably."

Nainoa thanks the Secretary-General and talks of the "light housed in the bottle." He talks of collecting declarations from communities around the world, communities committed to caring for the oceans that border their homes, commitments that he has bound in a koa-framed book that he now gives to the Secretary-General. Nainoa explains that the greatest wealth of his island's nation and culture is the health of the water that surrounds their home. Beyond time zones, latitudes, and longitudes, the element that binds us all is the ocean.

"We brought back the bottle," Nainoa tells the Secretary-General, returning it to him now. "We give it back to you on this day, as our promise to you to be in perpetual care for our ocean and our Earth."

A CROWD HAS FORMED along a pier railing overlooking the Hudson. There appears to be something bobbing, blowing air, in the river. It floats up, then dips back down to fully disappear under the brackish water.

"It's a whale!" someone announces. Someone else says, "It's a dolphin." "Maybe it's a seal?" someone else asks.

A quiet reverence overcomes those awaiting its next breach. But then, it lifts to the surface to reveal its true nature—a walrus-sized plastic pipe floating, spinning, in the river.

The crowd disperses. The moment becomes a reminder of the connection between the health of the waters and the health of the land.

That connection can be felt on a day like this, where hundreds of paddlers from around the world have come to paddle six-man outrigger canoes up and down the New York waterways in the Liberty Challenge outrigger race. It is midafternoon. The men's and women's competitions have been completed, and it's now time for the co-ed race.

Nainoa is committed to the race. His crew includes his sister, Lita; brother-in-law, fellow *Pwo* navigator Bruce Blankenfeld; Bruce and Lita's children, Tia and Nai'a, and a *Hōkūle'a* crewmember, the greatly respected retired Army Major General Darryll Wong. Their canoe is made of fiberglass and painted a glossy white. She is built with modern materials but her essence is purely traditional. *Wa'a* were originally created to carry people exploring new and known lands. Back then and still today, she must be paddled and steered with *pono*, the right intention.

Nainoa knows the challenges. One challenge is to paddle as one. *Pūpūkahi i Holomua,* Unite to Move Forward.

Climate change—the multiple stressors of hypoxia, dead zones, acidification, rising sea levels—these disconcerting issues Nainoa has spoken of in his time here in New York. These are the issues that you will sail around the world for, to seek out stories and people and solutions to unite canoes, countries, and continents.

And with this in mind, the captain now navigates the river. Through channels and currents, past islands, under bridges, around the Statue of Liberty, stopping for ferries, yielding to tankers, and pausing for kayaks, he steers the canoe wisely, efficiently, and respectfully. The crew paddles as one.

When the canoe reaches the finish line, she is greeted by a flock of fireboats, spraying a rainbow-wide salute. She glides by, like a white flower offered to the great waters.

Opposite: Solomon Aikau helps sail the canoe into Manhattan. His brother Eddie gave his life while trying to find help for the crew of the *Hōkūle'a* when she flipped in the Moloka'i Channel in 1978.

Above: One of the crews *Hōkūle'a* entered into the Liberty Challenge, holding onto second place as the Statue of Liberty comes into view.

—

Local Voices
Tadodaho Sidney Hill
Member of the Haudenosaunee Nation

Tadodaho Sidney Hill is the spiritual leader of the Haudenosaunee nation, sometimes referred to as the Iroquois Confederacy or the Six Nations. The Haudenosaunee are an influential confederacy of Indigenous Nations and are often sought out by Indigenous peoples around the world for guidance and support. In 1142, the Great Peacemaker brought five warring nations together on the shores of Onondaga Lake and gave them the message of peace, power of the good mind, and righteousness, thus forming the Haudenosaunee Confederacy, led by a Grand Counsel consisting of chiefs from each nation. This democracy became the structural model for the United States and has been acknowledged as the birthplace of democracy by Congress. Tadodaho often speaks to the members of the United Nations, expressing his concerns about global warming and the urgent need for all nations to act with unity. Sitting on a bench by the East River, with a wide view of the New York skyline, he discussed his people's philosophy. He is known to sign his letters and end his speeches with this simple reminder, "While we deliberate, the ice is melting."

In His Own Words

YOU HAVE ALL THIS HERE, AND YOU JUST WONDER, what's going to happen? What's going to happen if things collapse? You have people upon people living fifty stories high.

The scientists say global warming is happening. Global warming is happening. But nobody pays attention until it affects them. It did affect them. It flooded Wall Street. But they went on to their business, "Oh, we'll go up to the next floor!" That's their answer. That's not good enough. You're not thinking about those people who suffer the most. They're the ones that can't move up to the next floor.

As a leader, you're given messages from the Creator—one message is about giving thanks and appreciating everything that is here. The Creator put everything here that we need, and we need to walk peaceably about the Earth.

We acknowledge water in our thanksgiving because water is everything. We acknowledge the water in our wells, in the springs, in the ocean. We believe that the salt sea was the protection for our lands at one time because nobody could get through there. The ocean protected us from outsiders. But when the Europeans broke through that, with their technology, they breached that protection.

When we give thanks, we acknowledge the great waters, and the grandmother of all the waters, the oceans. You can't give any more respect than to your grandmother. This is how high we regard the ocean.

We're given names as a child through our ceremonies, through our clans. The clan mother has the names. She has a basket of names for her people. This basket of names is given to the child when he or she is born. When the name is given, the elders will say, "Now, your name has been like a drop in the water that's going to go all over, every trickle of water circulates and goes into the ocean, and it feeds all the medicines and the animals and the plants, everything, so now all those elements know who you are. So when you need them, you can ask them for help. That's how connected you are to the water."

That's the connection that we have, and the respect. It's not just a stream, and the attitude of, "Oh, I own this stream, and you don't, you can't have it." This is different. Nobody owns this. It's for everybody and you don't have a right to destroy it. Or contaminate it. It's all about respect.

If you don't restore your own environment, you're not going to survive. You're not going to survive. You shouldn't have to depend on something outside of your realm.

Where are you? How sustainable are you? If you can't take care of yourself, what condition are you in, really?

That's where we are today. You talk about hope. You have this doom of global warming, climate change, all this destruction, high winds and the storms. But then you have people, like the Hawaiians, who are bringing that ancient sustainable knowledge back, so they have hope. They have hope.

Most Indigenous people are sustainable. They sustained themselves for thousands of years. It's only since the last five hundred years that we started going down this path of destruction. A lot of people call it "progress." Yes, people live longer but how are they living and who's living longer?

We call ourselves survivors now. We survived. We survived through time. We endured. As a people connected to the land, we see if everything fails, now we have to go back to the land.

Because if you can't drink that water, what are you going to do? What are you going to do if you can't eat the fish?

We have to clean this up. We have to clean this up for the people depending on these waters, on these lands, on these plants, on these medicines. That's our purpose now—to make sure we don't stray too far off where you can't come back, where you can't survive.

But how do you educate seven, soon to be nine, billion people about the connection to the land and where you need to be? The technology, it's there. It's the will of the people, whether it's too late or not.

Local Solutions
The Billion Oyster Project

In 1605, when Henry Hudson sailed into New York Harbor, you could harvest fish by simply lowering a basket over the rail of your boat. Over 220,000 acres of oyster reefs lined the harbor's floor. For the next three centuries, these reefs provided sustenance for the inhabitants of the growing city. But by the early 1900s, nearly all the oysters had been harvested. Dredging had scraped the remaining reefs, and silt from increased farm runoff had discouraged any native repopulation. Pollution and sewage had made the remaining oysters dangerous to eat. When typhoid and cholera breakouts were traced to the oyster beds, health officials shut down the harbor for fishing and harvesting.

Oysters are natural water filters. Oysters are also a native keystone species: The shells and reefs provide habitat for other species. With the depletion of this species, the entire equilibrium of the harbor was disrupted. In 1972, the Clean Water Act put an end to unrestricted dumping of industrial pollutants and mandated cleanups of the New York waterways. While this allowed the harbor to begin its slow recovery, the restoration of oysters would require additional assistance.

In 2014, the Billion Oyster Project (BOP) was created as a large-scale restoration of the oyster beds in the harbor. The goal: to restore one billion oysters into the harbor by 2035. By restoring oysters, the project will improve water quality, revive fish and wildlife, and engage the next generation in the care and protection of the local waters.

The Billion Oyster Project was born out of the Urban Assembly New York Harbor School. Located on Governors Island, this public charter high school teaches students various maritime skills, including aquaculture, boat operations and repair, scuba diving, marine biology, and ocean engineering. Students then use all these skills to carry out the work of the Billion Oyster Project.

Reef restoration is a complex process. BOP collects used oyster shells from fifty-eight restaurants around the city, gathering an average of four tons weekly. To prevent any pathogens from entering the harbor, these shells are cured at a site on Staten Island for a year and then brought to the aquaculture lab at the Harbor School. In the lab, students and BOP staff induce adult oysters to spawn. The free-swimming larvae that subsequently form are introduced into water tanks filled with bags of cured oyster shells. The larvae find a home on these shells, latching on to them, and creating what is known as the "spat on" shell stage. Students then place these shells onto plastic trays. The trays are lowered into the water of New York Harbor at one of several nursery sites, including one beneath the school's main dock which was built from the recycled legs of a former water tower.

Students monitor these oysters. Once oysters have grown big enough, they are placed on one of a growing number of reefs around the harbor. These reefs are various structures. The most common one is an oyster cabinet: a ten-foot-long, box-shaped structure made of rebar, designed and built by students. Each cabinet has several wire mesh sleeves into which the spat-on-shell oysters are placed. If the oysters were simply dropped into the water, they would be buried in the mud on the harbor's floor. The cabinets allow the young oysters to remain in the water column where they can feed and grow.

In addition to building reefs, BOP is also involved in the Living Breakwaters project, a response to damages from Hurricane Sandy. Funded through the federal Rebuild by Design program, BOP is helping to install 13,000 linear feet of oyster reef on top of breakwaters constructed off the shores of Staten Island. These living breakwaters support local species, creating "reef streets," which will become habitat for other marine animals. The breakwaters also absorb some of the energy of incoming waves, helping to mitigate damage during superstorms.

By World Oceans Day 2016, the two-year-old project had restored 16.5 million oysters to the harbor and had reclaimed 400,000 pounds of shell. Since its inception, sixty other schools have teamed up with the project. BOP has engaged more than 4,500 urban schoolchildren in the care of their waterways, creating a viable way to correct past mistakes by enlisting the future stewards of our planet.

Opposite: Tools of the trade.

Next spread: *Hōkūle'a* passes in front of the One World Trade Center building, also known as the Freedom Tower.

CREW STORY

Jason Kaholokai Tseu Patterson

Apprentice Navigator

Jason Kaholokai Tseu Patterson is an apprentice navigator on the Worldwide Voyage. His middle name was given to him to honor his maternal grandfather, Kaholokai, which translates as "one who travels on the sea." When he is not voyaging, he is a photographer and editor for ʻŌiwi TV. Sitting on a pier beside Hōkūleʻa in Lower Manhattan, New York, Jason talked about how his own experience aboard the canoe has clarified his perspective of what it means to serve the common good, and how the original vision of 1975 has grown to become the global mission of Mālama Honua.

I WAS FIRST INTRODUCED to Nainoa in 2003. I was taking a marine science class at Kamehameha Schools and one of the field trips was to Nainoa's house, where he shared his idea about educating a new generation of students about *Hōkūleʻa*. Then, a couple of years later, I was taking an honors science research class where we had to develop a science project and present it at the State Science Fair. I was presenting my project to a group when Nainoa recognized me and came up. He was wearing a name tag that read "Celebrity Judge" and had a rolled-up science fair pamphlet in his hand. As soon as he saw me, he said, "Hey, what are you doing here?" So I gave my presentation to him and to the others that had gathered. After I finished, he tapped me on the shoulder with the pamphlet and said, "We're going to Nihoa, and you're coming!"

I didn't know what to expect, but I knew that it was going to be an adventure. There wasn't any doubt whether or not I'd go. Nainoa didn't give me that option. He just said, "… you're coming!"

That first voyage was the first time I felt the connection to my culture that I had been searching for, for so long. I was very lucky to go to Kamehameha Schools—a college preparatory school for those with Hawaiian ancestry—from kindergarten through high-school graduation. But I often felt like an outsider looking in at a culture that was supposedly my own. *Hōkūleʻa* gave me that connection to my Hawaiian culture. I fell in love with the canoe on that sail and that love grows deeper with each opportunity the canoe provides.

After that first sail, I didn't see Nainoa, or the rest of the crew, again for a couple of years because I went to college in California. Then after returning home, I went with my sister to her friend's graduation, and Nainoa was the commencement speaker. After the ceremony, he had all these spotlights on his face and everybody was swarming him. He could barely see anything, but he still pointed to me. He was full of joy to see me and my friend Waimea McKeague, a fellow crewmember on my first sail. He said, "Hey, good to see you! We're going around the world, we start training on Monday. Get down to the canoe!" Nainoa's like that—totally direct, and that little bit was all he had to say.

I went down to the canoe the next Monday and started training. The first person I saw was Kaʻiulani Murphy driving in the gate. Kaʻiulani had really helped us younger students on that first sail, and in a few months, she would become our navigation teacher at the University of Hawaiʻi. Everything was coming together. That was in May of 2008, and I haven't left the canoe since.

The notion of the Worldwide Voyage began with an idea from NASA astronaut Lacy Veach. Nainoa and Lacy were close friends, and both are pioneers of exploration. After *Hōkūleʻa*'s Voyage of Rediscovery in 1985–87, PVS leaders were talking about what the next voyage should be. It was Lacy's idea that *Hōkūleʻa* needed to sail around the world, share the love and kindness of Hawaiʻi with the world, and inspire other native peoples to reconnect with their ancient wisdom and knowledge of caring for Earth.

It all started from Lacy seeing the Hawaiian Islands from the space shuttle and relaying that moment to Nainoa, explaining, "You have no idea how incredibly beautiful our planet is until you see it from space." He saw the planet as an island floating in the sea of space and made the connection of Earth being our island, our canoe. He had that experience and later wanted to connect schoolchildren to the space shuttle and to the canoe, and was able to have a radio call between the canoe, a classroom, and the space shuttle all at the same time.

As *Hōkūleʻa* went up the East Coast of the mainland in the spring of 2016, we made a special stop at NASA. It's always great to meet like-minded people. These two voyaging platforms—NASA and PVS—are alike in many ways.

Some see *Hōkūleʻa* as an oceanic space shuttle. The Polynesian migration, colonizing islands throughout the vast Pacific, was like the original space shot. Even though our *kūpuna* were very intelligent and knew how to navigate to new lands, on their first voyage they probably didn't know what exactly was out there. With NASA and the moon shot, they saw their target and they had to figure out how to get there. Getting to the moon was incredibly difficult and challenging, but they could see where they were going. Our ancestors—on the first sail out in search of new islands—were heading to a target they couldn't see. That took a massive amount of courage.

And each mission, that of NASA and that of the first voyaging canoe, was to serve the common good.

When you're on the canoe, it's not about you: It's about the canoe, and what the canoe has done for you and what the canoe has done for others, and what the canoe will potentially do for the future. Many of the core crew have this same mindset and same attitude toward the work that needs to be done. We all subscibe to this philosophy. We have to, for us, and for the future.

Above: The rigging for *Hōkūleʻa's* mast needs to be well maintained to withstand the rigors of the Worldwide Voyage.

CREW STORY

Russell Joshua Amimoto

Captain

Russell Amimoto has been sailing on Hōkūleʻa for more than half of his life. Born on Kauaʻi, Russell was raised on Oʻahu near Sandy Beach, his childhood playground. Growing up, Bruce Blankenfeld was his paddling coach and he did more than a few channel crossings with Nainoa as his steersman. He was sixteen years old the first time he sailed on Hōkūleʻa, and from that day forward, the canoe became what he refers to as his "Great Teacher." His many years of sailing have shown him the need for conservation in Hawaiʻi and have led to his current role as community marine monitoring manager with The Nature Conservancy of Hawaiʻi. As a father of two young boys, Russell had not yet sailed on the Worldwide Voyage until his wife encouraged him to do so, knowing how important the canoe was to him. About to set sail from Rapa Nui to Tahiti, Russell took a moment to reflect on his mentors, his own role as a captain, and the way the canoe guides everyone home.

BY 2009, I HAD ALREADY done a lot of interisland sails. So when Bruce invited me to sail from Hilo to Marquesas, I thought, *Oh, yeah, I'm ready, no problem!* But that first night out at sea, I was eating *lau lau, taro* leaf wrapped around pork. They were really good, so I ate a lot of them. But it was super-rough seas, and when I went digging down below looking for some medical supplies it turned into a long, miserable night. I got really sick.

This big wave came over the front of the canoe and soaked me in my bunk and it got everything I had wet—my nice, warm sleeping bag, all my dry clothes, everything. And so, I put my foul-weather gear on and slept in it that first night on the canoe, and I was thinking, *Oh my gosh, what did I get myself into?*

Three days later, I snapped out of it and I felt good, "Oh, okay, here we go!"

Bruce was the captain and navigator on that sail—most of my sailing has been with Bruce. Bruce has always been a mentor, a father figure. Now as a captain, being like Bruce is what I strive for—but those of us who sail with Bruce know that's not really possible. Bruce is Bruce. There is no way to reach those standards. Bruce is always so calm, knowledgeable, and thoughtful. He's such a good teacher. He's good at sharing. His base—with the ocean, with the canoe, and with the culture—is so solid, and the way he deals with stress in extreme situations is amazing.

One of my most difficult sails was a captain's training sail from Palmyra to the Big Island of Hawai'i. Bruce was the navigator, Kaleo was the watch captain, and I was the captain. Before we sailed, the feeling amongst us was, *No big deal, Hawai'i, it's just right there, a thousand miles north of us.*

So we were towing out the channel on a sunny day, and I was grinding down sausages—cold, straight from the cooler. There were some really big seas on the way out of the channel. We were both eating this stuff. Kaleo and I get sick together sometimes. I think we had a bet to see who would throw up first—I won, easily.

Then, after we untied our tow and started sailing, the sun disappeared. The weather was switching in every direction around us, and Nainoa was on the radio, "You guys have these big storms forming about one day away from you, and you need to turn around and go back. You are in serious conditions out there."

"Yeah, we know we're in serious conditions!" The waves were breaking our blades, but we just kept sailing—dropped the rig, threw up a storm sail, and kept moving forward. The moon disappeared. The stars disappeared. We were looking at Bruce, "Do you know where we're going?"

And Bruce said, "Yeah, we're fine, I'm gonna take a short nap. If you see some stars, wake me up."

So, we're looking up and there was one break in the cloud cover and we could see one star peek out. Everyone's like, "Oh, a star, a star! Let's tell him!"

We wake him up, "Bruce, Bruce, we see a star!" He opens his eyes and he looks at it and says, "Okay, good, keep going." And he goes back to sleep. Bruce was basically sailing by the wind, and whenever the wind would switch from that dominant east-northeast swell, he would have us adjust our heading.

It rained the whole time. We were taking waves over the side, waves ripping our canvas. We were closing sails, opening sails, constantly changing things around. We were wet for ten, eleven days straight. Soaking wet. The wind was coming straight down out of these clouds. It was so cold that I was expecting it to hail. We were heating water on the stove and warming our hands over the boiling water to stay warm. We hadn't prepared for cold weather.

We all slept on deck in our foul-weather gear. There was water sloshing around in my foul-weather gear almost the whole time. Almost the entire palm of both my hands had blistered and then the skin peeled off—same with the soles of my feet—from being worked over and wet for that many days straight. It showed me how small we were in this huge, vast ocean, and how unpredictable things can be—how we should be prepared for anything.

And I kept looking at Bruce. Crazy things would be going on and he remained so calm. He deals with everything so calmly and everything turns out fine. He had the steadiest demeanor the entire time and just worked through things.

And the canoe is solid—she's built so well. *Hōkūleʻa*, she just does her thing out there.

As we got nearer to Hawaiʻi, we got into some voggy areas so we thought, *Okay, it's got to be nearby*. So we kept looking. I was envisioning seeing Mauna Kea and Mauna Loa coming out of the clouds. I kept looking for the mountains. Then the swell started to die out, *Oh, this is weird. We must be in the swell shadow of the island.*

Turns out, we were just seven miles offshore before we saw the Big Island. It was the hardest sail, but also the most rewarding. I learned just how fragile we are and how powerful the ocean is—and how the canoe took us right to where we wanted to go.

Opposite: Russell at Hanga Piko Harbor, awaiting a ride out to the canoe, Rapa Nui.

"The planet will continue without humanity, but if people want to be a part of this planet, we need to live with nature and wildlife respectfully. The people in Galápagos are a good example of how to live. We can learn how living this way can help us take care of our islands. We want our children to experience the beauty of our planet. That's why we voyage. We voyage this traditional way so we can relearn and reconnect to the ocean and then share our experience with the children—so that they, and the next generation, and the next, can survive and thrive on planet Earth.

Tamiko Fernelius
Crewmember

GALÁPAGOS

CHAPTER 8

The turtle is a representation of the universe

—

*Si el cielo fue siempre una bóveda hemisférica y la tierra una planicie circular, enten-
demos por qué en la mitología de algunos pueblos la tortuga es una representación
del universo. Entre el cielo estrellado que es el domo y la tierra que es su vientre, está el
mundo intermedio dónde viven los hombres.*

If the sky was always a half-dome cavern and the Earth a circular plain, we understand why in the mythology of some peoples the turtle is a representation of the
universe. Halfway between the starry sky that is the dome and the earth that is its
belly, there is the world where humans live.

JOSEPHINO IS INVITED INTO THE AIR-CONDITIONED LOBBY OF A
hotel overlooking Playa de Oro in San Cristobal. The hotel's hostess calls him by
name as she stands holding the tall sliding glass door open. "Josephino lives here,"
she explains. It is unclear who Josephino is until she points down to the dainty
grey-feathered finch on the outside sunlit patio carpeted with sleeping sea lions.
"He's very smart," she says, snapping her fingers, and just like that, Josephino comes
hopping toward her.

His mother, Josephine, lives inside here too, the hostess says. She lives in the
lobby's palm tree that extends from the ground straight up through three floors to
the roof where its leaves offer shade to sunbathing tourists by day, and shelter for
sunburnt divers tossing back beers by night.

Just beyond the hotel's terrace, children, dressed in their school clothes, hurl
head over heels into the water off a small dock. The children know the rules: No
stepping, jumping, or splashing within two yards of an animal. And no flash photog-
raphy; it disturbs the animals. No worries, the children know the island and its oceans
belong to the indigenous tribes of finches, fur seals, sea lions, marine iguanas, giant
tortoises, flamingos, penguins. The Hawaiian philosophy of *mālama*, to care for, is
intrinsic in every regulation for those living in and those visiting Galápagos. These
regulations ensure that all boats, planes and humans entering this UNESCO World
Heritage Site take precautions to avoid bringing any dangers to the archipelago.

This natural heritage site is so heavily protected that *Hōkūleʻa* was nearly forbidden entry. Midway between Panamá and Galápagos, the words of warning came
through an electronic hurricane on the Internet: The canoe had not gone through
the proper biosecurity protocols to be allowed entry. The canoe had been properly
inspected and fumigated in Colón, Panamá, and then after passing through the
Panamá Canal to Balboa in the Pacific, the hulls were professionally scrubbed by a
scuba diver. But the canoe should also have been fumigated again in Balboa. Luis
'Champi' Rodriguez, a Galápagos licensed naturalist guide and the shipping agent
responsible for helping the canoe obtain the proper permits to allow entry into the

Opposite: The multilayered textures of the Galápagos.

Galápagos protected areas, discovered the mistake and sent an e-mail to crewmember 'Aulani Wilhelm. Prior to her role as senior vice president for oceans at Conservation International, for fifteen years, 'Aulani has helped to stand guard in protection of another World Heritage Site, Papahānaumokuākea, in the Northwestern Hawaiian Islands.

"The confusion was that there was supposed to be two fumigations and we only had one. One was to get you to the canal, the other was to get you to the Galápagos," Nainoa says.

"The whole process showed us how complex it is to move this canoe around the world without damaging anybody's environment that we go through," he explains. "So when you look at risk, the risk of hurting somebody's special and sacred place that these people fight so hard to take care of."

As true practitioners of *mālama honua*, no one wanted to disrupt a most delicate ecosystem where a third of the plants, and most of the land birds and reptiles are endemic.

"The dilemma was that we were breaking the single rule that we made a promise never to break, right?" Nainoa continues. "So I said, 'OK, we're turning around. We're gonna go back to Ecuador.' And I was just so, so sorry, and I aplogized to the crew and the people in Galápagos."

"Your people have a cultural link to the ocean that our people are missing," Champi would later recall. "We need your knowledge of the oceans, the way seafaring people have made the ocean their means of thriving and surviving. In Galápagos, people live with their backs to the sea, only acknowledging the land and the volcano they live on without realizing they are surrounded by the largest playground on Earth and the greatest provider of life."

"How can we protect the Marine Reserve if we don't know it? How can we call ourselves islanders if we don't reach out to the sea? Galápagos could be lost if locals don't learn more about the ocean, if they don't experience it, if they don't take care of it and nurture it for the future."

Champi helped to convince Nainoa that the crew could and should do the work to clean the canoe to pass inspection and bring her needed inspiration to Galápagos. The sails were dropped. The sea stood still. The crew got to work.

On deck, the crew dug in, on elbows, knees, and shins, cleaning the deck, catwalk, *manu*, sails, rails, sweep, and all fourteen holds. In the water, wearing snorkels, masks, and fins, Nainoa, watch captain Archie Kalepa, and photographer John Bilderback scrubbed the hulls of what 'Aulani referred to as "freeriders" that may have attached en route from Panamá.

Respect and permission: two key precepts of the voyage shined through in every slipper scrubbed, every zipper inspected, every crawl space scoured.

"That crew worked to make sure we were not going to damage anything," Nainoa says. "They were completely dedicated to the crisis and to doing the right thing. It was a beautiful lesson that came out of the solution."

After three complete cycles of sunrise to sunset, Nainoa deemed the canoe ready for inspection. The officers—twelve in total—came on board, representing customs, immigration, port authority, antinarcotics, biosecurity, and the national park. So clean was the *waʻa* that the inspectors deemed *Hōkūleʻa* one of the cleanest

Opposite top: Nainoa Thompson checking the set of the headsail while sailing to the Galápagos.

Opposite bottom: After three days of cleaning the canoe, the crew rests awaiting inspection and permission to enter the Galápagos.

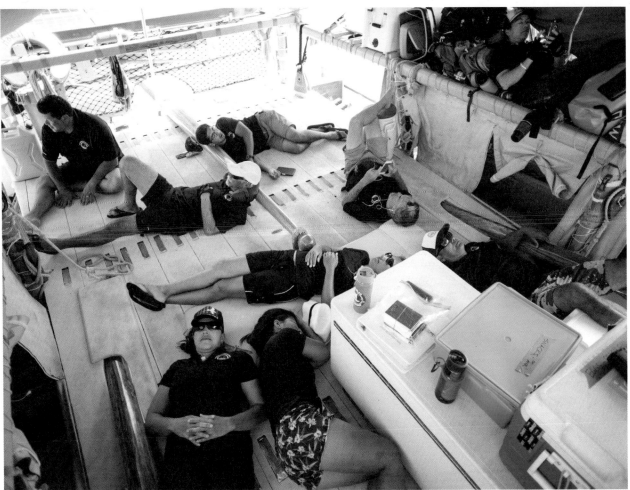

vessels they had ever boarded. But when one of the officials noted, "Hawai'i is what we hope to not become," the mood shifted from uplifted to sober.

That statement was cause for reflection. What ancient practices has Hawai'i abandoned? What can be done in Hawai'i to protect the islands the way Galápagos continues to protect their own? How can Hawai'i reclaim its role as a custodian of the oceans and lands—and perhaps even become an example for preserving resources? Crewmember Sam 'Ohu Gon III, a senior scientist of The Nature Conservancy of Hawai'i, posed these questions and later observed that the answers to these queries are "the hope—and the promise—of the Mālama Honua Worldwide Voyage."

Such queries loom with every step you take. One sign on the beach reads:

CAMBIANOS DE CONDUCTA?
CAMBIANOS DE PLANETA!
CHANGE YOUR BEHAVIOR?
CHANGE YOUR PLANET!

As Josephino hops into his hotel home, the hostess slides the door closed behind him so as to not lose any precious chilled air, and it becomes clear that humans may well be the most invasive species of all.

PRE-COLUMBIANS VOYAGED ON RAFTS built with balsa and bamboo, tied together with reed cords, and with sails of hemp. These early voyagers, the Manta Huancavilca people who lived along the Ecuadorian coast, skillfully sailed against the currents along the coast of South America. It is believed these people ventured as far west as the isolated archipelago some 600 miles offshore. The nineteen islands, spread north and south of the equator, are situated in the confluence of three ocean currents flowing across geologic hot spots, some still volcanically active.

The first Old World explorer to document these islands was the Bishop of Panamá, Fray Tomás de Berlanga. On a mission for the King of Spain in 1535, de Berlanga was sailing from Panamá to Peru to inspect the land recently stolen from the Incas. When the winds went slack off the coast, his vessel drifted and was pulled into a current that led to the islands. He would later describe the steep volcanic peaks rising above the horizon "as if God had rained down stones" into the ocean.

Those "stones" were later named Insulae de los Galápagos, or Islands of the Tortoise, a tribute to the once-dominant land species. The tortoises themselves are believed to have traveled here, flowing along the Humboldt Current, riding on drifting vegetation after heavy, land-washing rains on the South American continent. Their buoyant bodies and ability to live for months without food and water allowed them to endure the perilous journey.

The dominance and resilience of this species was threatened by the arrival of pirates and buccaneers in the sixteenth century. Sailors used the uninhabited islands as a stopping point for fresh water, ship repairs, and provisions. The defenseless giants were stacked on their backs, like bricks, one on top of the other, on the decks of ships, providing fresh meat on long voyages. The sailors, and later settlers, also brought pigs, goats, and rats to the islands—all of which have changed the landscape and threatened the tortoises. Tortoise oil was used for lighting street lamps on the continent and, two oceans away, in Europe. By the late seventeenth century, whalers

Opposite: Tamiko Fernelius, quarter master and cook, organizing provisions in her hotel room in Panamá.

arrived to tap the profits gained by harvesting whales and seals. In 1790, the British ship *Emilia* returned to London with 140 tons of whale oil and 888 fur seal pelts.

In 1859, naturalist Charles Darwin offered the world a different perspective on the riches of these islands when he published *On the Origin of Species*. Nearly twenty years earlier, Darwin, a young naturalist aboard *HMS Beagle*, had spent a few weeks exploring Galápagos when the islands were still known as the Enchanted Islands and when Ecuador was still referred to as the Republic of the Equator. Darwin viewed the islands as "a little world within itself," a "satellite attached to America," possessing its own vibrant "creative force." On his return to England he was later intrigued by the difference in the mockingbirds he had collected in Galápagos. A colleague, John Gould, later confirmed that they were separate species. This was a catalyst for Darwin's theory of evolution by natural selection.

On the Origin of Species proposed that all species of life evolved from a common ancestral thread and that any changes were the result of the need for survival—natural selection. The struggle for existence is an ongoing battle here. Since Darwin's visit, hundreds of plants, insects and marine organisms have been introduced. These compete with the endemic plants and animals found only in Galápagos, causing the loss of some species completely and pushing many others to the brink of extinction.

Just as ocean voyaging and navigation were practiced by Polynesians long before European ocean exploration of the world, the science of evolution was also well entrenched in Hawaiian oral traditions a century or more before Darwin was born. Ancient Hawaiians described the evolution of the universe through the *Kumulipo*, a sacred creation chant over 2,000 lines in length that recounts the birth of all living things from the universe itself to the first coral polyps, to all the plants and animals from sea and land, and eventually human beings.

"The cosmogonic genealogy of the *Kumulipo* teaches us that we are all related, but humans are the younger sibling to all other life in the world, including the land itself," explains cultural liaison Maya Saffery. "Therefore, we have a *kuleana*, responsibility, as younger siblings to care for and respect our older siblings so they can in turn care for us. This lesson is right in line with Mālama Honua."

The *Kumulipo* and the lessons embedded therein is yet another reason why modern scientists are turning to indigenous peoples and cultures to try to understand how to better care for our oceans and natural resources.

Scientists refer to the current geological age as the Anthropocene Epoch—where humans are viewed as a force of nature altering the natural environment. Our influence is written in coral cores, in the mud of ponds, and in the sands of beaches. Galápagos invites us to look at the Earth, how it was formed millions of years ago, and where our responsibility lies in our continually evolving physical presence on this planet where younger islands continue to form and older ones continue to erode.

In 2001, the *MV Jessica*, carrying 160,000 gallons of diesel oil and 80,000 gallons of bunker oil, ran aground near San Cristóbal, en route to nearby Baltra Island to deliver fuel to a tourist ship, *Galápagos Explorer*. This event was the catalyst to ban the use of bunker fuel in the archipelago. As more planes and boats arrive daily, more goods must be imported to feed the growing tourism industry, adding to the risk of another environmental disaster. Tourism numbers have grown steadily in the last thirty years. Six-wheel, twenty-eight person "Eco-tourism" buses are a common sight

Opposite: The marine iguana is endemic to the Galápagos where several subspecies live throughout the many islands.

here. There's a new cement pier being constructed in San Cristóbal, which will be a launch pad for the many day tours that venture forth from here to other islands. But the Ecuadorian government is looking for ways to preserve and conserve this World Heritage Site. Immigration, tourism, and population control are key to the future sustainability of these islands.

The Galápagos National Park rangers play an important role in the control of the impacts from tourism. If you're on a boat and about to slip into the waters, a ranger may suddenly appear, zipping by to check that you are with a certified naturalist guide. If you're walking a long, isolated path to a snorkeling bay, a ranger may pedal by on his bike, stopping to ask if you have enough water on hand. On the beach, where the popcorn salesman strolls, a park ranger may remind you not to feed the birds.

A recurring sign along the shoreline reads:

EL MUNDO ES SALVE, SI UNO HACE DEL PARTE.
THE WORLD IS SAVEABLE, IF EVERYONE DOES HIS PART.

THE TORTOISE RAISES HIS HEAD, neck telescoping out of his shell, sensing the nearby presence of his friend, the finch. This movement sends a signal to the finch and it begins picking parasites from the tortoise's neck and legs. Known as the "finch response," the relationship benefits both—the tortoise gets cleaned, and the finch gets a meal. This behavior is only seen in some Galápagos tortoises, and you can find several of these most patient creatures in the lava-rock corrals of the Fausto Llerena Tortoise Rearing Center on Santa Cruz Island. Nearby at the Charles Darwin Research Station, scientists provide results from research that helps make decisions about best practices for the conservation of land and marine environments.

In a place without an indigenous people, the *tortugas gigantes* can be considered the indigenous elders of these islands. Believed to have colonized the Galápagos some two to three million years ago, the tortoises grow to around 1.3 yards in length and can weigh over 880 pounds. They are believed to be able to live more than 150 years. Giant tortoises are found in only two places on the planet, here in Galápagos and on Aldabra, an atoll in the Seychelles in the Indian Ocean. Yet the Galápagos tortoise remains the largest living species of its kind. In a place where there were once fourteen identified species of tortoise, only eleven remain today.

Re-establishing natural ecological conditions can sometimes require uncompromising actions. In 1997, multiple agencies joined together to remove feral goats from three islands: Pinta, Santiago, and Isabela. Overgrazing had caused massive ecosystem degradation that, among other things, was destroying the tortoise's natural habitat. Similar issues have come up in other islands, such Lāna'i, Hawai'i; San Clemente Island, California; and Auckland Island, New Zealand. In Galápagos, this meant eradicating the goats. By 2006, the eradication was complete, and this effort is considered one of the largest ecosystem restoration projects in history.

Still, many of the Galápagos tortoises remain endangered, and one species, the Pinta Island tortoise, recently became extinct.

This last living individual of Pinta Island tortoise was known as Lonesome George, an icon for conservation and also a popular theme for souvenirs. You'll see images of the hundred-year-old tortoise on T-shirts, hats, and magnets, and there

Opposite top: Galápagos National Park Director Walter Bustos presents Nainoa Thompson with a baby tortoise, which Nainoa names Hōkūle'a.

Opposite bottom: Baby tortoises, hatched in the breeding center, live a protected life until they are strong enough to be released into the wild.

are various stores, hotels, and even cocktails named after him. You can also read his story typed and wallpapered on hostel walls.

In 1905, the Californian Academy of Science collected what was thought to be the last three tortoises from Pinta Island, the northernmost island of the archipelago. But then in 1971, a group of park wardens and scientists discovered Lonesome George on Pinta. He was brought to the Charles Darwin Research Station, on Santa Cruz Island, with the intention that he would reproduce. A worldwide search in zoos and private collections for a Pinta female turned up none. George spent his last decades accompanied by females from similar species but he demonstrated little interest and no young were ever produced. Fausto Llerena, one of the park wardens on the field trip that found George, went on to supervise the Santa Cruz tortoise rearing center, which was named after him in 1999. He was George's devoted caretaker for over forty years. Even on weekends, Fausto would come to visit George.

"He came to meet me and stood in front of me, stretching his neck and opening his mouth," Fausto would tell a reporter for *Mongabay*, an environmental news agency. "And there he stood … without blinking, as if he wanted to say something."

"I had a lot of affection for him. Whenever I went to the center, my first stop was always checking on him," Fausto would recall.

After George's death in 2012 of natural causes, the Galápagos Conservancy arranged for the frozen remains of Lonesome George to be shipped to an expert taxidermist in New York. Once preserved, George went on display at the American Museum of Natural History in New York City for several months. George was supposed to come home sooner, but there were several years of discussions between Ecuador and Galápagos about where his final place of rest should be. Five years after his death, George finally returned home.

While the options for George were being debated, the Galápagos National Park Directorate and partner Galápagos Conservancy up-scaled the Giant Tortoise Restoration Initiative—a massive program to restore the population of tortoises. One initiative is genetic research to identify tortoises with DNA from the extinct species from Floreana Island. A current project aims to return tortoises carrying the original genes back to Floreana where they have been extinct for over 150 years.

On a day where the sun seems to stay stuck in the peak of the sky, Nainoa visits the center on Santa Cruz. To enter, you must first clean your shoes on mats soaked with an antiseptic solution. Once entering the open-air center, you will find dozens of baby tortoises cruising around in pens covered with a mesh wire roof to protect against predators. The tiny tortoises are each categorized by island and by species, with an identifying number painted on its shell. When they are large enough, they will be returned to their original habitat and set free.

The director of the Galápagos National Park, Walter Bustos, is there to greet him. Nainoa is moved to see the tortoises, the children of the land, a glimpse of the future.

"The Galápagos Islands are the star," he tells the director, "shining love and care for nature, guiding us toward peace for Earth and all of humanity." After a few moments of quiet reflection, the director honors Nainoa by naming him the godfather of tortoise #82. Nainoa blesses the tortoise by naming it Hōkūleʻa.

Hōkūleʻa is now carefully returned to the pen. As the tortoise makes its gentle way across the lava, each measured step is a reflection of what hundreds of people have done to restore these original landowners. The name, Hōkūleʻa, binds the tortoise for the century ahead to an archipelago much like its own—isolated and rare and in need of protection.

DESTINATION: GUAYAQUIL, ECUADOR
CARRIER: LATAM AIR FLIGHT 539 JFK
WEIGHT: 232 Kilos
ORIGINS DIETL: 158 West 27th Street, New York, New York

THE COMMERCIAL AIRLINE STICKER gives the information. All that's missing is the name of the traveler. The crate, too large for the planes that fly into Galápagos, has been flown to Guayaquil and then placed on an Ecuadorian Air Force jet to arrive on Baltra Island, Galápagos. A delegation led by Walter Bustos, Fausto Llerena, and Washington Tapia, Galápagos Conservancy's director of the Galápagos Tortoise Restoration Initiative, are in Baltra, along with five Air Force security officers to meet George and escort the crate onto a truck headed directly to the Fausto Llerena Tortoise Rearing Center on Santa Cruz Island.

The Ecuadorian Minister of the Environment cannot contain his excitement. "The illustrious son of our islands returns home," he announces on Twitter.

George's final resting place is a specially constructed building in the center; with an expected 150,000 visitors a year. The museum, the "Hall of Hope," is the principal attraction along the "Path of the Tortoise," an interpretation trail designed to remind us of our responsibility to live in a sustainable way.

"George's extinction shows us that humans have the power to destroy our future," says Washington Tapia. "His presence reminds us human beings not to commit the same mistakes of the past."

After a ceremony of dance, story, and song, Washington escorts a handful of visitors into the hall. Only small groups are allowed in at a time to ensure that the experience of seeing George is not crowded.

The temperature is a carefully monitored 66 degrees Fahrenheit with 55 percent humidity. The lighting—fifty lux of light—is in place. Once inside, all you see is a curtained wall.

After Washington explains how long it took George to find his way back home, the curtain is slowly drawn open. Behind spotlessly shined glass, there he stands—what some may view is a reminder of destruction, conservationists are determined to see as a symbol of *esperanza*, hope—Solitario George.

George stands poised, one foot in front of the other, his neck fully extended, head held elegantly high.

—

Local Voices
Norman Wray
Conservation International for Galápagos

Norman Wray was the former program manager for Conservation International for Galápagos, during Hōkūleʻa's visit to the islands. He is now living in Cambridge, England, volunteering for BirdLife International. Norman grew up in Quito, Ecuador, where he earned a law degree, devoting his time to helping indigenous people of the Ecuadorian Amazon defend their land against mining. Norman was also elected to the Asamblea Nacional Constituyente, the Constituent Assembly in Ecuador, and was widely known as a defender of the rights of nature. On a terrace overlooking the bay of Puerto Ayora, with iguanas pacing the wall beside him and magnificent ʻiwa, frigatebirds, gracing the sky above, Norman spoke of his concerns and his hopes for the future of Galápagos.

In His Own Words

THE STORY OF GALÁPAGOS IS A MIX OF STORIES. THE pirates, the whalers, and the fishermen all have different stories. The first colonies of people came in the 1920s. Each island has its own history. People decided to move here for different reasons—maybe as a unique economic opportunity, maybe because they wanted solitude and distance from civilization, or maybe because nature is so amazing here. You have this mixture—it's not one culture. And when Galápagos was declared a national park in 1959, the story grew another layer.

The one story they all share is they were always trying to live in a tropical environment with difficult conditions. Galápagos is not an easy place to live.

The relationship between the conservation of nature and the needs of people has always been a source of conflict. The first colonists struggled to live here, and people today still struggle. You have to clear the land of rock to build your house. You have to get your water from far away. And so on. But in the end, people here have to be connected to nature because nature is how you earn your money to live.

The economy in Galápagos is based on tourism, and all the tourism is based on nature. But the tourist business generates a lot of individual competition. You need cooperation between people. You have to generate more agreements between people around the things that people really care about—for everybody. And you always have to know that you're making decisions around nature—nature by itself, and also nature for human beings.

When I was in the Constituent Assembly in Ecuador, I brought what I learned from my experience working with indigenous people of the Amazon. I supported them in the defense of their rights, traditions, their ways of living with nature. One of the concepts in the constitution is from them: it's called *Buen Vivir*, good living. It's about the relationship between nature and humans, and how you can live in harmony with nature. That has been my approach to defending the environment.

The people of Galápagos are always asking: "What is our identity? What are the things that connect us?" There is always a big discussion about how we build things. When we tell people that they can't surf or fish at a certain beach, they say, "I can't live here as I can live in other countries!" But that is part of the difficulty of living here. Many of these restrictions have been added to take care of this natural heritage by the people of Galápagos since the islands have been designated as a park and a marine reserve.

Another question comes up: Is Galápagos for the people of Galápagos?

I have a big commitment to nature. I have a big commitment to people also—to make sure people are happy. But, maybe not everybody can live here. Maybe Galápagos decides how many people can live and work here. Conservation scientists say that Galápagos doesn't need incentives for the people to come here. Galápagos is the place where nature drives the incentives.

The problem is that right now you need people to understand what's going on with nature. There is often a struggle between man and nature. But nature is first. We need nature. Nature doesn't need us. And in the end, nature will decide. Climate change is the way nature responds to our reality. Man produced climate change, so nature finds a balance. In the end, maybe the balance is against human beings on the planet. Maybe that is the balance.

Most of the people here don't know about the incredible things on the other islands because it's too expensive to travel to them. They have to exercise their right to be connected with nature, to be connected with the sea. You need to generate a process where the people know and love the place they are living in. And want to defend it. You have to work a lot with the young people. You have to generate a commitment in them to their island because, in the end, they will be the ones protecting this place.

Nature is vulnerable, vulnerable to human beings. All the things that make Galápagos so important are vulnerable. We need restrictions. We need to realize we can't do the same things that we can do on the continent. And then, we have to act with love. That is the way of finding a human connection. You have scientists. You have the tourism industry. You have conservationists. You have fishermen. You have politicians. you have a people with a huge range of experiences. The question is, how do we build "us"? Solidarity and responsibility to nature. And, in the end, that is the challenge of any society.

We have a lot of things to learn from the *Hōkūleʻa* experience. We have to learn more about the connection with the sea. Maybe you only understand the wind when you sail without an engine. Maybe you only understand the stars when you sail without navigational instruments. How do you understand something that is more important than you? That is the lesson.

Local Solutions
Giant Tortoise Restoration Initiative

IT IS UNKNOWN PRECISELY WHEN THE GIANT TORTOISE first arrived in Galápagos, but documentation from the 1500s notes the predominance of these docile reptiles. It was once estimated that there were more than 300,000 tortoises throughout the archipelago. In the sixteenth and seventeenth centuries, sailors discovered tortoises to be a prime meat source for long voyages. These creatures were able to survive without food or water for months. Whalers, pirates, sailors, and settlers brought with them a collection of destructive animals—pigs, dogs, and rats—all of which altered the natural environment. Some, like the black rat, preyed on tortoise hatchlings in the nests. Others, like goats and donkeys, overgrazed the grassland and trampled nests. Through the past several centuries, out of all the animals in Galápagos, the giant tortoise has been the most devastated by such invasive activities.

In 1959, the Galápagos National Park and the Charles Darwin Foundation conducted a review of tortoise populations across several islands. They found that only eleven of the original fourteen populations remained and many were endangered. In 1965, in collaboration with the Galápagos National Park Directorate, a rearing and repatriation program was created at the Charles Darwin Research Station—to rebuild giant tortoise populations. The breeding program led to the first transfer of tortoise eggs from Pinzón Island to the Fausto Llerena Tortoise Center on Santa Cruz Island. Today, the Giant Tortoise Restoration Initiative is a multi-institutional project run by the Galápagos National Park Directorate, fueled by the collaborative work of international scientists and the technical support of the Galápagos Conservancy.

Breeding season runs December to May, with tortoises laying eight to sixteen eggs per nest. At the Tortoise Center on Santa Cruz, eggs and hatchlings are brought from the wild and others are bred in captivity on site. The eggs are collected and placed in an incubator heated by a simple hair dryer. The incubation period lasts up to 120 days. Once hatched, the eggs are placed in a dark box to re-create the natural underground nest. There, the hatchlings remain for four weeks during which time they feed on their own yolk. They are then moved to protected outdoor pens for two to four years, and then into the adaption pens before being released to the wild.

There are now tortoise centers on three islands: Santa Cruz, Isabela, and San Cristóbal. Through these centers, 7,000 tortoises have been repatriated to their island of origin across the archipelago, including the islands of Española, Santa Cruz, San Cristóbal, Pinzón, and Isabela. In 2016, a tortoise was born on Pinzón Island, marking the first recorded natural birth in over 100 years.

To restore the tortoise populations, the land must also be restored. Tortoises are herbivores, and their presence maintains the balance of vegetation for themselves and for other herbivores. Tortoises are also natural architects and gardeners; they clear through vegetation and impact plant distribution by eating plants and then later passing the seeds, which then grow in the following season. Helping to fully understand their impact on the earth, one project on Santa Cruz tracks the tortoise movements using GPS tags on their shells. It's been learned that these creatures are long-distance trekkers, some even traversing tens of kilometers—sometimes up and down volcanic peaks—in their search for food and breeding sites.

The Galápagos National Park Directorate and collaborators are also working to restore other threatened species, including the mangrove finch, Galápagos petrel, Galápagos penguin, Floreana mockingbird, and endemic flora.

Opposite: The Galápagos tortoise's life expectancy is more than hundred years.

Next spread: The thriving underwater world of Galápagos.

CREW STORY
Lehua Kamalu
Apprentice Navigator

Lehua Kamalu is the second-born of six sisters, four of whom have sailed on the Worldwide Voyage. Fluent in Hawaiian, Tahitian, French, and English, Lehua is also multiskilled. With a bachelor's degree in mechanical engineering, Lehua is comfortable balancing on a slippery rescue board over crocodile-infested waters to fix the solar panels on the canoe. She's equally at ease singing a solo in Hawaiian to the Dalai Lama for his eightieth birthday. In the fall of 2009, Lehua became involved in the Mālama Honua mission and, the following year, she began assisting with the creation of the worldwide sail plan. While the task was daunting, her approach to data collection earned her the nickname 'Spreadsheet Lady.' She also introduced the PVS team to Google Earth, offering the full potential for visualizing both geographic and oceanographic information across the planet. Lehua spoke about her upbringing as a Hawaiian as she sat in the shade of a banyan tree at the foothills of Diamond Head.

WE MOVED A LOT AS KIDS because our dad was in the Navy: New York, Utah, Puget Sound, Arizona. But my dad really wanted us to grow up in Hawai'i; something he didn't get to do even though my grandfather, his dad, is originally from 'Aiea, the Pearl Harbor area. My mom is from Kaua'i and both my parents wanted us kids to live in Hawai'i when we were really young. So we moved to Hawai'i when I was four and my parents put us into the new immersion program for learning the Hawaiian language at a young age.

Our school was in Kāne'ohe. We didn't live anywhere near there. We lived halfway across the island. My parents would drive us to school five days a week, almost two hours each way, from kindergarten all the way through the sixth grade. Our family moved every year, ever closer to the school. The teachers spoke only in Hawaiian. You learned math, science—all your subjects—in the Hawaiian language. Many of the parents were very involved in the school because a lot of them didn't hear any Hawaiian language growing up. There was an entire generation, like my parents and Nainoa, who didn't have Hawaiian spoken to them as kids. And now, twenty-five years later, you have Kaleo Wong, who is fluent in Hawaiian … and when Kaleo speaks, it's like listening to Shakespeare.

Hawaiians traditionally learned everything by memory, by singing, chanting, dancing. At school, we would chant up the sun every single morning. The chant would talk about where the sun comes from and how it bursts into the sky. It was our way of honoring, thanking, and welcoming the sun for the coming day. I remember that long drive back and forth to and from school, my sisters and I would chant the entire time. My parents loved it. We would sing a song about Hawaiian pride, and every time we sang it, our parents would say, "Sing it again!" And I would say, "Guys, we just sang it five times in a row!" All those chants, a good chunk of them, I do now with *Hōkūle'a*.

I'm an engineering student, but back in the early times, maybe I would have been a voyager. Building the canoes for voyaging was the engineering feat of that time. Partial differentiation and thermal dynamics—I'm pretty sure that's not how Hawaiians talked about building and designing and sailing. But they thought about this in some way, and with very rudimentary tools they designed the canoe and made it work, and then set off on these very intense voyages.

The family name on my mom's side is Nu'uhiwa. From what I understand, many Hawaiians trace their ancestry back to the island of Nuku Hiva—the origin of my mom's name—in the Marquesas from the early migrations to Hawai'i. Who were those first voyagers? There's no Ellis Island of Polynesia. There's no verbal record. I think that's what first led me to *Hōkūle'a*—the idea that you are looking for where you came from to find out where you're going. This is the same philosophy we use in navigating.

Above: Lehua charts a course through the many reefs, cays, and shipping lanes of the Great Barrier Reef.

When you're navigating, you're tracking where you've been and your progress—constantly. You're looking as far back as you can and as far forward as you can. To look forward, you have to know where you came from. It's the whole idea of history. Studying what's happened, to know where you are, and what's likely to happen next. Why did we migrate here? How hard was it? You can stand on the deck of *Hōkūleʻa* and ask those questions.

If I'm looking at what we have done in the last few years as an indication of what's going to happen next, I'm reinspired. Having gone around the world, you really see the powerful levels of awareness, action, and education. I've sensed an urgency. You also see that some people can't even have a conversation about the Earth. They're just trying to find something to eat, they're trying to sleep and wake up tomorrow in a safe place, trying to just get their kids to school.

I remember these two kids who were on board with us in Durban. They were survivor kids, running around the streets of Durban. One of them was fourteen and the other was twelve but looked seven. I asked them, "Do you guys have food?" They didn't. So they ate dinner with us every night. I don't fault people for not having the ability to care for the Earth. But I tell people they have the privilege to care about the Earth. It's a privilege and a responsibility, because there are those who are digging through the garbage just to find food to eat.

When my very rational engineering mind does simple arithmetic, there are a lot of people on this planet. And the numbers are only getting bigger. And the number of trees is not getting bigger. And the number of fish is not getting bigger. We all need to step up. We need to figure this out on all fronts, whether it's technology or education—or even outrage—to get it done.

One lesson I learned as a kid in a Hawaiian school, and especially in my Hawaiian family, is you have to step up—you don't step back. If you are asked to share a song or a *hula* there is no option to say no. There are two reasons for this. One has its roots in an ʻōlelo noʻeau, a wise saying, that goes *ʻAʻa i ka hula, waiho ka hilahila ma ka hale*. Though this refers specifically to *hula*, the meaning is that when you show up to dance, or to sing, or to learn, or to work, you fully engage in the experience. The second reason you step up goes back to the fact that the previous generation never had the opportunity to step up in this way. They weren't able to experience such a level of active Hawaiian immersion or to express pride in their culture. But now, as they have been able to give this opportunity to their children, they want to see their culture fully embraced.

This was particularly challenging for me when Nainoa asked if I would study navigation. It is something I always wanted to learn about, but he didn't ask me without the understanding that there is significant *kuleana* attached, a responsibility, to continue to teach the skills and perpetuate the values of navigation.

Being raised the way I was, I couldn't help but say yes. If someone asks me to do something, I will step up, I will do it.

CREW STORY
Brad Kaʻaleleo Wong
Apprentice Navigator

Brad Kaʻaleleo Wong works for the Office of Hawaiian Affairs (OHA) as the specialist for the Papahānaumokuākea Marine National Monument. Also known as the northwest Hawaiian Islands, the monument is a marine reserve, encompassing 583,000 square miles of ocean waters, including ten islands and atolls. Brad first sailed on Hōkūleʻa in 2010, the same year Papahānaumokuākea was named a UNESCO World Heritage Site. As a competitive paddler, Brad has joked that his hardest lesson on Hōkūleʻa has been that each leg is not a race. It is a journey. The waʻa travels at the speed nature allows. But reading the ocean in a six-man canoe, as it crosses currents and channels, has helped transition him into the role of apprentice navigator. In the early evening in Honolulu, after a full day of work, Brad spoke of the need to protect the national monument for both marine and cultural conservation.

PAPAHĀNAUMOKUĀKEA was a sacred place to our ancestors for both voyaging and traditional religious practices. Archaeological evidence has shown that voyaging to the northwest Hawaiian Islands began at the same time that voyaging to Tahiti and the South Pacific stopped. There is a wealth of ancestral knowledge in the stories, chants, and place names of Papahānaumokuākea, linking our ancestors to this place. Our people were there.

For Native Hawaiians, the Hawaiian archipelago is split into two realms—*pō*, meaning darkness, is the realm of our ancestors and gods, and *ao*, meaning light, is the realm of man. Metaphorically, *pō* is where all life springs from and returns to after death, and literally encompasses most of the northwest Hawaiian Islands. Metaphorically, *ao* is the realm of light and the living, and literally includes the main Hawaiian Islands along with Nihoa. This metaphorical and literal division is marked by an important navigational marker, *Ke Ala Polohiwa a Kāne*, or the Tropic of Cancer. It is not only a spiritual division, but a physical one, as the islands change geologically from high basalt rock islands to low-lying atolls and shoals.

Nihoa is the first island up the northwest chain and was a stepping stone to get to the realm of *pō*, which starts at the island of Mokumanamana. Due to its close proximity to Niʻihau and Kauaʻi, Nihoa was a perfect navigational test for training navigators and a seasonal stop for adventurous fishermen. Mokumanamana, the second island up the northwest chain, lies directly on *Ke Ala Polohiwa a Kāne* and is the gateway to the realm of *pō*. An abundance of archaeological and historical research indicate that Mokumanamana is an incredibly important and powerful spiritual *piko*, or center, for Hawaiians. In ancient times, yearly voyages were made to Mokumanamana to care for the numerous *heiau*, religious sites, on the island.

Through my work with OHA, I have been able to visit Nihoa and Mokumanamana for research and also cultural practices. I have been able to spend some time on Nihoa and, on several occasions, slept on the island while assisting in research projects. Being an apprentice navigator, it was very humbling to observe the sky behind the ancient upright stones once used by my ancestors as navigational indicators. It was such an amazing experience to watch the south-pointing stars of Māui's fishhook, *Ka Makau Nui a Māui*, slowly travel across the sky to align directly with these stones. I get chicken skin thinking that this is the same sky my ancestors watched, the same stones they touched.

Being in the northwest Hawaiian Islands, you feel spiritually connected with the elements around you. It's very different from here on Oʻahu. Papahānaumokuākea is a place that feels totally free from man's reach. You begin to see what your ancestors saw and think the way they did. It is a place that can reset your baseline for what defines abundant natural resources. This is one reason why it has always been considered a sacred region.

Today this area is a conservation zone where large predatory fish roam free and millions of seabirds nest, creating the world's largest seabird rookery. When you think about it, a conservation zone is a sacred region. It is an area protected for the special resources within and the personal experiences that we, as people, have there.

The purpose of the Polynesian Voyaging Society's Mālama Honua Worldwide Voyage is to bring greater awareness and importance to protecting our oceans, as well as to build a global community focused on the simple question of—what can you do to care for Earth? Trying to answer that question brings up another question—what are we going to do here in Hawaiʻi to care for our islands? Finding those answers is one of the reasons why expanding Papahānaumokuākea was important

to me. The expansion was a way for Hawai'i to show that not only do we believe in the meaning of *mālama honua*, caring for Earth, but also that we will take action to preserve areas for future generations. The expansion quadrupled the original size of Papahānaumokuākea and created the second-largest protected area in the world. A related action also elevated the Office of Hawaiian Affairs to co-trustee, the highest level of management, and effectively solidified advocacy for traditional practices and Hawaiian interests within the area.

I feel blessed that the purpose of the Mālama Honua Worldwide Voyage is a key function of my everyday job. It is important for me to continue to help protect our natural resources in Hawai'i because they feed us in more ways than we know, and they remind us of our traditions and history.

Hōkūle'a has reawakened pride in Native Hawaiian traditions and has been a symbol of where we come from as a people. *Hōkūle'a* has shown us the importance of being steadfast in our culture and to remember our past while also moving foward in both our cultural and voyaging traditions. I'm very fortunate to have had opportunities given to me by the leadership of *Hōkūle'a* to be a watch captain on several voyages and to navigate through the Caribbean to Panamá. Navigating was overwhelming for me at first as I don't know the stars well, even though I had been studying with them for several years.

But, navigating is about being confident in the skills that you do have and knowing where you are and where you are going. During the voyage, Uncle Bruce taught me many different aspects of navigation that I hadn't learned before, from clouds, to storms, to stars, and by the end of the trip I felt like I could see the sky the way he sees it. I admire him for the captain and navigator that he is, and the confidence that he shows in the people around him. These experiences have been so important for me, for my personal growth as the leader I hope to be.

Someday, I hope that I will have the opportunity to navigate to Papahānaumokuākea and experience this sacred place by pulling these islands up from the sea. It is important that all the *'ohana wa'a*, the voyaging canoe families from across the Hawaiian Islands, reopen these voyaging pathways. Papahānaumokuākea is a reminder. Remember where you came from.

Above: Brad, along with fellow crewmembers, conducts an interactive livestream discussion using Science on a Sphere to show planetary interconnections, American Sāmoa.

"Our sail to Rapa Nui was the first time a *Pwo* navigator was not on board. But from the time we left Galápagos, the crew had gelled. The spirit of the crew proved that the next generation could do it. There were thirteen leaders on board. Any one of them could have been a captain. I just had the title."

Archie Kalepa
Captain

RAPA NUI

CHAPTER 9

*Ka tatou te tupuna
o te ta'u nei.*

—

We are the ancestors now.
We are the *tupuna*.

– Mahani Teave
Rapa Nui Musician and Activist

IN THE FOURTEEN DAYS SINCE LEAVING GALÁPAGOS, NINETEEN hundred nautical miles have passed under the hulls. *Hōkūle'a* is sailing south. Thirteen crewmembers in all. No *Pwo* navigators on board. Four apprentice navigators—with the support of the crew—are being called upon to pull a small island up from the Pacific—Rapa Nui, Easter Island. Rapa Nui marks the southeastern corner of the Polynesian Triangle.

"I looked around and said, 'Okay, who's going to teach me now?'" says one apprentice navigator, Noelani Kamalu, of sailing without a *Pwo* on board.

Training the next generation of navigators has been a keystone of the Worldwide Voyage. For several years, the plan has remained firm. The master navigators would step into the background in Rapa Nui, allowing the students to sail the canoe home. But that plan changed in Galápagos when Nainoa was suddenly called back to Hawai'i. Another principle of any voyage: "You need to remain flexible."

Before leaving Galápagos, Nainoa expressed his full confidence in the Leg 28 crew, Captain Archie Kalepa, Billy Richards, Max Yarawamai, Nā'ālehu Anthony, Russell Amimoto, Keahi Omai, Rex Lokeni, Tamiko Fernelius, and Dr. Dickran Boranian—all seasoned sailors. His confidence flowed into the four young apprentice navigators: Haunani Kane, Jason Patterson, and sisters Noelani and Lehua Kamalu.

"Before we sail, Nainoa has overthought everything—the strengths of the currents, the size of the line, which storm sails to use," Lehua says. "Nainoa is thinking 24/7 about everything. Then when he said he wasn't going, I told him, 'Nainoa, can I just run through a few things with you before you leave so that I don't go crazy?'"

Then came another shift in the sail plan, the satellite terminal, responsible for all communications to land, failed. So while Nā'ālehu worked on getting a replacement terminal, the gang of four navigators had a couple of extra days to create a course line, working closely with Keahi—who has years of experience on the canoe—as an advisor. Because Rapa Nui is so small, they chose what Haunani refers to as a buffer by adding the sighting of Isla Salas y Gomez, a low-lying volcanic island—known in the Rapa Nui language as Motu Motiro Hiva—only a hundred feet high and roughly 220 miles east of Rapa Nui. Navigating toward Gomez would expand the land target of Rapa Nui to the east, greatly increasing the chance of a successful landfall.

Opposite: There was no protected anchorage for *Hōkūle'a* within the harbor so she anchors outside, Hanga Roa, Rapa Nui.

On day fourteen, the navigators observe from the stars that they are shy of twenty-seven degrees south—the latitude of Rapa Nui, and the team calls for a right turn, west toward Rapa Nui. The apprentice navigators and crew grow increasingly sure that they have missed the sighting of Gomez, and now it is time to start looking for signs of Rapa Nui.

The team enters into what Haunani describes as the Three Days. "Three days of intense concentration. Three days of questioning the decisions we made. Three days of combing the horizon for shadows. Three days of monitoring the ocean for land debris or changes in color. Three days of minimal sleep."

Add to that, three days of wanting cake. The crew was craving cake. Chocolate cake. They had cake with the *ono* caught a couple of days ago, the *ono* that lifted everyone's spirits because it offered not only a fresh meal but also indicated shallower waters. Now, within a few days of reaching the island, Tamiko, the cook, cuts a deal.

"No island? No cake!" Tamiko, a former Japanese Coast Guard officer, says jokingly, while joining the crew's 360-degree horizon search for land.

"I have a question," Noelani says to her sister Lehua. As the least experienced apprentice navigator, Noelani has to rely on her younger sister to teach her now. "What are we looking for?"

"We're looking for something that's not quite like everything else," Lehua tells her sister. "You've got all these clouds everywhere. You've got some that definitely don't look like the others. So let's look underneath the clouds that are different. Is there rain under there? Are there dark patches? Are there edges? You've got to spend some time sort of scanning each section, take a break, don't look at it, go back again, take a look, take a break ..."

Taking a break, Jason tells Lehua, "I think we are two houses down," meaning two houses south in the star compass, two houses south of the course they had originally set in Galápagos.

"I think we are too," she tells him. "Should we correct it?"

"No, I think I like it," he says, and she agrees. "I like it too."

This marked the beginning of what may be the most difficult lesson of all in learning to navigate without modern instruments. This is the final lesson of letting go of the math, the science, and the measurements. It is a lesson that cannot be taught, one that comes to navigators at different times in their journey. It is a lesson that is invaluable and, as Nainoa has said, a personal one. This is the step toward true knowing. This is the moment when you let go and allow the island in.

At one point, on the bow, Lehua stands beside Billy. Lehua has lost her sunglasses. Billy gives her his. Now with his polarized glasses on, she can discern something.

"Hey, Billy, look at all that orange over there."

Orange clouds, cotton ball shaped, hover above the horizon. "Why would a cloud be orange?" Lehua wonders aloud. It's not sunrise, not sunset. Nainoa never talked about orange clouds. He talked about dark clouds, and green clouds, and brown clouds, and even blue clouds that reflect off the ocean around atolls. But he never talked about orange clouds.

She takes off the glasses to see if the cloud really was orange and just as she does, a full wide-arcing rainbow appears.

"Hey, Billy," she says to him, "wouldn't it be cool if the island was just right there, right now, behind that rainbow?"

Billy has sighted several hundred landfalls in his more than forty years of sailing on *Hōkūle'a*. He nods and smiles, and looking toward the rainbow, tells her, "Yeah, wouldn't that be nice?"

Time passes. One day. One night.

When Haunani spots a shadow on the horizon, Max tells her, "Be patient, watch it and see if it changes." Max was born and raised on the very small and flat island of Ulithi in Micronesia and moved to Hawai'i when he was young. His senses are fully aligned with oceanic deviations and he's been known to discern an island long before others.

"I had an overwhelming fear that every time I closed my eyes, I would potentially miss spotting land," Haunani remembers. "The night before we spotted Rapa Nui, Max, Billy, and Nā'ālehu reminded us that navigation is more than science, math, distance, speed, and all the other numbers. Navigation is spiritual and instinctual. We need to see the island not with our eyes but with our *na'au*, our gut."

The following day, Max is on the steering sweep. He's focused in on a particular cloud. "Look at those edges," Max tells the crew, "keep watching that cloud!"

At this point, Lehua steps down from the bow and goes to the stern. She grabs a bucket to scoop up some ocean water. She does what she always does once the destination is seen. She washes her clothes. She adds her Dr. Bronner's to the water and then tosses her dirty clothes in and digs in with both hands, and as she does this, she thinks to herself, *This is crazy. I'm washing my clothes. We haven't even seen the island yet, and I'm washing my clothes.* But she continued on, as she knew in her *na'au*, that Rapa Nui was indeed right there.

Above: The crew, with local help, ferries themselves and all provisions in and out of the narrow passageway of Hanga Piko harbor.

Still out on the bow, Uncle Billy leans in toward Noelani and offers her a little experienced advice. "You know, in all the time I've done this, the island has always come up right between the *manu*."

By sunset, the island rose into view. By working together, the thirteen crew-members had pulled Rapa Nui up from the sea.

Some cried, some screamed, some grew quiet, many hugged. Tamiko got out the cake pan, and the next day the anchor was dropped just outside Hanga Roa fishing harbor.

"There is something to be said for how you find islands beyond just the mathematics of it all; it is the spirituality of it all," Lehua will later say. "The idea of seeing the island before it actually is there is something I totally believe now."

"There were doubts here and there, but I never lost faith we would find Rapa Nui," Jason recalls. "There was doubt when we couldn't get a good latitude fix the couple nights before we made the turn west to look for Isla Salas y Gomez. There was doubt when we didn't spot Isla Salas y Gomez, and doubt when we didn't spot Rapa Nui when the numbers we calculated indicated we would," he admits. "But through all our trainings, this confidence builds in you—and the canoe wants to get to these places, too."

Within time, a handful of locals arrive, on a skiff named the *Star Line*, to give the crew *lei* and fresh water and watermelons. One of the locals is Auntie Mahina. She embraces everyone but gives Nāʻālehu the longest embrace of all. The last time she saw Nāʻālehu was nineteen years ago here in this harbor, when he was twenty-four years old and about to embark on his first deep-sea voyage. That was nearly half of his lifetime ago, and the profoundness of this moment is shared between him and Auntie Mahina as he continues his *kuleana*, snapping images of all those around him, sharing *aloha* and *mālama*, in honor of their safe return home to Polynesia.

Soon, Rex and Haunani are jumping off the canoe, getting their first taste of Rapa waters, and the rest of the crew is finger scooping the last remaining crumbs from the cake pan. The waves are picking up nicely, too.

"I keep going back to when we first sailed to Tahiti at the start of the voyage," Noelani says. "I feel like I did after that first leg; *Hōkūleʻa* was guiding us then and she guided us here to Rapa Nui. We were just helping her to get to where she wanted to go."

RAPA NUI IS KNOWN AS *Te Pito O Te Henua*, the Center of the World. Fourteen miles long and seven miles wide, this small, solitary island is 2,300 miles from South America, and 1,100 miles from the nearest island. Its first volcano, Poike, erupted some three million years ago. Two more volcanoes, Rano Kau and Maunga Terevaka, erupted several hundred thousand years ago. All the volcanoes have erupted from hot spots two and a half miles below on the ocean floor. Their peaks create the mountainous outline of the island where lava fields, prairie grass, and gentle hills weave throughout the terrain.

It is believed that the first Polynesians arrived here from Marquesas, led by a chief named Hotu Matuʻa, sometime between 400–1200 CE. With his wife and two canoes, Hotu Matuʻa sailed into the small cove now known as Hana Rau O Te ʻAriki, the Bay of the King—the only white, soft-sand beach on the entire island. Within a few hundred years of the chief's arrival, the people were organized into *mata*, groups

Opposite top: Traditional dancing begins with the young in Rapa Nui.

Opposite bottom: Specific protocols have to be conducted to welcome the crew of *Hōkūleʻa* and the escort vessel *Gershon II* ashore, Hana Rau O Te ʻAriki, the Bay of the King, Rapa Nui.

with ownership and stewardship of the land extending from mountaintop to sea. This division of land is a Polynesia-wide concept similar to the *ahupua'a* in Hawai'i, where land is divided into self-sustaining sections. With these natural boundaries, communities can live off of and care for all that is offered from the mountains, the rivers, and the sea.

Studies have shown that Rapa Nui was once the main breeding island for Polynesian marine birds. Twenty-five to thirty species nested here, but their numbers slowly declined due to the introduction of the Polynesian rat, which preyed on bird eggs. Before colonization, the island is said to have sustained fourteen tree species. It is believed that fire, beetles, and the rats—and the people themselves—created massive deforestation. But Rapa Nui never had the biodiversity of flora and fauna of other Polynesian islands. Today, the center of the crater of Rano is the main area where conservationists are working to preserve natural flora.

"This Island's ecosystem is very fragile," says Sergio Rapu Haoa, an internationally known archaeologist and Rapa Nui native. "Balancing the entire ecosystem has always been a challenge." Sergio acknowledges that while this island has inherently been challenged environmentally, humans could have had a hand in creating "the system collapse."

There are many interpretations to the causes of ecosystem collapse here on this island that seems to exist in its very own time zone, a place where saddleless horses stroll the streets and dogs swim in tide pools, hunting for snacks. What everyone can agree upon is the dignity of the *moai*, the ancient stone carvings of former chiefs of clans. There are some 900 *moai* on the island, standing an average of thirteen feet high and weighing an average of fourteen tons each. The largest one is uncompleted, lying down, with a length of 69 feet and a weight of 270 tons. Some are carved from basalt, or pressed volcanic ash, or red scoria.

Above: Lehua Kamalu engages with a young artist at Toki School.

These *moai* were erected on an *ahu*, a platform that held and protected the *iwi*, or bones, of prominent chiefs. *Ahu* were constructed in villages and the location of these *ahu* were determined by the geographical nature of each site. When Polynesians first settled in Rapa Nui, the earliest communities were located along the coastline where there was access to the ocean and its many resources. The *ahu* were built directly beside the water's edge because this land was less valuable for agricultural purposes. The *moai* situated on *ahu* are always facing directly toward their villages. Rapa Nui have always understood that the greatest resource is the strength and relationships within the community. Today, feasts and rituals and customs continue to support the importance of collective solidarity.

The word *moai* means "to exist," Sergio explains. "Invest in the ancestors" was the philosophy in the sixteenth century when the statues were created. At Tongariki, fifteen *moai* stand in a line on an *ahu*. Each one bears a slightly different physicality, yet all exude a dignified force. In time, the passionate diligence that created these statues was inverted to the dispassionate disorder that toppled many of them, leaving them face down, and sideways, on the hills of grass.

Petroglyphs in caves depict the story of the Birdman Cult. While the exact dates are unclear, the cult is believed to have been a cultural response to the island's limited food reserves. Every year, men from around the island would compete in a race to collect the first sooty tern egg from the islet of Motu Nui. After collecting the egg, competitors would then swim back to Rapa Nui and climb the steep, 800-foot cliff of Rano Kau to the village of Orongo. The winner would be hailed as the *Tangata Manu*, Birdman, and his feat would allow his clan control of the island's resources for the coming year.

By the time a Dutch navigator came upon the island on Easter Sunday in 1722, the island was grossly suffering from a depletion of natural resources. And when Captain Cook visited in 1774, he noted only a few canoes, all in various degrees of disrepair.

In 1862, a fleet of seven Peruvian slave ships arrived, taking only the strongest with them, and instantly diminished the population by more than 50 percent. The last Rapa Nui king died as a slave in the Peruvian mines in the late 1860s. By 1877, the population had dropped from 18,000 to 111. The Rapa Nui people had endured internal warfare, famine, cannibalism, introduced diseases, and, now, slavery. The island was annexed by Chile in 1888. After annexation, Chile leased the island to Enrique Merlet. It was during this period that a wall was constructed around Hanga Roa within which the Rapa Nui people were forced to live.

The magnetic *moai*, however, would help lead the island back to recovery. In 1914, a British archaeologist arrived on a sailing ship named *Mana* and began surveying the island and its *moai*. They arrived to find that while the natural terrain was devastated, the last remaining thread of a culture was still fully intact—the *moai*. The archaeologists began excavating, studying, and restoring the *moai*, and in the coming century, more archaeologists would arrive to restore and study the statues.

Archaeologists have noted that only *moai* situated on the *ahu* have carved eye sockets. Unfinished *moai* in the quarry do not have this feature. According to Sergio's daughter, Julianna, carving eye sockets and the placement of the eyes is the final step in completing "*te aringa ora o tupuna*," the living faces of the ancestors.

In 1978, during archaeological work at Ahu Nau Nau, Sergio discovered several white coral fragments that would answer the question as to why the statues had deeply carved eye sockets.

These fragments were then fitted together to reveal the almond-shaped portion of the eye of the *moai*. The pupil of the *moai* is made by red scoria and resembles the *'ulu maika* of Hawai'i.

"This is the power of the eyes looking over you," Sergio explains. "The eyes of our ancestors, a *hunaunau*, are watching over what we do today."

"Easter Island is a microcosm of what is happening to our planet," Sergio says. "On our planet, we are playing the same game."

Like our planet, Sergio says, Rapa Nui is currently going through a difficult transition. With over 150,000 tourists visiting each year, the locals are trying to accommodate the masses while also protecting their island. How can this island sustain the many physical footprints of tourists? How can the planet sustain the burgeoning footprint of modern industrialized man?

"Sustainability is a nice word," Sergio says. "We can try to control nature, but nature will kick us around in many ways."

THE UNWAVERING INTENT OF THE *Moai* guard the coastline as you head along an unpaved, dusty road. As you pass by Ahu Tahai you will see one *moai* with his eyes fully restored, fully awake and ever watchful over you as you continue up toward the hills, though a grove of tall, swaying eucalyptus surrounding a ferrous-rich soil sprouting taro, yucca, and melon. When you reach the end of the road, there is building shaped like a flower with patio petals blossoming in eight separate directions. Sage is being burned and water is poured along the steps where a woman waves palm leaves and chants, "*Hare mai*," welcoming the crew and a group of Hawaiian schoolchildren into Toki, the only nonprofit, tuition-free music and art school in Rapa Nui.

"We wanted to create a place where we could take care of our culture, because our culture was dying out," says Mahani Teave, one of the school's founders. Along with her husband, Enrique Icka, she formed the school for the sole purpose to resurrect a people who had nearly passed into extinction.

Born in Hawai'i to a Rapa Nui father and a Colorado mother, Mahani grew up in Rapa Nui. As a child, she studied piano and had the gift of playing, but, after a year of study, the only piano teacher on the island moved to Chile. So she and her parents followed the teacher there, where Mahani pursued her passion and became a concert pianist. She returned here to revive for the children what was once taken away from her, as she knows music is the one universal language. She also knows that through music, the Rapa Nui language can be revived. With the language reborn, the tools will come to revive the culture, and eventually, the sailing canoe. In the forty-two years *Hōkūle'a* has sailed throughout the Pacific, Rapa Nui remains one of the few islands that has yet to revive its traditional sailing practices.

"Our dream is to build a canoe. We want to bring back that knowledge which was on this island and then disappeared."

To carve the canoe, they will need a *toki*, an adze like the *ko'i* Billy Richards ensured to be on the canoe the entire length of the Worldwide Voyage.

Opposite top: The crew pitches in to help build a seating area constructed entirely out of rubbish at the Toki School.

Opposite bottom: Archie Kalepa prepares the towline on the foredeck.

"We are all *toki*," Mahani says before offering the crew a concert on the piano. "We are all like this rock, this chisel, which in old times, they used to carve a canoe, and draw the petroglyphs, and make the *moai*."

The school was built of recycled materials collected from the local recycling center, using 2,000 tires; 40,000 aluminum cans; 25,000 glass bottles; 10 tons of cardboard; and 10 tons of recycled plastic. Minimal cement was used to seal walls. Designed by Michael Reynolds, a sustainable architect, the school was built with the help of over seventy volunteers from around the world.

A sky-lit atrium sits at the center of the structure. It is here where the upright piano stands. Mahani and Enrique and a few of the school's children circle around the piano. Enrique holds their ten-month-old girl, Tahai, in his arms, wrapped in a *pareo*. "Breathe," he says to the group, and everyone takes three, consecutive, unified breaths. Then the prayers blow through, like a wave riding through the circle, in both Rapa Nui and Hawaiian.

Everyone sits on the floor. After a harmony on *'ukulele*, the group sings a song that seems to introduce the melody that will come next. Mahani takes a seat at the piano, sweeping her long hair behind her. Some of the crew hold up their cameras to film her as she begins to play, but soon the cameras are lowered, as the delicate song grows and ascends into an anthem. A solemnity overcomes the space as everyone witnesses the true grace of the pianist who knows the keys as intimately as her own baby's breath.

Mahani refers to her work as "rescuing our patrimony." To rescue the language through music, through dance, through body painting, through ancestral chants, in order to rescue the communal soul that was once alive in Rapa Nui.

"I always dreamed that there would be a place where the children could develop their talents," she says later that day. "To have opportunities to develop their talents."

Her childhood piano instructor is now teaching at the school, something Mahani refers to as a beautiful circle. Adding to that circle are the recyclable gifts the crew have brought to the school today—all the nonbiodegradable materials from the sail from Galápagos to here—to help build a tiered seating wall for the school's outdoor amphitheater.

While Mahani tends to Tahai, Enrique leads the crew to work. Enrique guides them as they take fifty-two tires and stack them into four rows. The tires are filled with dirt, then the trash, packed down hard with more dirt, and then, later, will be covered with cement. On the roof, some crew are helping to plant a lemongrass garden. On the land, some are planting taro.

"You know how the archaeologists say that we depleted the island instantly, and it's an example of what the world is doing today?" Mahani asks. She is now seated in the shade in one of the flower petals, a stained-glass wall behind her; before her are the *taro* fields and the ocean far below.

"At one point, there had to be a balance. To reach the level of living here on this island in the middle of nowhere, so far from everything, where they made astronomical calendars aligned with the solstice and equinoxes, and where there were petroglyphs, and actual writing, the only place in the whole Pacific with writing. I think there was a level of balance, an equilibrium; that is the only way that someone can make art, and be inspired. That's where we should navigate to, to try and find that balance, where you live in harmony with your environment, with yourself, and with the people around you," Mahani concludes.

In a few days she will travel to Tahiti to perform and teach as a guest of the Tahitian Music Conservatory. For now, it is time for the baby's nap. Wrapping the *pareo* securely around Tahai, Mahani stands. With a mother's knowing expression, she says, "We are building the present and the future. We are carving the world we live in, and the one that we're going to give to our children."

STANDING ON A PATH ALONG THE UPPER RIM OF A VOLCANO, Bruce, Kaleo, and a handful of Hawaiian students have come to learn about the stars. *Makaleha*, fascinated, are those who stand tonight with heads lifted, gazing up, listening to Bruce unfurl the pathways of the sky. The children are stewards of the Hawaiian culture through *hula*, chanting, and song, each chosen to share these gifts with the Rapa Nui people at a ceremony tomorrow. *ʻIke kupuna mau*, to perpetually return to ancestral knowledge, is the promise among those here.

"The typical night is clouds. The typical night is not like this," Bruce says. "This is a beautiful night."

Bruce talks about the sky as if it were his own family. He refers to individual stars as "this guy" and "that guy," and to the four Hawaiian star lines as if they are ancestors, and the thirty-two houses, the directional points, are the neighbors across the way. Bruce makes it seem as if this celestial guidance is alive in all those who stand around him; it has just been dormant in a thick, fog-drenched sleep.

"If you can find one point on the star compass, you can find any point on the star compass to keep yourself oriented to what direction you're going," Bruce says of the Hawaiian star compass that has been used to sail the entire way around the world. "You really just need to stay oriented by one star. Then you plan for where you want to arrive—what stars do you want to see along the horizon when you are arrive?"

Bruce points out directions and quadrants, all in Hawaiian. *Lā*, sun; *ʻāina*, land; *noio*, the tern; *manu*, bird; *haka*, empty; *nālani*, the heavens; and *nāleo*, the voices of the stars speaking to the navigator.

"And there's *Hikianalia*, reflecting the light of the sun," he says, pointing up to the sky with a laser penlight.

"And *Hōkūleʻa*," someone asks. "Where's *Hōkūleʻa*?"

"She has yet to rise," someone says, and then Bruce explains that stars rising and falling are an illusion. It's a fixed field of stars and we are rotating. "We're standing on this piece of *honua* and it's spinning pretty quickly."

Somebody notices that since we've been standing here, *Ka heihei o nā keiki*, Orion, has moved from here all the way to over there.

"These guys are like thousands of light years away from us," Bruce adds.

"So what we're looking at might not even be there anymore," someone says, and then someone else says, "It's like we're looking into the past."

Everyone grows quiet. The crickets chirp.

Then one of the students asks about Papa Mau. "How did Papa Mau teach?"

"His wisdom was so deep," Bruce replies. "Mau had such a different way of observing. He could tell weather by the stars, the nuances and the hints of things, by the twinkling of the stars."

"Right now, it comes out as really science-based, but it's really just this different way of explaining in a language that people are more familiar with," Kaleo explains. "Our ancestors understood the same movement of the moons and the background stars, but they spoke about it in a different way than we do now."

"How do we take what we've learned from all these decades of sailing, from Mau and through Uncle Bruce, and then apply it to our *kūpuna* system of navigation?" Kaleo asks. "That's part of the next project, recovering all that information and how it was passed down through generations."

The sky seems to have grown taller. *Hōkūleʻa* can now be seen hovering along the horizon of the crater. Everyone pauses to regard and consider and respect the Star of Gladness.

And for this moment, there is a drinking in of the sheer magnitude of where we are, standing on the precipice of a volcano—on one side a sheer cliff, on the other a lake-filled crater, staring at the star that a *waʻa* is named after, a *waʻa* that has allowed for what Bruce calls "a rediscovery of our common bond across the Pacific."

"What a gift to have this canoe built and be a part of this journey and this rediscovery," Bruce says. "It's really a rediscovery of ourselves."

"THE RAPA NUI PEOPLE WILL FIND THEMSELVES," Billy Richards says, sitting on a bench overlooking the ocean, nearing the end of his more than two-month stretch on the canoe. "They will find themselves, but it's not on land," he reflects. "It's out there," he says, gesturing toward the ocean.

Billy knows about the anchoring of self that can be found only out on the ocean. Billy offers this anchoring in a ceremony at Hana Rau O Te ʻAriki, the Bay of the King.

This ceremony is an exchange of *aloha* between one people, Hawaiians and Rapa Nui, separated by the vast ocean. The ceremony begins with the crew swimming ashore from the canoe and onto the beach, and then up to an *ahu* where the Rapa Nui feed the crew the sacred white chicken served on a paddle. The ceremony then continues to another *ahu*, Ahu Nau Nau, where seven *moai* preside over a stretch of grass. There, the dancing, chanting, and drumming rolls on as the sky fades from sun-streaming bright to cloud-filled dark. The ceremony has brought together elders and children, women and men, dancers and chanters and drummers—the collective force that is Rapa Nui yearning to find their center in this Earth. Part of this centering is listening to Billy share story, share heart, share *mana*. Listening to Billy is an invitation to return to the source.

"My first voyage on *Hōkūleʻa*, I was twenty-seven years old," Billy begins. "I'm sixty-nine now."

Billy holds the *koʻi*, the *toki*, in his hands. The basalt is from Taputapuātea, the ancient navigator's *marae* in Raʻiātea. The wood is from the island of Hawaiʻi. The sennit, binding the adze to the wood handle, is from Mau Piailug's island home of Satawal.

"Back then, there was one canoe in Hawaiʻi, *Hōkūleʻa*," Billy explains. "Now there are eight canoes in the Hawaiian Islands."

Billy speaks of the even larger *ʻohana waʻa*, the *ʻohana waʻa* of the great Pacific that has been created due to the birth of *Hōkūleʻa*. He tells the story of ten years ago, when *waʻa* from Sāmoa, Tonga, Cook Islands, Fiji, Tahiti, and Aotearoa all voyaged together to unite in Hawaiʻi.

"We joined together as one family," he says of that day the *koʻi* was bound. "All of the navigators from each *waʻa*, each island, took a turn, wrapping the adze to this handle to bind us as one people."

Billy raises the *koʻi* up to the sky, and slowly, like the Earth on its axis, he begins to turn. "I say to all of you," he says, "this *toki* waits for you."

Opposite: Under a canopy of stars, Hawaiian students learn the pathway home.

——

Local Voices
Enrique Icka
Rapa Nui Musician and Activist

Enrique Icka is a native-born Rapa Nui whose family has lived on the island for generations. Enrique received his degree in engineering in Santiago, Chile, where he reconnected with his childhood friend, Mahani Teave. Enrique and Mahani grew up in Rapa Nui. Their reconnection as adults further solidified their lifelong bond, joined as partners in love and in a shared devotion to care for their island home. While widely known as a songwriter and a musician in Rapa Nui, Enrique is also increasingly known as a man who has committed his life to helping to build a music school for the children of his native island. Enrique sat on the edge of the patio at the Toki music school, overlooking the plateau where he envisions someday building a Rapa Nui sailing canoe. In a measured voice, Enrique told the story of how his shared dream with Mahani grew into the reality of Toki School.

In His Own Words

IN THE FIRST MONTH OF 2012, I HAD JUST FINISHED studying construction engineering in Chile, and a voice inside of me took my heart and said to me, "You need to talk to Mahani."

And I said, "Yes. Yes."

And the voice said, "Not tomorrow, now!" But I'm a little shy and couldn't talk to her, but also couldn't eat, couldn't sleep, and the voice kept saying, "Talk to her, hug her!"

Finally, Mahani hugged me and my chest went boom! We felt connected, and I knew she would be my wife.

Once Mahani and I connected, we said, okay, we have to start. And we, along with other youthful people on the island, made this NGO to build the music school. We did some research on how we wanted to build it. We learned about an architect who constructs buildings with garbage, things he calls Earthships. He lives in New Mexico. So we sent a message to him and he wrote us back, and Mahani and I went to meet with him.

Driving in the United States is different than here. It's fast. As we were driving there, the American Indian people would ask us, "Who are you? Where you from?" And we would say we're from Rapa Nui. "Ah, okay," they would say. Because they know Rapa Nui.

The architect agreed to come here to teach us. And people from all around the world came here and camped here, and together, we built this school. We've been working on this for about a year and a half. We had to stop at times and wait for more money.

It's been a very powerful project. My ancestors are directly connected with the wise Rapa Nui Hotu Matu'a, the first voyager to arrive here, the *ariki mau*, the supreme chief. That chief brought the good kind of power. I call it *mana*, good *mana* that connects the people to each other.

Many years ago, the family of Mahani and the family of my ancestors met in battle. But now, Mahani and me, and our child, we are the peace. And this voice guides me, this protector told me, we had to connect again with the aboriginal Rapa Nui of the world. The voice told me that Rapa Nui is the bank of energy for the world. I always have to listen to that voice, the voice of my *tupuna*, my ancestors.

This school, this project, we helped build to connect the people of Rapa Nui with each other. We need to reconnect with our heritage—the art, the dancing, and the music, and this is the first step: to make this school.

Music is humility. It is the key to open all hearts. It's the universal language.

We have thousands and thousands of engineers with PhDs and doctorates in the world, but look what is happening to our planet. With the tools they have, they still cannot save the planet. But if you open the mind and the heart, together, I think you can—a world united. We need a world united to save the world, because the planet is really, really tender.

When my baby was born—in our house, not in the hospital—I cut the umbilical with a *mata'a*, an obsidian stone warhead. The doctors had told me, "No, no, you can't cut it with that, you need scissors." But I cut it with a *mata'a*, like my *tupuna*. After her birth, the desire for our people to navigate and to sail started to grow in my heart. I heard the song of the dance, the *haka*, and this *haka* told me how to navigate, and about the canoes of our ancestors.

I want to talk with Bruce [Blankenfeld] and ask him how we can make this happen. We need help, we have forgotten how to build canoes. But our ancestors knew and it's in the blood of our children.

We want to build this *vaka*. Maybe bring the trees up and plant them here, and when they are big enough start cutting, and carving, and building.

But this is just the beginning, and these are all dreams. In Rapa Nui, we have a lot of dreams to dream. But the most difficult thing is how these dreams become a reality for our children.

Local Solutions

Planta de Reciclaje Orito

SOME ISLANDS, LIKE DENSE URBAN CITIES, ARE IN DIRE need of assistance in disposing of waste. The more isolated the island, the higher the cost for removing these materials and the greater the challenge to finding a sustainable approach to waste management. Modern packaging and the Western disposable lifestyle exacerbates the problem.

As an isolated island, some 2,300 miles away from the South America, Rapa Nui remains highly dependent on outside resources—including relying on companies to help transport their waste to recycling centers on the continent. The island has one recycling station, Orito, and two landfills. Orito was the supplier of the raw material for the Toki music school construction. The recycling center's main office is built in the same manner. Known as an Eco Hare, an ecological house, the building was built using cans, plastic bottles, and tetra packs.

Back in the 1990s, a local leader, Carmen Luz Zasso Paoa, created Orito as a first step in addressing the problem of waste on the island—waste that has been imported by air and sea, as well as the waste generated on the island itself. This involved a major effort to get the island community aware of a growing environmental concern. Initially, Orito's groundwork involved door-to-door education on the value of recycling. Then came advertising campaigns on radio and TV, and hands-on workshops in both Spanish and Rapa Nui to teach the basic practices of separating waste. By 2005, one van was in service—to gather separated trash from twenty-five homes involved in the recycling project. After collecting the waste, the plastic, aluminum, paper, and cardboard are compressed with a hydraulic press—donated by the European Union—into bales to be sent to the continent to be properly recycled.

In 2014, an agreement with LATAM Airlines and the local Rapa Nui government led to the free weekly transportation of bales of recyclable materials to Santiago, Chile. Each bale weighs about six tons. In Santiago, the cardboard is received by Recupa, the aluminum is received by Metalum, and PET 1 (plastic bottles) by Greendot. The companies process these raw materials and turn them into recycled containers. Today, 30 percent of the recyclable waste is dispatched from Rapa Nui via LATAM Cargo. A portion of the profits from recycling these materials will go toward the building of an Ecopark in Santiago.

There are many tireless activists such as municipal worker Piru Huke who has picked up trash along the coastline for nearly thirty years now. Ocean currents funnel debris from the continent and the discarded nets of tuna trawlers in the waters. Much of the debris is plastic, a worldwide ecological plague. Piru organizes trash pickup days with children: daily trolls with volunteers, where as much as two tons of trash have been collected along the shoreline. Her work has brought her recognition as a Water Guardian by the Race for Water Foundation, a group dedicated to preserving water ecosystems. "I was born without trash and want to live without trash," Piru has said. Like Piru, local authorities realize the need to increase the awareness of recycling in children through education programs in the local schools.

With only fifteen full-time employees, the Orito facility still lacks infrastructure, equipment, and personnel. All the processing tasks—including sorting each item—are done by hand. In 2017, Orito has grown to include 900 homes committed to recycling, and waste is now collected daily, reaching between ten and twelve tons of material. Still, only one fifth of the island's waste is sent for recycling, the rest is sent to the dump. The prime objective of Orito is creating a waste management plan that encourages reuse and recycling and, for now, removing it from the island.

After centuries of devastation, Rapa Nui is still in the early stages of environmental recovery. Having their own plant to recycle their own waste is one key to the future sustainability of Rapa Nui.

Opposite: Recycling, packed tight, stacked high, in Rapa Nui.

Next spread: A *moai* serves as a sentry to the gateway of Ahu Tongariki.

CREW STORY

Bruce Mealoha Blankenfeld

Pwo *Navigator*

Bruce Mealoha Blankenfeld was a high school student in 1974 when he first learned about the building of Hōkūleʻa. While bodysurfing on Hāpuna Beach on Hawaiʻi, he saw her for the first time: the canoe's big white sails fully open while sailing offshore. By 1977, Bruce was volunteering on training sails and construction and repair work of the waʻa kaulua in dry dock. Since then, Bruce has voyaged thousands of miles throughout the Pacific and now throughout the world. He also led Hōkūleʻa's recent, extensive renovation and serves as the voyaging director for the Worldwide Voyage. As a fisherman, paddler, paddling coach, and the president of the Board of Directors of Hui Nalu Canoe Club, Bruce is widely respected for his laid-back demeanor. When he is not sailing, he works as a stevedoring contractor. He is married to Lita, Nainoa's sister, and they live on the Thompson-Blankenfeld family homestead in Niu Valley. Before a dinner gathering of family, crew, and friends, Bruce sat at the long table on his porch, while his grandchildren ran happily and freely around, and talked about the principles of teaching, learning, and leadership.

FIRST TIME I GOT ON BOARD *Hōkūleʻa* was in 1977; that's when I started working on her, too. The lashing we did back then was basic. Nobody was real confident about the lashing for that big of a canoe—that we would get out there and that it would be solid. Then Mau's son, Sesario, came to Hawaiʻi with a group of Micronesians to do the lashing for us.

To learn, I have to sit back and watch, observe, and listen. So I watched them do the lashing. There was nothing complicated about it, and I thought, *Shoot, we can do that.* And we have lashed everything after that.

I've always enjoyed learning and teaching on the canoe. Learning is really the student's willingness to take it to the next level. What it comes down to is whether you have a true intention of learning. It's what we call *ʻimi ʻike*, seeking knowledge.

You're going to see that in students: see them trying to figure it out, and then when it's time, you take them to the next step and watch the person grow. In a student, there are a few things to look for. One is values. You need to get a sense of who they are and how they work with others. If students have respect and love, they're going to be good—you can see it. But, as a teacher, you have to give that back, too.

I like a teaching style with a lot of interaction, very hands on, very casual. I think that's a nice way to learn—by doing it. But, you have to keep it relaxed. And when you're out in the open ocean, in the heat of all the excitement, with chaos and everything, that's an even better time to teach.

On the Tasman Sea, it was rough, and cold, and a lot of the guys were new. They had no idea how they were going to steer the canoe in those conditions. So I just took it one step at a time. I told the guys, "Okay, let's close those sails, leave that one up, change those sails to the smaller ones." And then once we got the smaller sails up, "Okay, now we need guys on the steering paddles and the surfing paddles." Then I tried to teach them how to surf the canoe. They had a great time. And they did good. We were surfing swells that were thirty, forty feet, and it was windy. It was radical.

You would think, "Wow, this is pretty nuts on the canoe in these big seas and cold weather, gnarly!" But, what it is about is giving good instructions and keeping calm. That's how they learn. That's the *kuleana*, the responsibility. I'm the captain, the guy everybody's looking to for leadership and a command for the next step to take. You've got this huge point of view. You can see it, you can see who is the best person for the job and then you just have to do it.

And the most effective way to do it is to be calm. Once the captain loses his head, it's chaos. You stay calm and keep thinking it through. Once you get excited, you lose it—everything gets tunnel vision, goes inward, and you're done. You're just done. But if you relax, think through it, and give clear instructions, everybody calms down and goes to work, and we move on.

Looking ahead to the end of the voyage, the Tahiti-to-home leg for the younger generation, we'll have someone experienced on board who can supervise the effort. Just like Mau did for us—he just supervised from a distance. You don't say anything. You don't get involved. You're not the captain. You're just there enjoying the fishing and playing around a bit. But if something unforeseen happens, you pitch in and help.

That's all it is. I don't have any doubts that they can do it. None. They'll be great. They'll be fine.

You know, with our own kids, when they were in high school, they didn't have a curfew. We knew they would always come home. They're smart, they're capable. It's about letting them grow. The more they experience, the more they grow. And you have

to trust them. You have to let them know that you trust them, too. You're saying to them, "Okay, you guys will do this. You're ready. You've got all the tools. You're going to be good." It's the same thing with the next generation of voyagers.

I'm building my grandchildren a canoe. I named it *Maua*, the name of the wind in this valley. Every valley on the island has its own wind and its own rain. The rain in this valley is different from the rain in the next valley. What's the name of the wind in your valley? It's important to know that and what it means. That's how you learn the deeper sense of your place and who you are.

You know, one thing *Hōkūleʻa* has taught me is that anything is possible. That which you can dream or envision, you can make happen. No matter how bad it gets, something can be done about it. And you just have to calmly think it through. You have to envision it even when other people can't envision it … but you can see it. You just have to push through and make it work. Even if the pushback comes from others who can't quite see it … eventually they're going to see it.

We've been around the world. We've been to so many places where people look at this canoe, and they say, "You guys got to be kidding me! You guys came from Hawaiʻi in that? You didn't ship it here?" They just can't believe it.

There are so many indigenous peoples we have met who have been hammered for centuries. Their numbers have dwindled. They're proud people and there's so much more they want to get done. I think *Hōkūleʻa* is a beacon to them, like, "Hey, you know what, we just got to do something."

Another thing that *Hōkūleʻa* has taught me—hope. There's hope—not only for Hawaiians but also for everybody in this world. We can do it. We can get it done.

Above: Bruce samples the swell in Coffs Harbour, Australia.

Opposite: *Hōkūleʻa's hoe uli* has been touched by many hands.

"In forty-one years, there are so many places the canoe has gone, and so many memories. This voyage around the world has been amazing for Hawai'i, but it has also brought a lot of hope to the people where the canoe has visited around the world. People need to understand this hope. You cannot do it yourself. You need everybody—no matter what color you are, no matter what religion you are. We need each other. This hope is for the future—for the future of our families."

Abraham 'Snake' Ah Hee
Crewmember since 1976

TAHITI

CHAPTER 10

E feti'i ana'e tatou, mai te tau e amuri noa atu

—

We are family, always and forever

ON THE DOCK, IN THE MIST, NAINOA SAYS, "LET'S *PULE*," AND EVERYONE gathers together. Palms open, arms extend, feet shuffle backward. The circle of prayer grows.

"We need to bring Eddie here," Nainoa says, and you can feel the collective breath expand even larger. Eddie. Eddie Aikau.

In the circle stand Eddie's brother and sister, Solomon and Myra, and his nephew Zane. Zane is about to sail on *Hōkūle'a*, upholding not just Eddie being here, but the whole Aikau *'ohana*, a family Nainoa says has shown the most grace and *aloha* of any Hawaiian family he has ever known.

Also in the circle are the men known in Hawai'i as the "Early Voyagers," the 1976 crew who journeyed on the maiden voyage of *Hōkūle'a*. Billy Richards and John Kruse sailed from Hawai'i to Tahiti. Abraham 'Snake' Ah Hee, Kainoa Lee, and Gordon Pi'ianai'a sailed from Tahiti home. Teikihe'epo 'Tava' Tapu, the former boxing champion who has been a part of the *'ohana* since 1978, is also here, along with three *Pwo* navigators, Nainoa, Kālepa, and Chadd 'Ōnohi Paishon.

Heads bow, eyes close, as Kālepa leads the *Pule Ho'omaika'i*, an incantation of gratitude for guidance and protection.

Today begins a sail of *mana'o*, intention, a pilgrimage to the *marae*, the temple of Taputapuātea on the island of Ra'iātea, anciently known as Havai'i. Taputapuātea was once the Polynesian center of voyaging and navigation where priests, navigators, and chiefs congregated to share story, history, and knowledge. To Pacific Islanders, Taputapuātea is the head of a *he'e*, an octopus, with its multiple arms extending like sail lines across a kingdom of islands covering ten million square miles. Some say the word Taputapuātea means "sacrifices from abroad;" some say the word means, "forbidden place," and to others "sacredness radiating outward." All agree that the *marae* was, for centuries, a place where Tahitian navigators would come to center themselves before undertaking long expeditions. It is a place where, before sailing home to Hawai'i, *Hōkūle'a* must visit to return the sacred *pōhaku*, stone, given to the canoe when they passed through here in 2014 at the beginning of the Worldwide Voyage. The *pōhaku* of Taputapuātea have provided mana to protect the canoe on its voyage around the world.

"The people in Taputapuātea told me, 'If you don't bring back the stones, don't ever come back,'" Nainoa tells the crew. "Don't come back."

No need to explain. The crew understands.

Opposite: The crew offers canoe tours at Ra'iātea.

"Taputapuātea is our heaven. It is our mecca," says Billy Richards, the *kāpena*, captain, of *Hōkūleʻa* for this sail. "Taputapuātea is who we are."

Before the voyage of 1976, a priest, *Kahu* Edward Kealanahele, a descendant of the Tahitian *kahuna* Paʻao, named Billy and John Kruse as spiritual guardians of the canoe. Both have held this *kuleana* close for over forty years, and as such, they are also the keepers of the *kiʻi*, the male and female images positioned on the *manu* at the stern of the canoe. Billy looks to John as a brother; they have shared much together on this canoe and on land, their bond further sealed by having both fought in Vietnam. Today, Billy carries the *koʻi*, in a drawstring pack, like a shield, guarding his back. Its adze stone is from Taputapuātea.

When Captain Billy grants you permission to come aboard, you gladly receive the invitation. Here to offer a hand on deck is a young man, self-described as "strong and tall," all sixteen years of him. He is allowed to refer to himself this way because it is true and because he is Keao, Nāʻālehu Anthony's only son. Keao has been sailing on *Hōkūleʻa* since before he entered grade school. Last night he crouched on the bow to ask his Auntie Pomai Bertelmann and Uncle ʻŌnohi, "How do I become crew? What do I still need to do? How fast do I need to swim Sandy's to China Walls?" The questions continued into the night. Everyone knows that Keao's devoted service will lead him to be a crewmember someday, and then his children, and his children's children, too. Today he is helping his father load camera gear on board.

Watching over it all is the knee-high sandstone *moai*, roped to the captain's box, a fiberglass trunk located in the center of the front deck. The *moai* is positioned perfectly to spot Raʻiātea when it first appears between the *manu*. He wears a fresh coconut-frond hat, woven this morning by Tava. Three *pōhaku* are tied on either side of the *moai*. Two of these came with Kaʻiulani from a stream in Hakipuʻu, the mountains above where *Hōkūleʻa* was first launched, and another one came with ʻŌnohi from Mahukona, Kohala on Hawaiʻi Island, home to Koʻa Heiau Holomoana, where he and Shorty Bertelmann continue to teach the traditions of voyaging.

Beside the *moai*, Lāiana Kanoa-Wong, a cultural specialist from Kamehameha Schools, has begun mixing *ʻawa* in a wooden bowl. Lāiana has shared ritual and chant and *ʻawa* for ceremonies in ports throughout the Worldwide Voyage. He travels with a select and ever-changing group of Kamehameha, Hawaiian immersion, and Hawaiian-focus charter school students who present hula to the hosting communities.

When the *ʻawa* is ready, Lāiana places the two *pōhaku* of Taputapuātea onto the lid of the captain's box. It is believed that *pōhaku* from Taputapuātea could be used to begin the building of a new *heiau*. The *pōhaku* can ignite the energy of the place and its people. In Hawaiʻi, scientists have found that some *pōhaku* on *heiau* have come from *heiau* and *marae* throughout Polynesia, including Taputapuātea. Lāiana places a third *pōhaku* beside the two. This one is from Nainoa's homeland of Niu Valley, a *pōhaku* chosen by his children. This one will be a gift.

"Everything in our *ʻāina* has life in it. We recognize it has a spirit," ʻŌnohi has said. "So when we are given the opportunity, we take care of it." This belief is expressed in the way Lāiana reverently pours the *ʻawa* onto the *pōhaku*.

As the *pōhaku* soak in the *'awa*, Lāiana chants a prayer to ward off any negative spirits that may have attached to the stones along the voyage and also to ask for growth and enlightenment to further inspire the community of Opoa at Taputapuātea once the stones are repositioned on the *marae*.

Lāiana then wraps the *pōhaku* in ti leaves, then swathes of cloth, and finally binds them with more ti leaf before placing them carefully on the navigator's bunk at the stern of the canoe.

You can now hear singing on the bow. It is Pomai, her deep voice carries. The daughter of a captain, the niece of a *Pwo*, and the wife of a *Pwo*, she is firmly devoted to her family while also carving her own path forward. On the sail home to Hawai'i, Pomai will be the captain.

Pomai frees the canoe from the dock. As she coils line, she continues the song, *hele 'e ka wa'a i ke kai ē*, and the crew joins in, everyone fully lifted as Tahiti grows smaller and the island of Mo'orea rises on the horizon.

As the morning swells past dawn, the sails are raised and Zane is everywhere on the canoe. With salty-blond hair and light blue eyes, Zane has a solidly built frame like his Uncle Eddie. On the bow, there's a bronze plaque dedicated to his uncle. "No greater love has a man than this, that he lay down his life for his friends. May 4, 1946–March 18, 1978."

Raising sail, dropping sail, catching the boom so it doesn't jibe, Zane knows what needs to be done next, reading it before needing to be directed. Zane is Eddie. Zane says he has never really sailed on *Hōkūle'a* before today. When asked how he knows what to do, he replies, "I'm just trying to think, what would Uncle Eddie do?"

Above: Provisions wait on the beach to be loaded in Taputapuātea.

TAPUTAPUĀTEA IS A DAY'S SAIL DOWNWIND from Tahiti, 110 nautical miles following the arc of the sun. The *marae* includes four low-lying temples overlooking the lagoon sheltered by a wide, sweeping reef. The *marae's ahu* is built of volcanic rock, and its floor is made of black coral woven with bright-white sand. This place was once the center of the *Te Fa'a Tau Aroha*, the Friendly Alliance, in Polynesia. Between 1100 and 1300 CE, scholars, warriors, and priests sailed from their home islands to meet here and observe religious ceremonies and engage in political discussions. But that alliance was severed when a local chief slayed a visiting priest. In retaliation, the high chief was attacked and the canoes from other island states sailed away, departing out of the *Te Avarua Pass*. A *tapu*, a spiritual restriction, was placed over the *marae* banning voyaging canoes from visiting again. For centuries, the island peoples remained an estranged family, separated by the vast seas.

By the time *Hōkūle'a* was launched in 1975, it had been more than 500 years since a voyaging canoe had sailed to the *marae*. According to historian Dennis Kawaharada, when the Pūpu Ariori, a Ra'iātean cultural group, learned that *Hōkūle'a* was sailing to Tahiti, the group reached out to the Polynesian Voyaging Society and asked that the canoe make a visit to the *marae* in hopes that this would help lift the *tapu*, revive the culture, and heal the wounds. At the time, a coconut plantation had been planted behind the *marae*, and there was talk of leveling the grounds to make room for a soccer field. In an essay titled, "The Sin at Awarua" in the journal *The Contemporary Pacific*, PVS cofounder Ben Finney described the arrival of *Hōkūle'a* as "an awakening of consciousness." Finney wrote, ". . . when the canoe finally arrived from Tahiti, the great mass of Ra'iāteans assembled there to greet their cousins from across the equator demonstrated that *Hōkūle'a* had indeed roused Taputapuātea from a long slumber."

Finney goes on to document the full day of ceremony, song, speeches, and *hula*, and how, when it all seemed over, a Ra'iātean elder stood to share one more story. His was a story no one had ever heard before, a story of how he had long waited for the canoe from Hawai'i to return here. He drew his words from a childhood tale his elders had often told him, of a voyaging canoe named *Hotu te Nui* that had left Ra'iātea with the strongest of all its community—sailors, healers, farmers—to settle a new land on a distant uninhabited island. But the canoe and its voyagers were never seen again, and there was a long-held belief that the *tapu* on "overseas voyaging would only be lifted when a canoe bearing the descendants of those long-lost migrants returned to Taputapuātea."

At first it seemed to this elder that the coming of *Hōkūle'a* would lift the *tapu* as these were the very descendants of those long-lost voyagers, but then the elder explained that *Hōkūle'a* had sailed into the *marae* through the wrong pass. The canoe had sailed through *Te Avarua*; they did not sail through *Te Ava Mo'a*, the Sacred Pass.

Until then, those in charge of PVS protocol were unaware of this Sacred Pass. This is the difficulty of piecing together history when stories are held in the few hearts and minds of those who are called upon to remember. It showed the way a valuable story of a people could disappear. The lesson was a strong one. Traditional knowledge and the historical rebuilding of this knowledge must remain secure.

Opposite: John Kruse, who helped build *Nāmāhoe*, a seventy-two-foot double hull voyaging canoe from the island of Kaua'i, bears a *pōhaku* at Taputapuātea.

For the next decade, *Hōkūleʻa* continued to inspire a voyaging revival throughout Polynesia, and in 1985, *Hōkūleʻa* returned to Taputapuātea with Gordon Piʻianaiʻa serving as Captain. This voyage through the Sacred Pass helped to properly lift the *tapu*, allowing for canoes to now return to visit the marae. And in 1992, *Hōkūleʻa* made its third return, with navigators from other islands on board, allowing for others to witness the sanctity of this space.

"We, as indigenous people, are commited to working to understand our culture, practices, and traditions to their fullest potential," Pomai says in regards to the canoe returning to properly sail through the Sacred Pass. "Sometimes doing something a second time is how we learn."

In 1995, Pomai sailed with her father, Clay Bertlemann, on *Makaliʻi*, the canoe he helped build for the island of Hawaiʻi, the same canoe she now watches over back home. Pomai is a student of the traditions of the *waʻa* and a child of ʻOhana Waʻa, the sailing communities that have grown in the South Pacific and on five Hawaiian islands, including *Moʻolele* and *Moʻokiha o Piʻilani* on Maui, and most recently in 2016, with *Nāmāhoe*, the canoe John Kruse helped build for the children of Kauaʻi.

John sees the *waʻa* as "a magnet." *Nāmāhoe* has drawn in hundreds of school kids who are eager to learn about the history of their people and about their own place in the voyaging history of Polynesia. Says John, "Mau told us, your job is to teach. Teach as best you can. That's what we're doing with *Nāmāhoe*. Forty years from now, these kids will tell their own story."

Forty-one years after *Hōkūleʻa* helped to revive Taputapuātea, the *marae* has been designated a UNESCO World Heritage Site.

WHEN THE SKY WIDENS and the sails snap open, the "you" that is "I" becomes "we." "It's not about me, or you, it's about everybody," explains Snake. "We are here to help each other and watch over each other."

So when Gordon tells Pomai, "Your father is here, he's with you," you know her father is with all of us, too. We all carry someone with us. Nakua Konohia-Lind has his great-grandfather Sam Kalalau Sr., who sailed with Billy and John in 1976. Gordon has his father, Abraham, a former master mariner who once walked barefoot across a path of burning stones in a ceremony on Moʻorea en route to Taputapuātea in 1992. Kainoa carries his late wife, Patricia, with him, wearing the red knitted cap she made for him only a year ago. And then there is Zane. Zane is carrying Eddie, his uncle. Eddie is carrying Zane. They are carrying each other.

The names of *nā ʻaumākua* are listed on a wood plaque at the stern, a reminder of those who once stood on this deck, but have passed, and who still watch over us now, sometimes in the form of sharks, dolphins, birds, rainbows, and even clouds. A recent name added to the list is Mel Paoa. Mel shares the surname of the last great Hawaiian navigator, Paoa, and he also kindly shared his soup in the rain in Aotearoa. Mel passed away suddenly at home in Molokaʻi in August 2015. His passing was felt by all who sailed with him, most especially by his friend Kawika Crivello, also from Molokaʻi, the watch captain today. Kawika tells the story of when the canoe crossed the Atlantic only months after Mel's passing. Mel's son Lohiao was on board, and on the day of Mel's birthday a *noio* bird flew around the canoe, and all Lohiao had to do was offer his hand, and the bird landed right on his finger and stayed a while. Everyone knew this bird was an *'aumakua* of Mel visiting his son.

Stories like these unfold like waves rolling from one side to the other, rocking us in the shared dream of remembering.

We pour water for the uncles, and the uncles show us how to *mālama pono*, take good care, of each other. If there's someone not feeling so well, get her a damp towel. If someone is tired, let him sleep. If someone is drifting, thinking, then give her the space. Someone missing someone, maybe there is a song to help the memory unfold. Singing, like salt water, heals. These are the lessons in taking care and then there are lessons in being fully *maka'ala*, awake. Those lessons are taught especially by Snake.

"If you love the ocean, the ocean will help you," Snake explains. A lifelong surfer, paddler, and sailor, Snake is fluent in language of the sea. "The ocean is helping

you put everything together, the ocean and the waves. If you don't understand the waves, you'll be lost."

"You got to be constantly watching. Look in the front, look in the back," he says. "It's almost like you're surfing, surfing downwind with the waves."

The canoe surfs along, sometimes smoothly, sometimes roughly. As Pomai would say, "Like a shark, the bow, the nose; the stern, the tail; the mast, the fin."

As the sun slowly slips down the sky, the winds shift. Sails are lowered, raised, changed, and then for a while things seem to reach a lull. There are squalls, sure, over there, far off, but for now 'Ōnohi pulls out the guitar and strums while Pomai

---

Above: Nainoa Thompson and crew return sacred pōhaku to the *marae* at Taputapuātea.

sings and Nakua softly drums the water jug. And then it comes. Like an earthquake is heard before it is felt. It comes in the sound of the sails and the boom suddenly whipping back and everyone springing up, some to hold the boom open, some to hold the sweep. It comes, full force.

Rain. Straight down. Sideways. Sun so low the rain is a blinding silver shine on the water all around. Gordon summons you, and you come stand beside him and hold the boom while someone else holds the other side. The rain seems to calm the waves to settle down. Sometimes nature seems to talk to itself and right now you are here to witness it.

And there you stand, Gordon and you in the shelter of the sail. Story time. Gordon talks, talks of how far the voyage has come since the days when he and Dave Lyman were selling books and T-shirts out of the back of Dave's Volkswagen to raise money to help maintain the canoe. When the deck was bamboo and when Herb Kāne would call in the middle of the night to ask you, "Hey, can you bring the canoe home from Tahiti?" A long way since those days when after sailing the canoe home, you simply wake up the next morning and return to work. No big show. Just doing your job, really.

Gordon is asked if he and his crewmates, in sailing the canoe back then, in reclaiming their language and culture, felt they were staking the spear in the ground and taking back what was once stolen, saying, "This is ours!"

Gordon pauses. He looks out over the waters for a good long while. "*Hōkūleʻa* wasn't a stake in the ground," he says. "*Hōkūleʻa* was removing the stake from our hearts."

POMAI IS CHANTING UP THE SUN, spreading across the horizon behind us, as we sail toward the Sacred Pass, the jagged peaks of Raʻiātea rising between the *manu*.

We raise the flags of Tahiti and Hawaiʻi, and a red-tipped, yellow-feathered *lei hulu*, feather *lei*, high up the mast.

"Steer to the mountain," Billy says, and Moani manages the *hoe uli* with Pomai guiding and encouraging her. Moani Heimuli is a twenty-six year old who captained the escort vessel up and down the entire eastern seaboard of the United States. Moani steers steadily with the sea pulling and the winds shivering as the canoe approaches the pass, an open channel through the reef. No conch shells blowing, no chants sung, as we sail through, only the quiet of us not breathing. Once the canoe is within the pass, the ocean calms. The embrace of the lagoon surrounds us, and you can hear our collective breath released.

"It made my spirit happy," Pomai will later say. "Seeing Uncle Gordon's, Uncle Snake's, Uncle Billy's, Uncle John's, Uncle Kainoa's spirits and how excited they were that we crossed into the lagoon over the threshold of the sea—that was burning inside me," she says. "It made all our spirits happy."

ʻŌnohi weaves *lei* for the crew to wear ashore. John hands a *lei* to you to place on the female *kiʻi* and you climb on the *manu* at the stern, and drape the *lei* around her neck and comb back her long black hair. Billy unwraps the *pōhaku* to carry ashore. This is Billy's fourth pilgrimage here. Twenty-five years ago he brought his daughter's *piko*, umbilical cord, as an offering to connect her to the navel of Polynesia forever.

Here come the canoes, two six-mans, bound together with a deck lashed between them, adorned with branches and flowers and *lei*. They look like small *motu*, traveling toward us. "Step aboard," we are told, this is your ride to the *marae*.

We can hear reeds being blown, inviting us in, and as we make our barefoot way across the rocky coral shore we see that this is a place like no other. This is a place where the elders greet us, where they are our future and not our past, and the familiarity of what once was and what was lost is now clearly found right here. Past, present, and future are all standing together in the warm, shallow waters of the lagoon.

Seeking permission to come ashore, we sing.

A honua, a hokua o ka ʻale,
> We have come from the troughs and crests of the swells,

A ka hoʻokuʻi ʻo Hōkūleʻa—
> Hōkūleʻa has reached the zenith—

Liuliu mālana i ka huʻa kai;
> We float readied here amidst the sea foam;

ʻEʻeʻina ka hoa waʻa
> The lashings creak

A lono ka heahea aloha;
> And the friendly tidings are heard;

He welina aloha ē.
> It is an affectionate greeting.

Come, children are waving palm leaves, welcoming us onto the *marae*.

The sun grows. It is a fainting sun, a heatstroke sun, a sun under which the children sing and elders speak in a language of union, Tahitian and Hawaiian. Keao stands behind Kainoa, holding a large palm leaf over the head of his uncle. Keao's full Hawaiian name is Koloikeao Honuaiākea Kanaʻiaupuni Heiariʻi Kuikuipua, meaning "to emerge into the day, [and] the Earth and the vast expanse, [from] Pele's *waʻa*, to conquer and unite the islands collectively, [and] to string many *lei*." Seeing him behold this ceremony, he embodies the journey his father placed in him when he named him at birth.

Come now, time for the elders and the captains to sit on seats of palm leaves stretched out on the sand in the shade, sharing *ʻawa*, sharing *pule*, sharing between many joined by one canoe.

The sun continues its sweep, and after the *pōhaku* are returned, the *pōhaku* from Nainoa's family's land will be gifted, rooting Nainoa's children's intentions into the *marae*.

Once the sun has settled and the food has been served and the drinks poured, some will take naps under the palms. Some will drink *ʻawa*. Some will talk story. And some will revisit the *marae*.

Everyone seems to need to take time here alone. We all do. A carved wooden fish, a long strand of *kukui* nuts, and a child's faded grass shirt are a few of the offerings encircling the tiki at the base of the altar's tall wall. These are the offerings you can see. The rest, the unseen, the unspoken, the ones still hidden under a rug in the

heart, those you can only vaguely feel as the sand whips your ankles, kneeling in the shadow of a wall built with stones that burned long, long ago.

Zane will have some quiet time here too. Zane will also have time to talk with an elder caretaker of Taputapuātea. This is the same elder who chose the *pōhaku* to place on *Hōkūle'a* three years ago. This man will share many teachings and many stories with Zane, and will offer up his vision as to why Zane sailed to Taputapuātea today.

"When Eddie left Hawai'i, he never finished his journey to Tahiti," the elder explains, "but you finished the voyage for Eddie by coming here."

"And I like to think that," Zane will later reflect. "It felt like that to me too."

A MASSIVE NAVIGATIONAL MAP is stretched out over the grass in the backyard of the home of Matahi Tutavae. Matahi has invited the crew of *Fa'afaite* to meet with Nainoa in preparation for their canoe's upcoming sail alongside *Hōkūle'a* and *Hikianalia* to Hawai'i. Sail lines from Tahiti to Hawai'i are drawn on the map. Nainoa and the crew sit on the grass along the borders. *Pwo* navigator Kālepa Baybayan and apprentice navigator Lehua Kamalu are also here.

"I think all the islands in the Pacific need the navigator back," Nainoa tells them. "Maybe we should start with Tahiti."

The crew is well aware they are in the presence of *Pwo*. Regardless of the many times Nainoa says, "I am not a master, I am a student of navigation," he is known throughout the Pacific as the man who has changed the modern-day course for Pacific Islanders. He has reclaimed what was lost and shown current-day Polynesians a deeper part of themselves and created a solidarity that is perhaps stronger today than it was when Ra'iātea was the axis of the Pacific. Tahiti has

Above: Veteran crewmember 'Snake' Ah Hee pauses on the dock before departure to Ra'iātea.

not had a traditional navigator in more than two hundred years. The last one was Tupaia, who could chart out 130 islands within a 2,500-mile radius from Tahiti. Tupaia helped Captain Cook navigate through the Pacific all the way to Aotearoa. Born in Raʻiātea and schooled at Taputapuātea, Tupaia was also a priest. His *piko* is buried in Taputapuātea.

No chart, no compass, no GPS. "You don't need it," Nainoa says of the modern sailor's instruments. "The moment you make the choice to pull out the GPS, the satellite's navigating you, not your ancestors."

For Nainoa, this meeting falls after his visit to Taputapuātea. For the Tahitians, the meeting falls after visiting the caves where Tupaia lived in Aoteaoroa. Just as a navigator needs to know where he is coming from to know where he is sailing to, a community needs to be firmly mindful of its past in order to move forward into the future.

Nainoa talks of a time when Polynesians chose the motor over the sail and the compass over the stars. There was a time when there were only six masters remaining and one was Mau Piailug. This was the time when Micronesia was forgetting the traditional practices. Forgetting is sleeping.

"Here's the problem," Nainoa says, "if you don't take command, you will go to sleep."

Sleeping is spiritual amnesia. The extinction of the navigator is an extinction of culture. The extinction of culture is an extinction of the soul.

Nainoa knows the dangers of losing the teachings and the loss of genealogy. He was thirty-two years old when he learned from his uncle that his own name was correctly spelled Naʻinoa and that it means "to overcome adversity, to take the challenge, to set thing to right." Nainoa's wife, Kathy, has made sure that their own son would have the name spelled the correct, traditional way, Naʻinoa, so that the genealogy of his story will never be forgotten again.

A Tahitian asks, "So what is a navigator?"

And now Nainoa leans in, confides. "Let me tell you, I didn't want to take *Pwo*." He told Mau this, and when he did, Mau said, "I'm not asking you. I'm telling you, you take *Pwo*."

"So, I asked him, 'What is *Pwo*?' It's the same question you just asked. What is *Pwo*?"

Mau answered in a thirteen-page document, translated into English, on the definition of *Pwo*.

"Where there is conflict between people, the *Pwo* needs to resolve. When there is a wounded seabird, the *Pwo* heals. When there is something wrong with the island, the *Pwo* takes care of the island. And the *Pwo* goes out to sea to bring the gifts back to his people," Nainoa explains of the document.

"And, at the end, the last paragraph read, '*Pwo* is the light, and the light is love.'"

"We have learned love from you, and I know, because I was here in '76. I know. So if you want, we could help you with the easy part, the navigating. Because the other part, the hard part, the love, you're already there."

Nainoa is speaking of the love extended to the crew when they came here in 1976. Tahitian families from the community of Tautira brought crew in to stay in their homes. Those same families still do the same today. As one crewmember, Maui

Opposite: Waterfalls bear fresh water from *mauka* to *makai* in Tahiti.

Tauotaha, explains, "Food on land, water for the voyage, housing in Tautira, trans-portation for wherever we need to go; the people of Tautira are always there for us." Maui has Tahitian roots. His grandparents were one of those Tautira families from 1976, and his parents eventually met because of *Hōkūleʻa*. Maui is an offspring of the canoe, and as the evening moves along it becomes evident that these sail lines on the map are simply *pilina*, connections between not only islands but people.

And tonight, the same *pilina* can be drawn directly back to Mau Piailug.

The last time Nainoa would see Mau, Mau was sick with diabetes. He was lay-ing on his bed, a piece of plywood, in his house in Satawal. Mau knew this would be the last time he would see his student, and the student knew the same. He told Nainoa, "When you put me in the ground, know that it's OK because that seed will grow. That seed will grow."

That seed is *Pwo*. That seed is *Hōkūleʻa*. That seed is the Worldwide Voyage. That seed is what is growing now.

"What you're doing on *Faʻafaite,* yes, it's for you," Nainoa says. "It's for Tahiti. But it's also for the world. That's why the responsibility is so heavy. But you cannot take just a part of it. You have to take the whole thing. You need to take it. It's your time."

The crew is ready to begin the lesson.

Nainoa asks permission for Lehua and Kālepa to be on board *Faʻafaite*: Lehua to teach navigation, Kālepa to help oversee. The crew welcomes them both in.

"Lehua, can you explain to everybody how to go to Tahiti from Hawaiʻi?" someone asks, and there are laughs, and she says, "No problem, just two sentences, right?"

"You can walk on the map," another crewmember says.

"OK," she says, carefully crawling across the Tuamotus, "how you plan a trip to anywhere—Aotearoa, Rapa Nui, Madagascar—you go through the same basic things. The first thing you have to think about is the canoe. How does she sail? Does she sail

Above: The hope for our future is with our children.

nice into the wind, against the wind, downwind, because the way you design to go to that island needs to work with the wind system you are going in. . . ."

And so, it goes. As the Worldwide Voyage nears completion, the student has become a teacher, and the seed that was planted decades ago takes root.

ON THE GRASS, IN THE PARK BESIDE THE DOCK, two women from Waimea take some time together. Pomai and Ka'iulani sailed together as crewmembers from Tahiti to Hawai'i seventeen years ago. But on the sail ahead they will serve as captain and navigator—one of the closest relationships on the canoe. These two view each other as sisters. And tonight, during the crew change for the final leg of the voyage, they pause to talk about sailing home together.

"I truly, truly believe the eyes of the canoe, the navigator, is the most essential part of the *wa'a* and is equally important as the hulls and the deck of the canoe. And I think the canoe needs to trust that person to do that," says Pomai. "That is Ka'iulani. Ka'iulani has been in and out, around, and up and down *Hōkūle'a* for years. There's no separation between who *Hōkūle'a* is and who she is."

"I also think *Hōkūle'a* chose her a long time ago. And, I think Ka'iulani knew that a long time ago. And, I think our teachers knew that, too."

"I would follow Pomai anywhere," Ka'iulani says of Pomai, whose father is one of her heroes. Ever respectful, Ka'iulani has a way of deferring any attention away from herself and toward honoring those around her instead.

"My job is to make sure that the team can work together to help give Ka'iulani the best opportunity to see the road," says Pomai. "That's my job. And, then to stay on the road."

The road home. The *Pwo* know the road well, not only as a vision in the mind but as a place in the heart.

"To find home, you have to feel home," says 'Ōnohi, a *Pwo*. "Mau said, 'You have to feel home in here [in your heart] to find your way to it.' It really is that relationship, that vulnerability to let yourself feel, and to really trust it, and then say, 'This is the way to go.'"

Tahiti is some 2,500 nautical miles from home, Hawai'i. That is 2,500 nautical miles of trust.

This is the same trust instilled in those who decided to undertake the Worldwide Voyage. This is a trust that knew it was more dangerous to stay home than it was to traverse the planet on a double-hulled canoe.

"What if we didn't go? What if we didn't go?" Nainoa has asked. "What if we tied the canoe to the dock and said, 'Hey, guess what, kids, it's too dangerous. Sorry, we're not gonna go. It's too dangerous. Because we're worried about fire or we're worried about a hurricane.' But we're honest with our children: the great voyage that we need to make is everybody sharing our relationship to Earth and to humankind. And *Hōkūle'a* made that promise when we left."

That promise has been kept. It is known as the Promise to Children, an agreement that educational leaders have accepted to apply the principles of the Worldwide Voyage throughout the islands. Over a hundred teachers have sailed on the canoe around the globe, taking the lessons of voyaging and incorporating them into curriculum, whether it is teaching students to engineer a *wa'a*, or applying the principles of STEM (Science Technology, Engineering, and Mathematics) to stabilize a deck, or learning how to utilize aquaponics on a canoe sailing across the oceans.

That promise is the University of Hawai'i connecting to every island *wa'a* with the intention to create a degree in navigation.

That promise is *Hikianalia's* captain, Bob Perkins, head of the Marine Education and Training Center, *Hōkūle'a's* dockside home, who hopes to convert the METC into a voyaging center.

That promise is the Mālama Honua Public Charter School where grade-school children are asked daily, "How can you live by the values lived on the *wa'a*?" And where teachers ask themselves daily, "How do you support students to live by those values?"

"*Hōkūle'a* is the spirit," says Laura Thompson, Nainoa's mother and Pinky's wife. "Mālama Honua is an extension of all these things that we've learned and put together by having *Hōkūle'a*. It's not just a hope; it is happening. It is happening now. It started long ago, all of us longing, wanting to care for each other and the Earth. We are perpetuating it, and I'm encouraged. I'm encouraged by what I see in my community. It's *aloha*."

Aloha. Aloha is eternal. *Aloha* is unchanging. *Aloha* is like a *lei*, a circle of prayer, sewn around the world.

Time to complete the *lei*.

The crew will say their farewells to their families in Tahiti.

They will release the lines from the dock, raise the flag of Hawai'i, and hoist sail.

They will reach the open ocean and the swells will rise and the squalls will hit.

And when they reach the place where the sun rises and falls quickly, that place that is known as Ka Piko o Wākea, *the equatorial navel of the Earth, they will lift the paddle and drop the sails. They will each take a part of themselves, in the form of a* pōhaku *from home, to the bow, and offer it up, and bless it, and let it go, allowing it to merge with the depths, connecting themselves directly to the ocean's core.*

The sails are hoisted. The paddle dipped in. Time to go. Time to follow the wind, trust the heart, home.

Opposite: *Hōkūle'a on the road to Taputapuātea.*

—

Local Voices
Matahi Tutavae
Cofounder of the Tahiti Voyaging Society

MATAHI TUTAVAE was born in Papeʻete, Tahiti, and raised on the island of Moʻorea. His love for the ocean began as a young boy, following his father spearfishing in Opunohu Bay; his love of the Earth began as young man, following his uncle's mission to protect the sacred valley of Papenoʻo, his maternal family's ancestral land. Matahi was steered into voyaging under the guidance of Pomai Bertlemann and Chadd ʻŌnohi Paishon in the ʻOhana Waʻa of Makaliʻi on Hawaiʻi Island. Since then, he has crewed on Hōkūleʻa, most recently as watch captain as the canoe crossed the Tasman Sea from Aotearoa to Australia. In the days before Faʻafaite set sail to Hawaiʻi, Matahi talked about how Tahiti has embraced its first voyaging canoe and his hopes for his country to reclaim its traditional navigational practice.

—
Next spread: With the wind in the high twenties and minimal sail up, *Hōkūleʻa* and *Hikianalia* sail into *Te Ava Moʻa*, the Sacred Pass to Taputapuātea.

In His Own Words

I THINK TAHITIANS HAVE DREAMED ABOUT A VOYAGING canoe for a long time. The first time I saw a voyaging canoe, I was in Hilo in the mid-eighties. Being there was one of the best things that ever happened to me. I met up with the Kanakaʻole family.

One day, Lehua, one of the Kanakaʻole daughters, asked me if I wanted to come to the other side of the island to study navigation with the *Makaliʻi* community. I was like a child being taken by the hand. I had no idea what was going to happen. They gave us cots outside to sleep on and told us, "In a few hours, we're going to wake you up and look at the sky." In the middle of the night, Uncle ʻŌnohi talked to us about how the stars move across the sky. Another night, ʻŌnohi left us with a young boy, he must have been thirteen years old—most of us were over twenty. The boy spoke about Kekāomakaliʻi, that star line, the bailer of Makaliʻi. This boy was so confident and eloquent. He knew who he was.

It changed my whole vision of the Hawaiian culture and ourselves. I realized how we take so many things for granted here in Tahiti. Our elders speak Tahitian fluently, and they grew up with that. We have news in both French and Tahitian. But we do little to maintain our culture. Our knowledge is slowly eroding away. When I came home I had a lot of things in my head. I was twenty-two.

And one day, I saw something that caught my attention. It was a notice for a meeting with a picture of *Te Rarotonga*, the sailing canoe from the Cook Islands. It was just a little picture of the canoe with an article saying that there was going to be a public talk about canoes and the protection of the ocean. I thought, *Oh, wow. Maybe we will now have an opportunity to have a canoe here.*

Then ʻŌnohi and Pomai came here for a school exchange. They were the people who influenced me most. We didn't have our canoe yet, we were just talking about it. And the way I was talking about it was as a "project." "So, we have this 'project.'" And Pomai came up to me and said, "Matahi, you're about to have a canoe and it is a big responsibility. A big *kuleana* for you, your family, your crew, and it's awesome. But you know, you just need to stop talking about it as a 'project.'"

"You have to stop talking about it as a project; if you talk about it as a project, you're putting in your head a limit. You have to see it as a lifestyle. It means your family has to be involved. Make sure that this is going to become a lifestyle, a community. And if you're not the right person to do that, then choose somebody else."

That was an interesting talk. I thought, *Wow, she's right. Makaliʻi is a family. Hōkūleʻa is a family.* I realized we have to create this canoe family here.

So we gathered a community of people who already were doing things—whether for the language, or land or ocean conservation. And, in March 2009 we founded *Faʻafaite i te ao Māʻohi*, and then, in October, we received the canoe from the Okeanos Foundation.

I had never really sailed in my life. I paddled, I swam, I surfed, and I fished. Our sailing teacher was Teva Plichart. Teva is a Tahitian captain who grew up on the ocean, sailing and racing. He's got this way of teaching; he makes sure you learn from when you make mistakes. It was cool to have him onboard because none of us really knew how to sail. It was all about safety and learning how to use the sails. It was a pretty steep learning curve for us.

This voyage to Hawaiʻi with *Hōkūleʻa* is not about us. It's not about proving a point. It's about starting something. I want to make sure that there are several of us who will benefit from the knowledge and the training. It's about starting something that will give us confidence.

When I sailed on *Hōkūleʻa* from Aotearoa to Sydney, I realized I was lacking confidence. It's about you choosing, or not choosing, to be confident. Having Nainoa and the Hawaiians trusting us is a big deal. When Nainoa tells me, "You can do this," I have to believe it. The first time he told me that, in 2014, when he came here at the start of the voyage, I was like, "Okay," because it didn't hit me. But then, I started thinking, *Can we really do it? What can we do to make sure that we can do it?*

The name of our canoe is *Faʻafaite*. The name was given by an elder, a preacher. We had been searching for names and we asked him to help us decide on a name for the new canoe. He asked us, "What are your goals? What is the purpose of the canoe?" Our objective, besides learning noninstrument navigation, is to help people embrace their culture, their history, and their ancestors. We were looking for a name that was accessible to everybody, anybody, not just a single community.

So the preacher said, *Faʻafaite*. I had never heard that word before. He said, "*Faʻafaite* means reconciliation."

I've been having the same dream for almost a year. It's a dream of a sailing canoe arriving at an island. It's a bare island, and there's an old guy, wrinkled and dark. He's standing on the island, and he's talking to us. He's speaking a Polynesian language. It's not Tahitian, but I can understand him. He's standing there, watching us sail in, and he's saying, "Finally, you've come. You guys are finally here. I've been waiting for you for a long time."

GALLERY IV
Homecoming

This spread: *Hōkūleʻa* turning downwind in the Kaiwi Channel and completing the final leg back to Honolulu.

Pages 340–341: *Moʻokiha o Piʻilani*, *Hikianalia*, and *Okeanos* round Diamond Head in the procession of voyaging canoes escorting *Hōkūleʻa* to Magic Island, Honolulu.

Pages 342–343: Thousands welcome the return of *Hōkūleʻa* into her home waters.

Pages 344–345: The Homecoming Celebration was held on Magic Island on June 17, 2017.

Hōkūleʻa
Star of Gladness

Named after the star Arcturus, which passes directly over the Big Island, *Hōkūleʻa* means "Star of Gladness" in Hawaiian. The canoe has logged more than 150,000 miles in eleven long-distance voyages, plus six statewide sails and numerous training voyages.

The traditional Polynesian voyaging canoe, designed by artist and historian Herb Kawainui Kāne, was launched from Kualoa-Hakipuʻu in Kāneʻohe Bay on March 8, 1975. The event not only revitalized voyaging and navigation traditions, it also inspired a new-found respect and appreciation for Hawaiian culture and language in the islands and beyond.

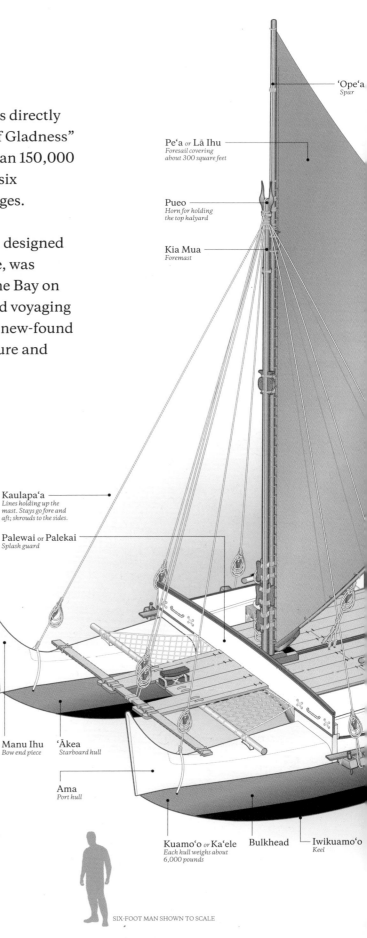

ʻOpeʻa
Spar

Peʻa *or* **Lā Ihu**
Foresail covering about 300 square feet

Pueo
Horn for holding the top halyard

Kia Mua
Foremast

Kaulapaʻa
Lines holding up the mast. Stays go fore and aft; shrouds to the sides.

Palewai *or* **Palekai**
Splash guard

Manu Ihu
Bow end piece

ʻĀkea
Starboard hull

Ama
Port hull

Kuamoʻo *or* **Kaʻele**
Each hull weighs about 6,000 pounds

Bulkhead

Iwikuamoʻo
Keel

SIX-FOOT MAN SHOWN TO SCALE

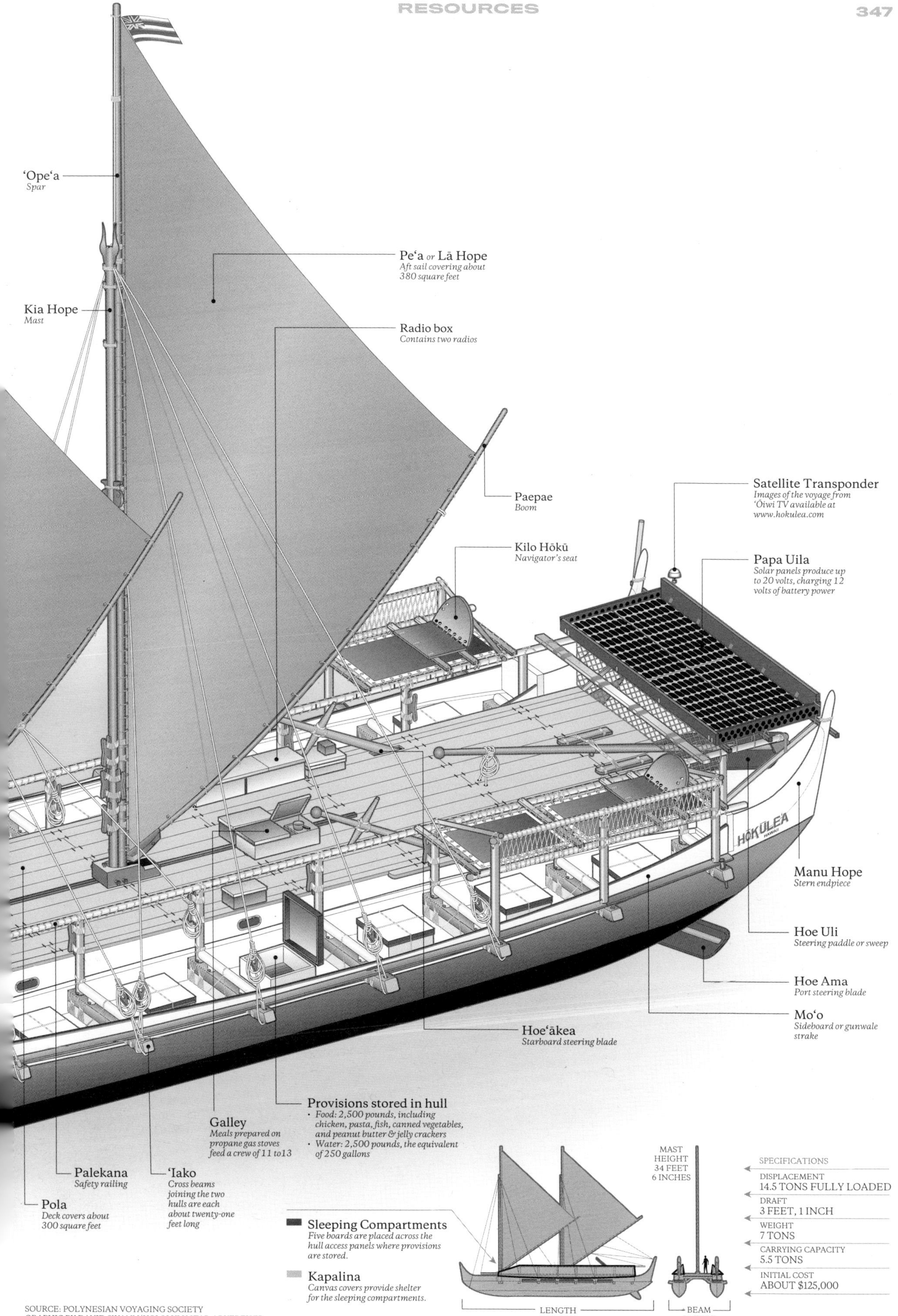

'Ope'a
Spar

Kia Hope
Mast

Pe'a *or* Lā Hope
*Aft sail covering about
380 square feet*

Radio box
Contains two radios

Paepae
Boom

Satellite Transponder
*Images of the voyage from
'Ōiwi TV available at
www.hokulea.com*

Kilo Hōkū
Navigator's seat

Papa Uila
*Solar panels produce up
to 20 volts, charging 12
volts of battery power*

HOKŪLEA
HAWAI'I

Manu Hope
Stern endpiece

Hoe Uli
Steering paddle or sweep

Hoe Ama
Port steering blade

Mo'o
*Sideboard or gunwale
strake*

Hoe'ākea
Starboard steering blade

Provisions stored in hull
· *Food: 2,500 pounds, including
chicken, pasta, fish, canned vegetables,
and peanut butter & jelly crackers*
· *Water: 2,500 pounds, the equivalent
of 250 gallons*

Galley
*Meals prepared on
propane gas stoves
feed a crew of 11 to13*

Palekana
Safety railing

'Iako
*Cross beams
joining the two
hulls are each
about twenty-one
feet long*

Pola
*Deck covers about
300 square feet*

Sleeping Compartments
*Five boards are placed across the
hull access panels where provisions
are stored.*

Kapalina
*Canvas covers provide shelter
for the sleeping compartments.*

MAST
HEIGHT
34 FEET
6 INCHES

SPECIFICATIONS

DISPLACEMENT
14.5 TONS FULLY LOADED

DRAFT
3 FEET, 1 INCH

WEIGHT
7 TONS

CARRYING CAPACITY
5.5 TONS

INITIAL COST
ABOUT $125,000

LENGTH
62 FEET

BEAM
21 FEET

SOURCE: POLYNESIAN VOYAGING SOCIETY
GRAPHIC BY DAVID SWANN/HOLOLULU STAR-ADVERTISER

Navigation

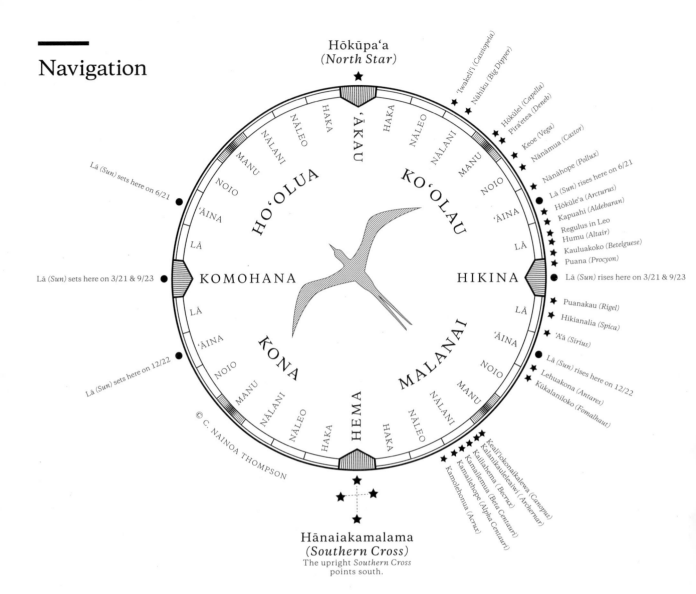

Hōkūpaʻa
(North Star)

'Iwakeli'i *(Cassiopeia)*
Nāhiku *(Big Dipper)*
Hōkūlei *(Capella)*
Pira'etea *(Deneb)*
Keoe *(Vega)*
Nānāmua *(Castor)*
Nānāhope *(Pollux)*
Lā *(Sun)* rises here on 6/21
Hōkūleʻa *(Arcturus)*
Kapuahi *(Aldebaran)*
Regulus in Leo
Humu *(Altair)*
Kauluakoko *(Betelguese)*
Puana *(Procyon)*
Lā *(Sun)* rises here on 3/21 & 9/23
Puanakau *(Rigel)*
Hikianalia *(Spica)*
'Ā'ā *(Sirius)*
Lā *(Sun)* rises here on 12/22
Lehuakona *(Antares)*
Kūkalaniloko *(Fomalhaut)*

Keali'iokonaikalewa *(Canopus)*
Kalanikauleleaiwi *(Becrux)*
Kailiahema *(Archernar)*
Kamailemua *(Beta Centauri)*
Kamailehope *(Alpha Centauri)*
Kamolehonua *(Acrux)*

'ĀKAU

KO'OLAU

HO'OLUA

KOMOHANA

HIKINA

KONA

MALANAI

HEMA

HAKA • NĀLEO • NĀLANI • MANU • NOIO • 'ĀINA • LĀ

Lā *(Sun)* sets here on 6/21
Lā *(Sun)* sets here on 3/21 & 9/23
Lā *(Sun)* sets here on 12/22

© C. NAINOA THOMPSON

Hānaiakamalama
(Southern Cross)
The upright *Southern Cross*
points south.

Noninstrument navigation relies on the senses and memory, not on modern devices like a GPS or magnetic compass. Hawaiians use a knowledge of the stars, winds, waves, current, seabirds, the concept of expanded landfall, and anything else that can provide a clue to where one is.

Sunrise and sunset are key times of every day at sea. Navigators study the swells, the colors in the sky, as well as cloud forms and the direction they may be moving. When the sun is low, it is also easier to see islands along the horizon. Some techniques and clues these navigators use are:

STAR COMPASS

Instead of a Western compass, Pacific Islanders use star paths as a way of direction finding. A certain star, upon rising, is used as a directional pointer to a particular island. This information, specific to each island group, was nearly lost by the time *Hōkūleʻa* was first built. Mau Piailug, from the island of Satawal in the Caroline Islands, was among a small group of navigators still practicing traditional navigation when the Polynesian Voyaging Society convinced him to teach a select few. Nainoa Thompson was among his students and, by studying with him and visiting the planetarium on Oʻahu, and studying with its director, Will Kyselka, Nainoa developed a star compass that is now used by traditional navigators aboard *Hōkūleʻa* and other Hawaiian *waʻa kaulua*.

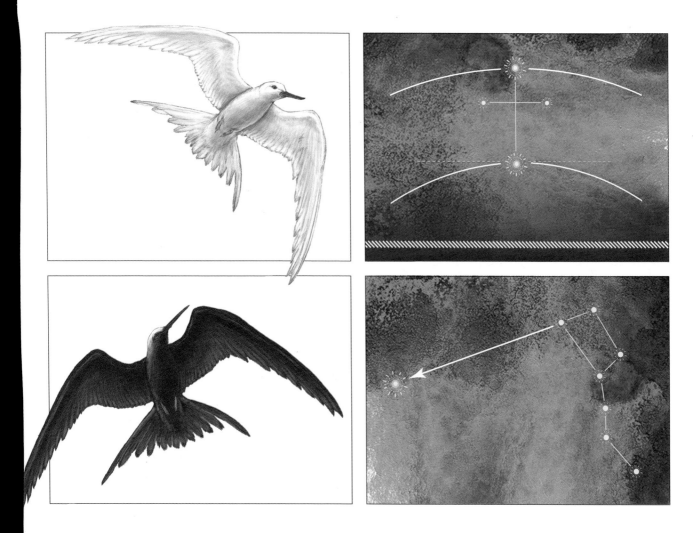

BIRDS

There are two key birds that help navigators know when land is near. The *manu o kū* (white fairy tern) has a range of roughly 120 to 200 miles from land, and the *noio* (black noddy) has a range of about 40 miles. Both birds return to land to rest at night. If the navigators see these birds around sunrise, they can assume they are coming from an island, and if they see the birds around sunset, they are returning to the island. Most other seabirds are less reliable indicators due to their ability to stay at sea without returning to land for several days, months, and at times, even years.

STARS

Hānaiakamalama (the Southern Cross) and *Hōkūpaʻa* (Polaris) are important for determining latitude. If you are sailing north on a line back to the east, upwind, of Hawaiʻi, once the distance between the top and bottom stars in *Hānaiakamalama* is equal to the distance between the bottom star and the horizon, you know that you are at the latitude of Hawaiʻi. Then you can turn downwind, an easier direction to sail, and be confident that you will see one of the islands in the expanded landfall that the Hawaiian Islands provide.

Hōkūpaʻa is also an important directional clue in the Northern Hemisphere. *Nāhiku* (the Big Dipper) helps navigators find *Hōkūpaʻa* and can also help determine latitude as the canoe gets south of the equator.

The Rebirth of Traditional Polynesian Voyaging

The successful voyage of *Hōkūleʻa* from Hawaiʻi to Tahiti in 1976 inspired the rebirth of noninstrument navigation in the Pacific and the birth of the ʻOhana Waʻa.

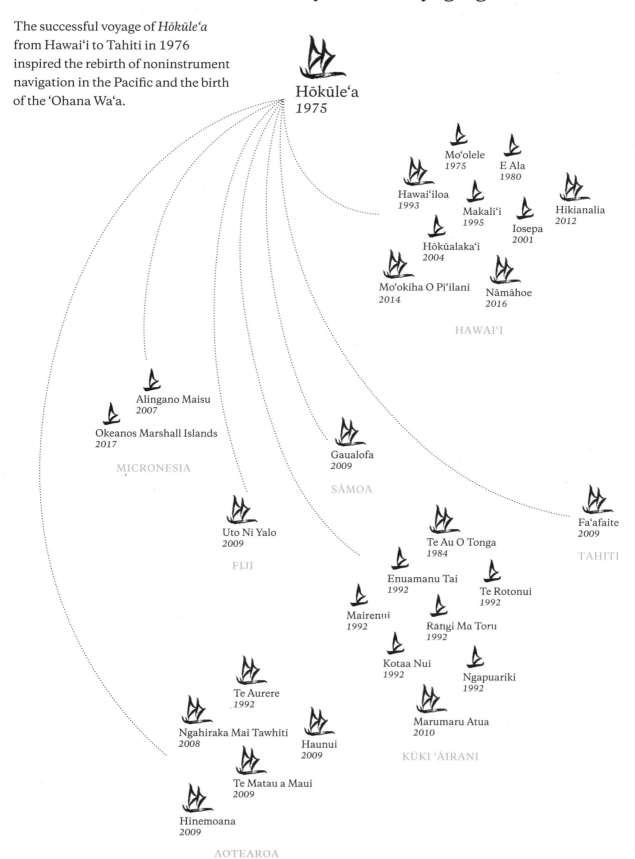

Hōkūleʻa
1975

Moʻolele
1975

E Ala
1980

Hawaiʻiloa
1993

Makaliʻi
1995

Hikianalia
2012

Iosepa
2001

Hōkūalakaʻi
2004

Moʻokiha O Piʻilani
2014

Nāmāhoe
2016

HAWAIʻI

Alingano Maisu
2007

Okeanos Marshall Islands
2017

MICRONESIA

Gaualofa
2009

SĀMOA

Faʻafaite
2009

TAHITI

Uto Ni Yalo
2009

FIJI

Te Au O Tonga
1984

Enuamanu Tai
1992

Te Rotonui
1992

Mairenui
1992

Rangi Ma Toru
1992

Kotaa Nui
1992

Ngapuariki
1992

Te Aurere
1992

Ngahiraka Mai Tawhiti
2008

Haunui
2009

Marumaru Atua
2010

KŪKI ʻĀIRANI

Te Matau a Maui
2009

Hinemoana
2009

AOTEAROA

Resources

BOOKS/MAGAZINES

Barlow, Cleve. *Tikanga Whakaaro, Key Concepts in Māori Culture.* Oxford: Oxford University Press, 1990.

Brougham, A.E., A.W. Reed, and T.S. Kāretu. *The Raupō: Book of Māori Proverbs.* Aukland: Penguin Books, 2012.

Buck, Peter H. *Vikings of the Pacific.* Chicago: University of Chicago Press, 1959.

Cantwell, Anne-Marie and Diana diZerga Wall. *Unearthing Gotham, The Archeology of New York City.* New Haven: Yale University Press, 2001.

Chartier, Clem, Alberto Chirif, and Nin Tomas. *The Human Rights of the Rapa Nui People on Easter Island, Report of the International Observers' Mission to Rapa Nui 2011.* Copenhagen: International Work Group for Indigenous Affairs, 2012: http://www.iwgia.org/iwgia_files_publications_files/0597_Informe_RAPA_NUI_IGIA-Observatorio_English_FINAL.pdf.

Chomsky, Aviva, Barry Carr, and Pamela Maria Smorkaloff, eds. *The Cuba Reader, History, Culture, Politics.* Durham: Duke University Press, 2004.

Cousteau, Jacques. *The Human, the Orchid, and the Octopus.* New York: Bloomsbury USA, 2007.

Ebrahi, Noor. *Noor's Story, My Life In District Six.* Cape Town: District Six Museum, 1999.

Finney, Ben. *Hōkūle'a, The Way to Tahiti.* New York: Dodd, Mead & Company, 1979.

Finney, Ben. "The Sin at Awarua," *The Contemporary Pacific.* V 11, # 1, Spring 1999, University of Hawai'i Press.

Henry, Teuira and others. *The Voyaging Chiefs of Havai'i.* Honolulu: University of Hawai'i Press, 1994. http://www2.hawaii.edu/~dennisk/voyaging_chiefs/voyagingintro.html.

Howe, K.R., ed. *Vaka Moana, Voyages of the Ancestors.* Honolulu: University of Hawai'i Press, 2007.

Johnson, Rubellite Kawena, John Kaipo Mahelona, and Clive Ruggles. *Nā Inoa Hōkū, Hawaiian and Pacific Star Names.* Bognor Regis: Ocarina Books, 2015.

Kawaharada, Dennis. "No Nā Mamo, For the Children: 1992 Voyage of Education." 1993, http://archive.hokulea.com/holokai/1992/no_na_mamo.html.

Kyselka, Will and Ray Lanterman. *North Star to Southern Cross.* Honolulu: University of Hawai'i Press, 1984.

Kyselka, Will. *An Ocean in Mind.* Honolulu: University of Hawai'i Press, 1987.

Lewis, David. *We, the Navigators: The Ancient Art of Landfinding in the Pacific.* Honolulu: University of Hawai'i Press, 1994.

Low, Sam. *Hawaiki Rising.* Waipahu: Island Heritage Publishing, 2013.

Marti, José. *José Marti, Selected Writings.* London: Penguin Classics, 2002.

McCalman, Iain. *The Reef, A Passionate History: The Great Barrier Reef from Captain Cook to Climate Change.* New York: Scientific American, 2014.

Turner, George. *Samoa, A Hundred Years Ago and Long Before.* Suva: University of the South Pacific, 1984.

Warne, Kennedy. "Sea Change," *New Zealand Geographic* (November/December 2014): https://www.nzgeo.com/stories/sea-change/.

ORGANIZATIONS

Abriculture
archive.hokulea.com
Billion Oyster Project
Conservational International
FOOD FIRST
Native American Law Alliance
New York Harbor School
Okeanos Foundation
The River Project
Sustainable Seas Trust
Tangaroa Blue

Acknowledgments

Blake McElheny for sending me to touch Hōkūle'a and planting the seed of this book. Kamaki Worthington for guidance at sea, and wisdom on land. Ian Anderson for constant support at home. Essex Waterhousings for decades of awesome gear. Dan Lin for encouraging me to become crew. Pam O for helping me steer by the stars. Jenna Ishii for somehow answering every single question. Nainoa Thompson for being the finest example of a human being I've ever met.

All the simply amazing people of the Polynesian Voyaging Society. And to my wife Alexis, for understanding how important this project was and what it would take; my incredible in-laws, for always helping; my brother, who taught me to love the ocean; and my sister, who taught me to love the universe. And finally my daughter Malia Keani, to whom and to whose future, I dedicate my work.

– John Bilderback

With a bowed head and lifted heart, I am grateful to Nainoa for permission to intimately witness and document the Worldwide Voyage; to Kauhi for blessings; for the support from the Polynesian Voyaging Society, most especially Maya for grace, Kaleo for guidance, Heidi for tracking, Jenna for clarity, Todd for sincerity, and Miki for quick-witted pep; to Nā'ālehu for being the getter of every possible thing; to Billy for the embrace of Aloha; to JB for enduring friendship; to Sylvia for aligning; to Patagonia for enabling the scope of this project to holistically unfold, most keenly Karla for direction and John for being a Buddha of an editor; to Mark, Roman, Deacon, and Anton for unflinchingly and unfailingly letting me go; and to the great healer known as *Hōkūle'a* for graciously allowing me in. *Me ka ha'aha'a, mahalo palena 'ole.*

– Jennifer Allen

MĀLAMA HONUA

Hōkūleʻa - A Voyage of Hope

Patagonia publishes a select number of titles on wilderness, wildlife, and outdoor sports that inspire and restore a connection to the natural world.

FIRST EDITION
Editor: John Dutton
Book Design & Photo Edit: Jeff Batzli and Christina Speed
Creative Director: Bill Boland
Creative Advisor: Jennifer Ridgeway
Project Manager: Jennifer Patrick
Production: Rafael Dunn and Michaela Purcilly
Woodcuts: John McCaskill

Printed in Canada on 100 percent post-consumer recycled paper.

Jacket photos: John Bilderback, John Bilderback's bio shot: Anthony Ghiglia

Hardcover ISBN 9781938340697
Library of Congress Control Number 2017948482

Patagonia wishes to thank the following people for their countless reviews of the manuscript: the crew of *Hōkūleʻa* for helping us get the story right; Jenna Ishii, Heidi Guth, Billy Richards, Sonja Swenson Rogers, Miki Tomita, Kaleo Wong, and the rest of the staff at the Polynesian Voyaging Society for accuracy of places, names, and dates, and answering other random questions; and especially Maya Saffery for volunteering her Hawaiian language expertise.

This book was developed in cooperation with the Polynesian Voyaging Society. A portion of the proceeds from the sale of each book will be donated to support PVS.

patagonia®

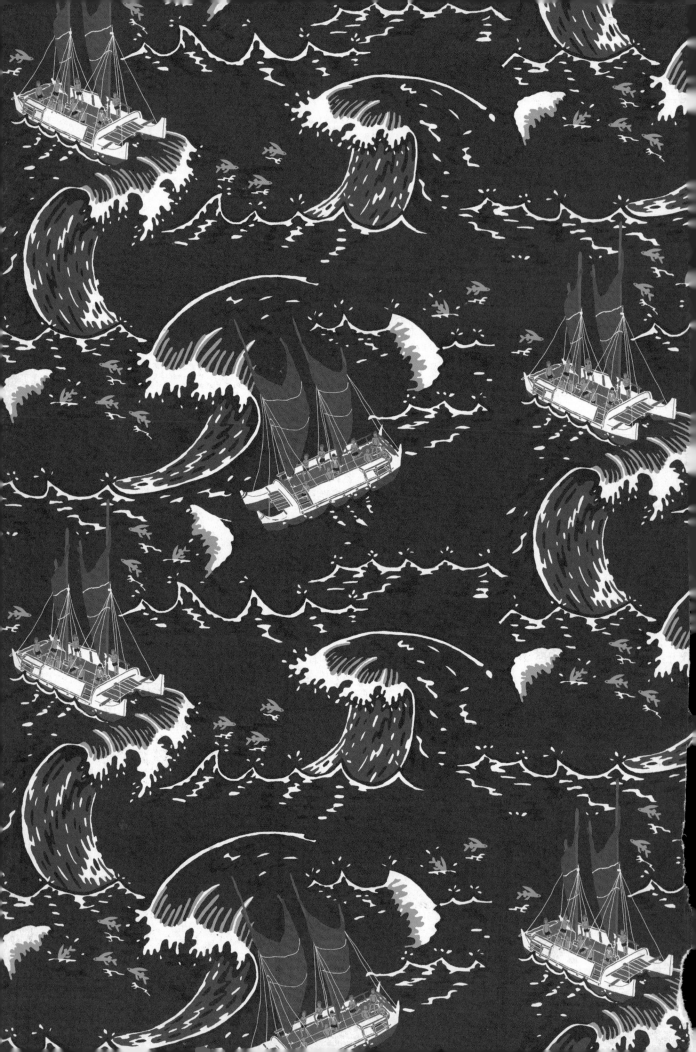